Liquid Asset

Liquid Asset

HOW BUSINESS AND GOVERNMENT CAN PARTNER TO SOLVE THE FRESHWATER CRISIS

Barton H. Thompson, Jr.

Stanford University Press
Stanford, California

Stanford University Press
Stanford, California

Printed in the United States of America on acid-free, archival-quality paper

Library of Congress Cataloging-in-Publication Data

Names: Thompson, Barton H., Jr., author.
Title: Liquid asset : how business and government can partner to solve the freshwater crisis / Barton H. Thompson, Jr.
Description: Stanford, California : Stanford University Press, 2023. | Includes bibliographical references and index.
Identifiers: LCCN 2023016822 (print) | LCCN 2023016823 (ebook) | ISBN 9781503632417 (cloth) | ISBN 9781503637351 (ebook)
Subjects: LCSH: Water-supply—United States—Management. | Water-supply—Government policy—United States. | Public-private sector cooperation—United States.
Classification: LCC HD1694.A5 T466 2023 (print) | LCC HD1694.A5 (ebook) | DDC 333.9100973—dc23/eng/20230627
LC record available at https://lccn.loc.gov/2023016822
LC ebook record available at https://lccn.loc.gov/2023016823

Cover design: Lindy Kasler

Cover photographs: Shutterstock

Typeset by Newgen in Minion Pro 10.5/14.5

To Grant and Charlie
and the next generation of problem solvers

CONTENTS

ACKNOWLEDGMENTS

There are many people who played an important role in informing this book and deserve my thanks. Matt Kline of O'Melveny & Myers LLP has co-taught "The Business of Water" with me at Stanford University since we created the class in 2016. Matt is exceptionally astute about the multiple roles that the private sector can play in water management and has continually forced me to think more deeply about the issues explored in this book. Matt is an outstanding teacher, colleague, and friend. I could never have written this book without him.

The scores of individuals who have visited and spoken to the class or participated in interviews have provided much of the substance and insight of the book. These individuals include Eleanor Allen (Water for People), Eric Averett (Renewable Resources Group), Ricardo Bayon (Encourage Capital), John Bohn (Deep Water Desal, and Water Asset Management); Ashley Boren (Sustainable Conservation); Nicole Neeman Brady (Edison Water, Renewable Resources Group, and the Los Angeles Department of Water and Power), Cat Burns (The Nature Conservancy), Don Cameron (Terranova Ranch), Jennifer Capitolo (California Water Association), Albert Cho (Xylem), Tom Ferguson (Burnt Island Ventures), Andre Fourje (AB InBev), Melissa Frank (Wonderful Company), Jon Freedman (Suez Water Technologies & Solutions), Brandon Freiman (KKR), Alison Gilbert (Gap), Mark Gold (UCLA), Hank Habicht (Water Finance Exchange), George Hawkins

(Moonshot Missions), Kelly Huffman (Poseidon Water), Gary Kremen (Santa Clara Valley Water District), Martin Kropelnicki (California Water Service Group), Clay Landry (WestWater Research), Jeff Langholz (Water City), Randall Martinez (Cordoba Corporation), Maria Mehranian (Cordoba Corporation), Taman Pechet (Imagine H2O and Upwell), Bill Phillimore (Wonderful Orchards), George Pla (Cordoba Corporation), Jon Reiter (Maricopa Orchards), Marc Roberts (Water Asset Management), William Sarni (Water Foundry), Ari Swiller (Renewable Resources Group), Rod Smith (Stratecon), Charlie Stringer (Renewable Resources Group), Richard Svindland (California American Water), Aaron Tartakovsky (Epic Cleantec), Ben Townsend (Google), Derrik Williams (Montgomery and Associates), and Richael Young (Mammoth Trading). I also have benefited from the wisdom and expertise of my colleagues in the water practice at O'Melveny & Myers, especially John Laco, Russ McGlothlin, Zach Smith, and Heather Welles, and at the Sustainable Water Impact Fund, especially Alyssa Go, Cat Burns, Ekat Alexandova, Lauren D'Souza, and Jordan Isken. Many fellow academics, lawyers, and clients also made comments on drafts of the various chapters or otherwise informed my thinking, including Newsha Ajami, Ashley Boren, Robin Craig, Peter Culp, Jennifer Diffley, Tom Eisenhauer, Brian Gray, Jim James, Michael Kiparsky, Jim Salzman, David Victor, and Philip Womble (who has written several particularly insightful articles on environmental water transactions).

I also owe thanks to those who have previously researched or reported on many of the issues discussed in this book. As my extensive endnotes indicate, my thinking has benefited immensely from this prior work. The reporting in *PublicSource* by Oliver Morrison, a Pittsburgh journalist, on the Pittsburgh Water and Sewage Authority was particularly valuable in writing the story that starts Chapter 3.

Geoff McGhee, who was the interactive graphic editor for *The New York Times* and who now works with the Bill Lane Center for the American West at Stanford, produced the wonderful figures and maps that are scattered throughout this book. Every author should be lucky enough to have a graphic designer like Geoff. Several excellent research assistants at Stanford Law School helped me in both my research and getting the book ready for publication. I particularly want to thank Hutchinson Fann and Andrew Keuler of the Stanford Law School Class of 2024 and Sam Joyce and Sam Wallace-Perdomo of the Class of 2023. I also want to acknowledge and thank John Greely, a close family friend, who came up with the title of the book as part of an after-dinner brainstorming session.

Finally, I owe enormous gratitude to my wife, Holly, who read through the entire manuscript and patiently helped me with everything from grammar to clarity. She also graciously put up with me and my frequent impatience as I wrote the manuscript, perhaps explaining why our marriage has endured for forty years.

About ten years ago, I was asked to give a speech on whether water is the "new oil." I thought the analogy was wrong then and still do today. Petroleum is a finite resource, while water is a renewable and sustainable resource if managed properly. Petroleum production and use are inherently harmful to the environment, while water sustains us and all other living things. Private companies produce oil and make a lot of money doing so, while municipalities and other public entities deliver most water, and few businesses have ever "struck it big" on water. Water is assuredly not the "new oil," nor will it ever be.

My speech, however, got me interested in why the private sector does not play a larger role in freshwater management. I knew that the private sector was involved to a limited extent in the water sector. In the late twentieth century, I had briefly looked at the efforts of several large international corporations to "privatize" domestic water supply systems in the United States and globally (an effort that did not appreciably increase the number of private US water providers). I also have long studied and written about private water markets in the western United States, Australia, and Chile. Yet as I looked more closely at the water field, I found that private involvement in water management was more sizable than I realized, and growing.

In the meantime, I became increasingly interested in the growing freshwater crisis facing the world and, more importantly, in how we might solve that crisis. Climate change, urbanization, unsustainable groundwater pumping, water pollution, long-ignored infrastructure needs, and other factors are threatening freshwater resources. Although it is easy to diagnose the problem and criticize current water management, it is more difficult to figure out how to solve those problems. The world will need a mix of rules, norms, new technologies, funding, and improved management and policies.

My separate interests in freshwater solutions and the private water sector came together in 2014 when the Brookings Institute asked me to give a presentation at a joint Brookings-Stanford water conference on how the United States can promote new technological solutions to the nation's water challenges. The paper that I prepared for the conference, co-written with Newsha Ajami and David Victor, found that even though new technological innovations are critical to improving freshwater management, the United States suffers from an "innovation deficit" in the water field. The paper identified problems that private technology firms face in the water sector and recommended public policies that can promote greater innovation.

I became hooked at that point on the question of what role the private sector might play in solving the world's growing freshwater crisis. Because water management can affect the human right to water and environmental concerns, this question is more difficult than it might seem at first glance. The question is not simply how the private sector is contributing or might contribute to effective solutions but also what risks a greater private role presents and how society can address those risks. Because the water sector is highly conservative and political and is dominated by public agencies, there is also the question of how easily private organizations can function in that sector.

To investigate these issues, I organized a class at Stanford in 2016 on "The Business of Water." Originally, I expected that the class would draw less than a dozen students (the cross section, I figured, of those interested in *both* water *and* business). I seriously underestimated student interest. The class, which is now in its sixth year, has proven enormously popular among law students, business students, engineering students, and other graduate students at Stanford, all of whom want to know how the private sector can help improve water management. The business executives who have visited the class have been passionate about their efforts to address water problems, and their ideas have been consistently creative and interesting.

I also have become more involved in the private sector myself in recent years. In my practice at O'Melveny, I have counseled private companies on how they can use their acumen to solve water challenges and better steward water resources. I also am a member of the Technical Advisory Committee of the Sustainable Water Impact Fund, an investment fund described in Chapter 5 that seeks to improve the environment through water-related investments.

This book is the result of the lessons that I have learned from working and researching in the water field for over four decades and teaching about the business of water. While the book focuses on the special value that the private sector offers, the book provides a broad look at the current water crisis and the actions needed to solve that crisis. The book also seeks to present a balanced picture of the roles of both government and the private sector in water management. Public water officials work hard to provide everyone with safe, reliable, and affordable water and to protect the environment, but they can accomplish even more if they actively find ways to partner with the private sector. While the private sector has much to offer, its involvement in water management can also raise concerns and challenges that public policy must address.

The book has multiple goals. One is to explore the freshwater challenges facing the United States and the world today and what will be needed to solve them. Another is to look at the roles that the private sector is playing, could play, and sometimes must play in addressing the challenges, particularly in partnership with government. A final goal is to engage with the difficult policy issues raised by the private sector's involvement with water issues.

I have written this book for both experts and generalists. Those with little if any fluency in water and business should find it readable, interesting, and informative. Most chapters begin with a story that illustrates the chapter's topic and introduces key themes and issues. Water experts, however, will not find the analysis lacking in detail or nuance.

Luna Leopold, who was the first chief hydrologist of the US Geological Survey, observed decades ago that "Water is the most critical resource issue of our lifetime and our children's lifetime." This book examines whether and how the private sector, working often in concert with government, can help ensure a sustainable water future.

Liquid Asset

Introduction

SOLVING THE FRESHWATER CRISIS: PRIVATE SOLUTIONS AND PUBLIC INTERESTS

This book is about the growing freshwater challenges facing the United States and the world. It is about how to solve those challenges. It is also about the important role that the private sector can play in solving them and the challenges and problems that will be raised by the private sector increasing its role in water management. Private organizations can contribute to a sustainable and resilient water future, yet private participation in the water sector raises questions about the appropriate roles of government versus the private sector in resolving water issues. Water is a distinctively public resource important to both human health and the environment. Private companies, in turn, have not always found it easy to work in a sector that is both highly public and highly political. To solve the freshwater crisis, the private and public sectors must learn to work together, each contributing its respective expertise and skills to joint solutions.

Freshwater is essential for human health and survival, for the environment, and for virtually every economic activity from growing food to manufacturing microchips. Along with air, freshwater is our most essential resource. Freshwater, however, is also in crisis. The frequency and duration of droughts have increased since 2000, and drought will likely impact three-quarters of the world's population by the middle of this century. Even without drought, two billion people lack access to safe, accessible, and affordable drinking water. While water quality has improved since 1970, many waterways remain heavily polluted, and water contamination kills two million people every year. As infrastructure ages, leaks are leading to unacceptably large water losses that in some poorer cities approach 65 percent of the water supply. Diversions and dams have seriously altered freshwater ecosystems, threatening a third of freshwater fish species with extinction. Our most essential resource, in short, is at tremendous risk.[1]

Governments have taken the lead in solving the world's water challenges for most of the last two hundred years. When concerns arose in the 1800s that poor water quality was causing cholera, typhoid, and other diseases, cities implemented new sanitary measures, often taking over water supply systems from private companies. When rapidly growing cities like New York and Los Angeles outgrew their local water supplies, they built aqueducts and pipelines to import more water. When farmers in the arid western United States demanded irrigation water, the federal government created the Bureau of Reclamation. When heavy rains led to floods, governments around the world rerouted and channelized rivers and erected flood-control dams. Private companies sometimes were involved, but in supporting roles as consultants or contractors.[2]

As today's water challenges grow, private organizations—businesses, non-profits, and philanthropic foundations—are playing an expanding and important role. Technology companies are developing innovative new products and tools to conserve and stretch the world's water supplies. Social entrepreneurs are helping to provide safe and affordable drinking water as well as sanitation services to the billions of people who lack those basic amenities. Water markets in the western United States, Australia, and elsewhere are providing water users with the flexibility needed to meet water shortages. Impact investment funds are buying water rights to improve the environment while earning financial returns. Private firms are helping to construct and finance needed infrastructure. Private foundations are funding the development of better water information for both water managers and the public. Corporations, through their water stewardship programs, are working to improve water management not only within their businesses but also at a societal level.

The shift toward greater private involvement has been slow, rocky, and largely incomplete. Twenty-five years ago, for example, private water suppliers looked poised to significantly expand their share of urban customers with a promise of better management, but their share has plateaued and the comparative advantages of public and private water suppliers is under active debate. Many cities are even retaking control of, or "municipalizing," their water systems. The growth in water markets, while real, has also been slower than many economists hoped and expected. Cities in the United States still look first to public coffers, not private equity, to fund water infrastructure. In multiple ways, governments still dominate water management. Yet the increasing involvement of the private sector, while gradual and sometimes halting, is also material and important.

This book examines four primary questions. First, does the private sector promise anything unique in solving the global water crisis? Second, what are the potential risks of growing private involvement? Given the "public-ness" of water, private engagement in water is often viewed with suspicion. What are the risks? And how do the risks vary among the different roles that the private sector is playing? Third, what are the challenges that private organizations face in working in a historically public sector? Not only is the water sector dominated by public organizations, but it is also conservative and highly political. Should governments promote greater private involvement and, if so, how? Finally, how can private businesses and governments better partner together to address the freshwater crisis? While the private and public sectors are often seen as competitors, they actually provide complementary competencies.

The rise of the private sector is a global story. To keep the narrative focused and manageable, however, this book looks primarily at the growing role of private organizations in the US water sector. The book occasionally provides examples from other countries, but anyone interested in the role of the private sector outside the United States will want to look more carefully at what is happening in their region of interest. Water is inherently local, and the challenges, institutions, and private involvement vary tremendously from country to country.

PRIVATE SOLUTIONS TO THE FRESHWATER CRISIS

Four examples from later chapters illustrate the promise of private involvement: technological innovation, water markets, private infrastructure financing, and universal water data. Start with the importance of technological innovation. Growing water scarcity calls for new sources of water. Few regions are running out of water. Instead, they are running out of inexpensive water, like the water they have historically pulled from surface streams and groundwater. To meet future demand, these regions will need to turn to recycled water, desalination, stormwater capture, and other alternative water sources. Each of these sources, however, will be more expensive than what they have now. Both water reclamation and desalination, for example, require enormous amounts of energy. Innovative technologies promise to lower the costs of these alternative sources while also increasing their reliability and reducing other technical challenges. Existing technology companies and startups are stepping forward to develop and commercialize these technologies (just as private companies have helped revolutionize the energy sector).[3]

Water markets and the private companies designing and supporting them will also be important. As water scarcity grows, conservation will be increasingly important, particularly in agriculture, which accounts globally for about 70 percent of freshwater withdrawals. Agricultural water use, however, is often unregulated. Regulations, where they do exist, often lag behind what is economically and technically feasible. Water prices are often subsidized, undercutting conservation incentives. Water markets can help to promote greater conservation by providing both an incentive to conserve (since those who save water can sell it) and the financial capital needed for conservation measures.[4]

Greater access to private capital will also be key. Cities are increasingly falling behind in new infrastructure. Public water suppliers have often failed to charge high enough water rates to replace aging infrastructure and install the new infrastructure needed to keep up with more rigorous drinking-water standards. At the same time, national and state governments have reduced their annual support for local infrastructure needs. Over the next twenty years, about $335 billion will be needed to meet water infrastructure needs in the United States, including transmission, treatment, and distribution. The 2021 Bipartisan Infrastructure Law provided an important infusion of new governmental funding, but it will not come close to meeting the financial gap. Private financing, including public-private partnerships in which private companies design, build, finance, and operate the infrastructure, can help to further reduce the gap, although private financing is still small and unlikely to meet the growing infrastructure need without significant policy changes.[5]

A final example of how the private sector can help is the provision of better water information. Given water's importance, the casual observer might think that water managers have ready access to accurate, near real-time data on how much water is available, the quality of that water, where it is needed, and how it is being used. The truth, however, is that governmental managers and regulators often work with incredibly poor information. Sometimes data is not available because it is difficult to collect or because the government does not have the funds to collect it. In other cases, the data is available but not in a usable or easily accessible form. Here again, the private sector is stepping forward. Technology companies are offering new ways to collect needed information, ranging from satellite imaging to AI-enhanced "smart" water meters. At the same time, private foundations are ensuring that water data is universally available to governments, businesses, and civil society.[6]

This book looks at the expanding role not only of for-profit businesses but also of foundations and nonprofit organizations. All are increasingly involved in water management, and all bring an innovative and sometimes transformative vision to their work. Foundations, which long avoided the water sector out of the belief that nothing could be accomplished, are now investing in efforts to improve the ability of both government and civil society to tackle water challenges. Charitable organizations are playing a vital role in providing safe and affordable drinking water to the world's poor. Many environmental nonprofits are using market mechanisms, among other tools, to improve and protect the freshwater environment.[7]

WATER: A PUBLIC COMMODITY

While the private sector is ready to help solve today's water challenges, the involvement of private organizations in water management raises unique concerns. Virtually every nation in the world recognizes water as a public resource to be managed in the public interest. Even in jurisdictions like the American West that recognize private rights to use water, the water itself belongs to the public. Colorado grants private "appropriative" water rights to farmers and other users, yet its constitution also declares that water is "the property of the public, . . . dedicated to the use of the people of the state." Other western states explicitly provide that governmental agencies must manage water for the "public interest."[8]

The public has a unique interest in the allocation, management, and use of water, a fact that separates water from every other resource. Water allocations can determine which communities thrive and which wither, which businesses grow and which fail, which households enjoy ample water and which must ration. Water management can impact the quality of a community's drinking water, determining whether the community is lucky enough to enjoy pure water or unlucky enough to receive water laced with contaminants like lead (Flint, Michigan) or nitrates (California's Central Valley). Water management also determines how well a community is prepared for droughts and long-term climate change and whether the community's water supplies are sustainable over time. Water management can determine the water quality of a region's rivers and streams, the health of iconic fish species like salmon and rainbow trout, and the availability of recreational opportunities.

Private water companies were a growth industry in the eighteenth century as newly formed water purveyors sought to meet the needs of emerging cities. But the unique public interest in water—the "publicness of water"—led to growing public ascendency over water in the nineteenth and early twentieth centuries. Worried about private companies' commitment to universal water access and safe water quality, many municipalities took over water supplies from private purveyors. In the United States, the percentage of private water suppliers fell from 60 percent in 1850 to only 30 percent in 1926. Only governments, moreover, were able and willing to invest the vast sums of money necessary to build the mega-water projects that would import water hundreds of miles to those cities and agricultural regions running short of local supplies.[9]

In recent years, the rise of two important legal concepts have further highlighted the unique public interest in water: the human right to water and the public trust doctrine. In 2010, the United Nations General Assembly formally recognized "the right to safe and clean drinking water and sanitation as a human right that is essential for the full enjoyment of life and all human rights." (No nation voted against this resolution, although forty-one countries, including the United States, Australia, Canada, and the United Kingdom, abstained.) A growing number of governments also recognize a human right to water under their local laws, including South Africa (by an express provision in its constitution), India (by judicial decision), and California (by statute). However reflected in the law, the human right to water dominates today's debates over water access, pricing, and quality throughout the world.[10]

The public trust doctrine emphasizes that the government holds water resources in trust for all members of the public, including future generations, and cannot abdicate its obligation to manage water in the public interest. South African law, for example, states that the government is the "public trustee of the nation's water resources" and must "ensure that water is protected, used, developed, conserved, managed, and controlled in a sustainable and equitable manner, for the benefit of all persons." In the United States and other countries, courts have used the public trust doctrine primarily to protect environmental interests in water. In a seminal 1984 case, for example, the California Supreme Court ruled that its state water agency could not permit water diversions that were drying up Mono Lake, the second-largest lake in the state, and must protect environmental interests in the state's waterways whenever feasible. While fewer countries have formally recognized the public trust doctrine than the human right to water, the doctrine enjoys an outsized role in water debates throughout the world.[11]

Some observers worry that the increasing role of the private sector threatens the public interest in water. Concern has centered on business involvement that can influence the allocation, use, and pricing of water. Efforts to privatize the delivery of drinking water, for example, have often fueled fears that private companies will raise prices, reduce access to water for the poor, and cut corners on water quality. Driven by such fears, residents and human-rights advocates have protested and derailed privatization efforts in many cities and regions around the world. Critics have similarly condemned companies seeking to promote water markets as "speculators" that would elevate economic returns over equity, fairness, and other public goals. In the words of one anti-privatization manifesto, "Water is a fundamental right and a public trust to be guarded by all levels of government." As a result, water "should not be commodified, privatized, or traded for commercial purposes."[12]

The international community, however, has also recognized that market forces can benefit water management and that, in at least some settings, water is an economic good. In 1992, over 500 experts from 114 countries, 38 non-profit organizations, and 28 United Nation agencies met in Dublin, Ireland, at the Conference on Water and the Environment, which was organized by the World Meteorological Organization. One of the conference's major goals was to develop strategies for more effective and sustainable water management around the world. In their final statement, the conferees concluded that water "should be recognized as an economic good." According to the Dublin Statement on Water and Sustainable Development, "Past failure to recognize the economic value of water has led to wasteful and environmentally damaging uses of the resource. . . . Managing water as an economic good is an important way of achieving efficient and equitable use, and of encouraging conservation and protection of water resources."[13]

Water, in fact, is neither a pure public good (best allocated by the government) nor a pure private commodity (typically best allocated by markets). Water is best described as a "public commodity," a resource critical to both public and private needs. Governments have an obligation to protect the human right to water and freshwater ecosystems. But once sufficient water is reserved for these public purposes, water is a commodity that generates economic value to society by enabling the production of food, energy, or other products. Private businesses and markets can help ensure that societies get the maximum economic value from the water available for those activities.[14]

With proper incentives and regulatory safeguards in place, private businesses can even advance the human right to water, environmental sustainability, and other public goals. Many communities without capital access, for example, have turned to private businesses for the funding needed to expand their water infrastructure and ensure water access to a higher percentage of their populations. Empirical studies have found that privatization of water systems has often led to accelerated capital investment in infrastructure expansion, although investments can also fall short of promises. To promote environmental sustainability, both nonprofit organizations and governments have increasingly turned to water markets to acquire water from farmers and other water users and dedicate that water to increased instream flows.[15]

Given the public value of water, however, private involvement in the water sector inevitably creates risks, particularly where businesses have direct responsibility for the allocation or delivery of water. The profit incentives of private businesses can subvert public goals where governments do not create proper incentives and regulations, are ineffective at implementing such incentives and regulations, or are subject to corruption. Privatization efforts have sometimes failed dismally even in developed countries. Water markets may work in California or Australia (although controversies have arisen there), but they are unlikely to work well in many regions of the world dominated by weak protections and enforcement systems. The private sector can sometimes bring immense value to water management. The trick is to understand where and under what circumstances it can do so safely.

Companies working in water also must recognize their responsibility to promote and protect human and environmental water rights. While many businesses have historically ignored this responsibility, the importance of the human right to water and the public trust dictates that water companies actively meet this responsibility.[16]

WORKING WITH THE PUBLIC SECTOR

Private companies wishing to promote better water management often find the water sector a tough slog. For multiple reasons, the public water sector is often not a hospitable environment for new private approaches or ideas. To start with, the public water sector is exceptionally conservative. This is understandable and beneficial to a degree. People want dependable, clean, and safe water and are far less tolerant of risks in the water sector than they might be in other areas. A malfunctioning smartphone is frustrating but tolerable; contaminated water is intolerable.

Other factors, however, have pushed the conservatism beyond what those risks alone would justify. Public water managers typically thrive by managing local politics, not by adopting disruptive new approaches with high but uncertain potential. Successful innovation offers little upside to managers, particularly when the managers are wrestling with short-term budgets and priorities and when the innovation's payoff is in the future. Failed innovation can attract unnecessary attention and even lead to managers losing their jobs. For these reasons, few public water agencies have anything akin to a research and development program, *creative* is not a word found in most agency job descriptions, and compensation and bonuses are seldom tied to innovation. Private businesses that seek to introduce new technologies or business concepts to the water sector therefore often meet skepticism or disinterest.[17]

Geographic fragmentation of the water sector also inhibits greater penetration by private firms seeking to introduce new innovations. Ninety percent of Americans receive water from one of approximately 152,000 water

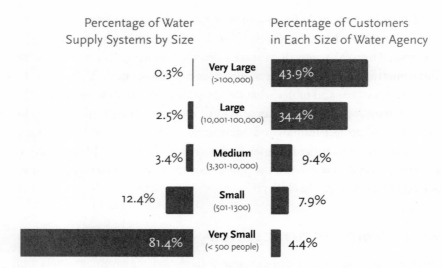

Percentage of Water Supply Systems by Size		Percentage of Customers in Each Size of Water Agency
0.3%	**Very Large** (>100,000)	43.9%
2.5%	**Large** (10,001-100,000)	34.4%
3.4%	**Medium** (3,301-10,000)	9.4%
12.4%	**Small** (501-1300)	7.9%
81.4%	**Very Small** (< 500 people)	4.4%

Figure I.1 Water Utilities by Size and Customer Base. Source: Data from the US Environmental Protection Agency, Safe Drinking Water Information System (2022).

supply systems in the United States. (The other 10 percent of Americans have private wells.) There are more water supply systems in America than public elementary, middle, and high schools and postsecondary institutions combined. Two-thirds of water systems are purely seasonal or, like campgrounds, serve changing populations; the remaining third are permanent community water systems with at least twenty-five customers. In some regions, all cities and even some individual subdivisions maintain their own water systems. While 40 percent of Americans receive water from large or very large water systems, over 80 percent of systems serve fewer than five hundred customers. Unlike in private industry, the many inefficient small systems seldom merge with the larger systems.[18]

This fragmentation can both drive and hinder private involvement in water. With diseconomies of scale and little in-house expertise, small public agencies often must turn to private consultants or service providers for help. Small water agencies, however, often do not have the time, expertise, or scale to identify and adopt recent technologies or new financial options. Private technology and finance companies also face a much more fragmented and diverse market and therefore higher transaction costs in marketing their products and services.[19]

The publicness of water supply systems also can undermine the economic incentives needed to attract private businesses like technology companies. Public water agencies, which are highly responsive to short-term public pressures to keep prices low, often do not charge consumers the full price of maintaining a sustainable water supply. For similar reasons, they also often underinvest in infrastructure. Rather than charge consumers the full marginal cost of the water they are receiving, public water agencies typically charge a lower average cost and sometimes also subsidize their water deliveries. To keep prices low and the public happy, public water agencies also often do not set aside adequate reserves for replacing and improving needed infrastructure, postponing to a future day (and a future general manager or board) the need to deal with an aging and inadequate system. As a result of low water prices, public agencies often do not have the funding needed to adopt innovative technologies or other private products and services, and customers often do not have an incentive to invest in new conservation technologies.[20]

For these and other reasons, private businesses often find it difficult to succeed in the water sector. When this happens, the water sector is robbed of the contributions that the private sector can potentially bring to improved water management. Key questions examined in later chapters are whether and how governments can lower the barriers to the private sector without undercutting public interests such as water affordability and how businesses can overcome the barriers that remain.

This book, in summary, is about the growing and important involvement of the private sector in the historically public function of supplying the world's population with clean, adequate, reliable, and affordable water. It is a story of the unique contributions that the private sector can bring to the global management of water, a resource increasingly threatened by population increases, economic growth, and climate change. But it also is an investigation of how far governments can trust the private sector in the management of the world's most important natural resource, a resource critical to both human health and the environment, and what oversight is needed. And it is a study of the cultural, political, and institutional clash between an incumbent and historically conservative public sector that views itself as a trustee of the public interest and an emerging and innovate private sector that believes it can improve on the old ways—and make money in the process.

Effective partnerships between the public and private sectors will often be the best way forward.

Section I opens the book with an overview of the world's growing water challenges and the reasons why businesses care about them. Section II examines the two areas in which private involvement has proven most controversial: privatization of municipal water systems and water markets. Critics have worried that both privatization and water markets will lead to an inappropriate commodification of water that threatens the human right to water, the environment, and other public interests. Section III turns to other important but potentially less controversial ways in which the private sector is seeking to improve water management: technological innovation, private financing of infrastructure, expert consulting, and efforts by foundations and nonprofits to promote environmental and equitable goals. Section IV brings the book to a close first by looking at how corporations are addressing the sustainability of their own water use (and, in the process, becoming involved in the public governance of water resources) and then by recommending steps that governments and private organizations should take to promote the beneficial involvement of the private sector in a way that is consonant with the public interest.

PART I
CONTEXT

Current water management is often failing to meet human and ecological needs and faces increasing threats from climate change, population growth, urbanization, and other factors. To overcome these challenges, water management will need to be more efficient, flexible, innovative, and responsive to real-time conditions, and adequately funded. The private sector believes that it can help meet these challenges.

Part I sets the stage for an in-depth examination of the private sector's role in water management. Chapter 1 introduces many of the major freshwater challenges facing the world today. Chapter 2 then examines both why businesses should care about these challenges and how the private sector can potentially play an important and valuable role in solving the challenges.

ONE

The Growing Freshwater Crisis

This book is ultimately about solutions, but it is important first to understand the serious and expanding challenges facing global water resources. It is these challenges that have attracted the private sector's interest and the call for new private-public collaborations. As water scarcity, environmental degradation, and other water risks grow, the private sector is naturally asking whether and how it can help solve the looming crisis. The story of Cape Town and its brush with "Day Zero" provides a useful introduction to some of the challenges as well as to the solutions the private sector might provide to help address them.

In January 2018, Patricia de Lille, the mayor of Cape Town, South Africa, announced that the city would run out of water on April 22 of the same year, a date that Cape residents quickly labeled "Day Zero." Unless the city immediately took extraordinary conservation measures, its reservoirs would drop to 13.5 percent capacity by Day Zero, jeopardizing Cape Town's ability to divert water into its distribution system. At that point, Cape Town would need to turn off people's taps. Capetonians would have to go with buckets in hand to one of 149 collection sites around the city to collect twenty-five liters (about seven gallons) of water per day per person, close to the minimum amount of water recommended by the World Health Organization for short-term emergency survival. As *The New York Times* reported, local officials warned that Day Zero presented a threat that would "surpass anything a major city has faced since World War II or the Sept. 11 attacks."[1]

Few people would have guessed that Cape Town would ever end up in this predicament. The tenth-largest city in Africa, the legislative capital of South Africa, and a tourist mecca, Cape Town enjoys a pleasant Mediterranean climate with dry summers but wet winters. When Portuguese explorer Bartolomeu Dias became the first European to arrive at the Cape in 1488, he even named the region the "Cape of Storms." In most years, it rains a third of the days. Rainfall in the Cape averages about 20 inches per year—not a lot, but enough when effectively managed and supplemented for a city of about four million people to thrive. In a typical year, Cape Town receives about the same amount of precipitation as San Francisco and significantly more precipitation than Las Vegas (4.5 inches), Phoenix (8.3), Los Angeles (13.2), or Denver (15.8).

Cape Town, moreover, had won national and international prizes for its water management—in particular for its conservation programs. As its population grew, Cape Town knew as early as the turn of the twenty-first century that it needed to do something to ensure that it could meet growing local demand. The city depended for its water on six reservoirs in the mountainous regions surrounding Cape Town that captured and stored local precipitation from a 300-square-mile area. A report by the South African Department of Water and Sanitation had warned that if water demand continued to grow unabated and local supplies were not supplemented, Cape Town would run out of water by 2015.[2]

Cape Town could have turned to additional sources of water, such as groundwater, water recycling, or desalination, to meet local needs or tried to limit local growth. Instead, Cape Town decided that it could and would conserve its way out of danger. This made a lot of sense to water managers at the time. As with energy, experts around the world argue that water managers spend too much time focused on supply enhancement rather than on demand management. Conservation is inexpensive and nimble compared to building new water infrastructure. The cheapest liter of water, many people observe, is the liter of water that you do not use. Controlling growth also would have been difficult and politically unpopular. As Cape Town grew, it therefore encouraged its residents to conserve water.[3]

Cape Town was amazingly creative and successful at conservation. It ran effective conservation ads. It reduced leaks from its water distribution system; while most South African cities lost over a third of their supplies to leaks, Cape Town lost less than 15 percent. Cape Town required that new real-estate developments incorporate water-efficient plumbing. It adopted "increasing block" price tariffs under which consumers paid more per unit of water the more water they used. It provided free leak repairs for low-income households. As a result of these efforts, Cape Town was able to meet its local water needs with virtually no increase in supplies after 2000. Between 1996 and 2017, Cape Town's population grew 67 percent, from 2.4 million to 4 million; during the same period, Cape Town needed to increase its reservoir storage capacity by only 15 percent. Cape Town became an international poster child for successful water conservation.[4]

There were major flaws in Cape Town's strategy. First, it ignored climate change. Like most Mediterranean regions—actually, like most of the world—Cape Town had always suffered from periodic droughts. But the droughts were typically short-lived and relatively mild, with one or two years of subnormal rainfall. Beginning in 2015, however, Cape Town suffered three completely dry winters. There had always been a small chance of such a severe drought, but climate change increased the odds fourfold. While the number of cold fronts passing through Cape Town had not changed over recent decades, the number of rainfall days had gradually been dropping. Second, as Cape Town pushed its residents to higher levels of conservation, their demand "hardened." When an exceptional drought occurred, Capetonians had already taken the easiest conservation measures. Third, the strategy assumed that Capetonians would continue to conserve as before. As the rain stopped and the weather got warmer, many local residents began to increase their water use.[5]

The result was one of the worst water crises ever faced by a major city. In 2014, reservoirs had been almost completely full. By the end of 2015, reservoir levels had dropped to 71 percent. And they continued to drop, to 60 percent in 2016 and 28.7 percent in March 2017. Throughout this period, Cape Town pursued still tighter conservation. The city imposed stricter conservation requirements, urged its residents to engage in additional voluntary conservation, adopted steeper water tariffs to drive down demand, and installed smart meters. The city also reduced pressure in its water mains, which lowered household consumption, decreased losses from water leaks, and reduced the risk of new leaks. Yet without new rain, reservoir levels continued to drop.[6]

By the end of 2017, Cape Town realized that it was time for drastic action. Reservoir levels were dangerously low but continued to drop 1.4 percent per week. Cape Town looked for ways to quickly increase supplies, but none by that point were feasible or economically viable. Cape Town, for example, considered purchasing nine temporary "containerized" desalination plants, but the cost proved prohibitive. Local groundwater was an option but could not be brought online quickly enough. Two academics and a local engineering firm even proposed towing an iceberg from Antarctica and then melting it for water. The city rejected that idea as both too risky and too costly.[7]

So, Cape Town doubled down once again on conservation. In January 2018, when it warned its residents of the coming Day Zero, Cape Town imposed "Level 6" water restrictions on its residents, limiting their water consumption to only eighty-seven liters per day. (For comparison, the average American uses 300 to 380 liters per day.) A month later, Cape Town imposed "Level 6B" restrictions of only fifty liters per day. Cape Town also increased the penalties for violations. To further promote compliance, Cape Town installed thousands of water-management devices (WMDs) in households that failed to comply with the restrictions despite written notices. The WMDs automatically restricted water flow once consumption levels reached monthly limits. Hoping shame might help, the city posted an online map of household water use, with red dots for households that exceeded their allowance and green dots for those that complied. Finally, the city appointed sixty water police to investigate water waste and illegal water sales.[8]

These conservation measures succeeded in delaying Day Zero. Cape Town first announced that the day of reckoning would not arrive until late April. It subsequently deferred Day Zero even further, to May. To help push Day Zero off even more, Cape farmers, who consume about 30 percent of the local water supply in an average year, agreed to reduce their water consumption beyond the conservation restrictions that already applied to them. Eventually, the city announced that it could get through 2018 without reaching Day Zero. And then it rained. And rained. By October 2018, reservoir levels had recovered to 70 percent. By 2020, Cape Town's reservoirs had returned to capacity.[9]

Cape Town's brush with Day Zero did not resonate the same with everyone in the region. To many impoverished residents of Cape Town, Day Zero seemed an ironic joke, because they were already living Day Zero every day. Millions of Black South Africans live in a series of crowded townships—Khayelitsha, Gugulethu, Langa, and others. The townships began as informal settlements during apartheid and now consist of street after street of mostly haphazard shelters made of scrap and salvaged materials. Poverty in the townships is endemic. Although water service is improving in the townships, many residents enjoy neither running water nor sanitation (despite South Africa's constitutional right to water). Many get their water by filling up buckets at central distribution sites and use public porta-potties for sanitation. To these residents, having to live on twenty-five liters of water per day would not have been a deprivation but merely a continuation of what they have endured for years. Nor did many residents of the townships believe that wealthy Capetonians would ever have to live on just twenty-five liters each day if the city reached Day Zero. The wealthy could always drill private groundwater wells, purchase water-storage tanks, and buy bottled water.[10]

In the eyes of some advocates for water equity, Day Zero was not just a slap in the face of the residents of the impoverished townships; it was also an effort to enrich the private sector. From their perspective, Day Zero was nothing less than a plot to justify replacing public water suppliers with private companies that would claim a better ability to plan for and manage droughts and to create a market for technological solutions such as desalination plants. The Water Crisis Council, a global advocacy group for water justice, went so far as to call Day Zero a "deliberate lie to justify the rapid privatization of water" throughout South Africa and the world, adding that water meters were just "technopolitical" elements of the same privatization agenda.[11]

Day Zero also put a critical spotlight on how much water farmers, beverage companies, and other businesses use. Protestors descended on the facilities of South Africa's largest brewing company and of Coca Cola with signs that read, "You [are] using municipal water while we the people have to stand in long queues for your gains," and "Hands off our water." Protestors also criticized agriculture for prioritizing exports of fruits and wine over the "right to water [of] ordinary citizens."[12]

The private sector, however, did not receive a free pass in the brush with Day Zero. Although the press's attention focused on domestic water reductions, business also suffered. Agriculture, the region's largest employer and revenue generator, ultimately bore the biggest impact. With irrigation water dropping to 40 percent of normal, production of major crops fell over 20 percent between the 2016–17 and 2017–18 growing seasons, leading to an estimated loss of thirty thousand farm jobs. Agricultural losses would have been even larger if farmers had not adopted a variety of new techniques to reduce their water need. Tourism declined about 10 percent, as potential visitors worried whether there would be any water when they arrived. Estimates of business losses range from $200 million to approximately $400 million.[13]

Private businesses played an active role in trying to reduce freshwater use and postpone Day Zero. In the process, they illustrated the role that the private sector can help play in improved water management throughout the world. As noted earlier, farmers found creative ways to voluntarily reduce their water use to meet urban needs. GrahamTek, a major South African engineering firm, built a $2.1 million modular desalination plant that would have offered 2,500 to 12,500 cubic meters of water per day; Day Zero ended before the plant went into use. The Westin Hotel on the downtown coastline of Cape Town realized that it could build its own desalination plant to turn the salt water that continually flooded the lowest level of its basement garage into potable water for both its guests and neighboring hotels as well. Maskam Water, a new Cape Town business, began to market systems for recycling the relatively clean, or "grey," wastewater discharged from sinks, dishwashers, and other plumbing fixtures and appliances in commercial and industrial buildings.[14]

Climate change threatens to further increase Cape Town's drought risk in the future. The severe three-year drought that triggered the city's Day Zero warning was a once-in-25-years event, up from a once-in-100-years risk in the mid-twentieth century. That's still only a 4 percent chance. But if global emissions of greenhouse gases follow what scientists consider to be an intermediate scenario, scientists estimate that the risk of such a drought will rise to 13 percent by 2045 and 25 percent by 2100. Even more troubling, the risk of a severe four-year drought, the type of drought that would have pushed Cape Town over the edge to Day Zero despite all the city's efforts, will rise to 15 percent by 2100 under a higher-emissions scenario.[15]

Cape Town's brush with Day Zero has focused attention on the concept of "water resilience": the need for cities and other regions to maintain water systems that can adapt and respond to change, particularly climate change. Water resilience benefits from supply diversity. Cape Town got into trouble partly because it relied on only one source of water—its local catchment basins. When it stopped raining, Cape Town had no alternative source of water to which it could quickly turn. The solution is to diversify supply.[16]

In March 2020, Cape Town announced a formal new water strategy, "Our Shared Water Future," that includes a diversification plan. Under the new strategy, Cape Town will augment its current surface water supply over the next decade by about 350 million liters per day (about a quarter of Cape Town's expected demand in 2030) at a cost of about $370 million. Cape Town has already begun to pump local groundwater, which will be available even during droughts when surface supplies disappear. It also plans to recycle seventy million liters of wastewater per day that it will supply for direct potable use after blending the recycled water with reservoir water. Finally, the city is looking at the option of building a desalination plant that could furnish another 50 to 150 million liters per day. The challenge of desalinated ocean water is that it is far more expensive than either groundwater or recycled water. Over time, however, Cape Town expects to make increasing use of desalinated water because, as the city explains, "it is scalable and not dependent on rainfall." The private sector will design and build much of this infrastructure.[17]

Cape Town also is looking at nature-based approaches to increasing its water supplies. Over the past 250 years, exotic species of trees that consume copious amounts of water (primarily acacia, eucalyptus, and pine trees imported by colonists in the nineteenth and early twentieth centuries) have taken root in many of the city's watersheds. These phreatophytic trees essentially "steal" water that would otherwise flow into Cape Town's reservoirs. A study by The Nature Conservancy has indicated that removal of these exotics could produce enough water to furnish Cape Town with four more months of water every year (and provide employment for hundreds of poor Capetonians as tree removers). The Conservancy is currently working with the city on an experimental test of the concept in one of the city's major watersheds.[18]

Day Zero provides multiple insights into global water challenges, starting with the critical importance of water. It is hard for most of us in the developed world to imagine what "turning off the taps" would mean. We are accustomed to water flowing freely whenever we turn on the faucet. Without running water, toilets would not flush. Even if people could pick up water at central distribution sites, they would spend hours each day waiting in lines to get a small volume of water. Limited water would lead to poorer hygiene and the accumulation of human waste, increasing the risk of disease. Violence could also flare as people fight over scarce water. The economy would largely cease to function. If Cape Town had run out of water, its two major business sectors—agriculture and tourism—would have collapsed. Productivity would have plummeted in all sectors, as employees waited in line for their water.[19]

Day Zero also illustrates an even more critical point: a growing number of cities and regions around the world are confronting the challenges of water scarcity as their populations grow. According to *National Geographic,* fourteen of the twenty largest cities already face significant threats from droughts and other water shortages. In 2008, Barcelona, Spain, suffered a drought so severe that it imported water by tanker from France. Water levels shrank so low in São Paulo, Brazil, in 2015 that the city could deliver water only twelve hours every day, forcing the closure of multiple businesses. Chennai, India, actually ran out of reservoir water in June 2019 and had to transport water by train from a water source over two hundred miles away. In the last decade, both Perth, Australia, and Rome, Italy, also suffered severe water crises.[20]

As Cape Town discovered, climate change is making matters even worse, and the situation will grow more problematic over time unless the world dramatically reduces its carbon emissions. Some regions like Cape Town already face lower average precipitation. Virtually all regions will face a greater probability of drought in the future, and many of those droughts will be more severe than anything the regions have endured in the past. As water becomes scarcer, higher evapotranspiration rates from increased temperatures also will escalate water demand.[21]

Day Zero also illustrates a central thesis of this book: the private sector's ingenuity can help mitigate these and other water challenges. Businesses in Cape Town adapted in numerous ways to reduce their water use in anticipation of Day Zero, from farming conservation to on-site desalination. The private sector also offers ways to increase Cape Town's water supplies going forward, from new desalination and recycling technologies to the removal of phreatophytes from the city's critical watersheds. The private sector will not solve local water shortages by itself, but it can be a powerful force, particularly in partnership with government. To become more water resilient, for example, Perth, Australia, has partnered with private consulting, energy, and technology firms to develop the Beenyup Advanced Water Recycling Plant, which can supply enough water for a hundred thousand households.[22]

THE UNEVEN DISTRIBUTION OF FRESHWATER

Earth actually has more than enough water to meet all human and environmental needs. The fourth planet from the Sun enjoys the moniker of the "Blue Planet" for good reason. Earth has roughly 1.26 quadrillion liters of water—or about 166 billion liters per person. That's the equivalent to providing each person on the planet with four Lake Meads, the giant reservoir of water behind Hoover Dam, for their own personal use. We also are not depleting our stock of water over time. The quantity of water on Earth is neither growing nor shrinking. Every liter of water that humans use, including the water that we drink, gets recycled back into the environment at some point.

Yet water often is in short supply for several reasons. First, humans cannot use much of the water on the planet without significant, often prohibitive cost and effort. Virtually all the water on the planet (97 percent of the water to be more exact) is ocean water, which is too salty for humans to consume or to use to grow crops or manufacture microchips. Humans can desalinate that water, as Cape Town is thinking of doing later this decade, but desalination historically has been a very costly proposition because of its energy consumption. As a result, humans currently use desalinated water to meet less than half of one percent of their water needs, and that percentage will increase significantly only with major innovations in desalination technology and cost reduction.

Not all the freshwater on the planet is easily usable. Over two thirds of the freshwater is locked in ancient glaciers, ice caps, and permanent snow. Humans once again could theoretically use some of that water (and might find more and more of it available if warming temperatures from climate change melt the world's remaining glaciers). As noted, several scientists and engineers proposed towing an iceberg from Antarctica to Cape Town as a solution to Day Zero. The idea was not new. In the 1940s, one California scientist proposed towing an eight-billion-ton iceberg to San Diego and then melting it for use during one of the state's frequent droughts. Yet even if technically feasible—the engineering issues abound—importing icebergs would be uneconomical.[23]

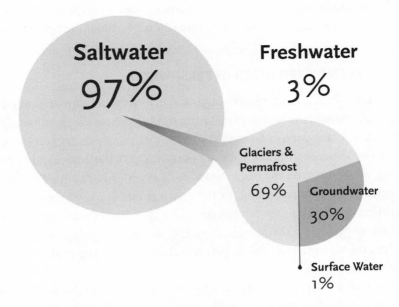

Figure 1.1 Global Water Distribution. Source: Igor A. Shiklomanov, "World Fresh Water Resources," in *Water in Crisis: A Guide to the World's Fresh Water Resources*, ed. Peter H. Gleick (Oxford: Oxford University Press, 1993).

The bottom line is that the freshwater that is easy to access—the world's rivers and lakes—is less than 0.3 percent of the freshwater on the planet (less than 0.01 percent of all water). Even this miniscule amount would supply each person on the planet with over 5.5 million liters of water, far more than a lifetime's supply. But humans are often not able to use that water when and where they need it. To start, the environment needs water too, limiting how much humans can extract for direct consumption or for production of tomatoes and smartphones. In California, about half of the state's water currently remains in its rivers and sustains the environment; environmental groups complain that even this is not enough.

Freshwater resources are also distributed unevenly across the planet. Much of the planet, such as Northern Africa and the Middle East, is arid. While that would not be a problem if no one lived there, the world's population and water needs are growing fastest in many of these arid regions, making existing water scarcity even worse. The United States also suffers from uneven precipitation, as Figure 1.2 shows. The 100th Meridian, has long divided the humid East, where farmers generally can grow crops without irrigation, from the arid West, where irrigation is typically essential. Nineteenth-century maps labeled the southwestern United States as the "Great American Desert." As climate change has increased aridity, the dividing line between humidity and aridity has moved east to around the 98th Meridian.

Americans unfortunately often like living in the arid regions of the West (think warmth and sun), and some of the best agricultural regions in the nation are arid. In California, for example, people like living in places with low rainfall, like Los Angeles and Orange County, and one of the most productive agricultural regions is the Imperial Valley, where summer high temperatures average close to 100 degrees Fahrenheit and yearly precipitation is three inches per year (compared to the national average of thirty-eight inches). So even though the United States sees substantial precipitation as a whole, many important US regions face significant water scarcity.

Not only is water not always available *where* people want it, but it often is lacking *when* people need it. Most regions enjoy wet and dry seasons over the course of a year, forcing the local population to figure out how to meet their water needs when the precipitation stops. Cape Town, as noted, enjoys

Figure 1.2 Average Annual Precipitation, 1991–2020, in inches. Source: Data from PRISM Climate Group, Oregon State University, prism.oregonstate.edu.

wet winters but dry summers. The wetter regions of California see ample rain from November through April but virtually no precipitation the rest of the year. The California growing season, however, starts when the rain ends—and *people* need water all year long.

Most regions are also subject to multi-year droughts, forcing local populations and businesses to cope for even longer periods without water. When droughts last long enough, local populations may have to migrate to survive. A series of megadroughts more than seventy-five thousand years ago may have triggered humans' first mass exodus from East Africa. Even shorter droughts can wreak havoc, as Cape Town's three-year drought illustrates. Indeed, droughts currently cause greater economic loss than any other form of natural disaster except hurricanes. Some scientists even link Syria's severe 2006–2009 drought to the country's subsequent civil war. The lengthy drought, coupled with poor water management, led 1.5 million people to migrate from rural to urban areas, overwhelming the local infrastructure and setting off social unrest.[24]

Regions use various strategies to try to adapt to these water challenges. Some water-scarce regions import water from hundreds of miles away with little regard to any physical obstacles. The Continental Divide bifurcates the hydrologic map of North America into eastern rivers that flow into the Atlantic Ocean and western rivers that flow into the Pacific. The Divide also splits Colorado into its "Front Range" to the east and its "Western Slope." Nineteenth-century pioneers settled the Front Range first. Within a few decades, utopian agricultural communities on the Front Range, like Horace Greeley's Union Colony, were vying with other farming communities and new towns for the Front Range's limited water supplies. To meet their water needs in the early twentieth century, Front Range farmers in the Cache LaPoudre Valley built an eight-mile canal, hand dug by Japanese laborers, to transport water over the Continental Divide from the Colorado River. Front Range residents thought even more boldly when the dust bowl struck in the 1930s: The Colorado–Big Thompson Project, built with federal funds, transports Colorado River water over the Divide and through ninety-five miles of canals to thirty cities and almost seven hundred thousand acres of farmland in eastern Colorado. Today, twenty-four diversion projects move water from the Western Slope to the Front Range, redrawing Colorado's hydroscape.

To overcome droughts and seasonal water variability, regions around the world have also constructed large reservoirs to store water when available for later use during dry periods. That was long Cape Town's strategy. To meet the water needs of Colorado River states, the United States built two large reservoirs on the Colorado River: Lake Mead (the largest reservoir in the United States, created by the Hoover Dam) and Lake Powell (Glen Canyon Dam). Together, the two reservoirs can hold over fifty million acre-feet of water—almost four times the annual yield of the river. (An acre-foot of water is the volume of water that would cover an acre of land to a depth of one foot. It is enough water today to meet the annual needs of about two to three households in the western United States.) California hosts over a thousand major storage reservoirs, with sufficient storage capacity to meet the state's water needs for an entire year.

These solutions have allowed water-poor areas of the world to grow and to thrive. But the solutions also have limits, which an increasing number of regions are learning. New reservoirs increasingly encounter environmental and political opposition. Construction of new reservoirs peaked in the 1970s and has declined since then. Most regions, moreover, have already used the best reservoir sites and built aqueducts or pipelines to the closest rivers. Additional reservoirs and import projects therefore generally yield less water and cost more money. While the world continues to build new reservoirs, total storage capacity has begun to level off as the amount of new reservoir capacity each year has declined (as shown in Figure 1.3).

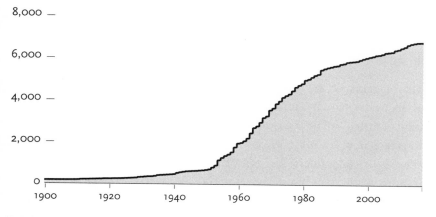

Figure 1.3 Global Cumulative Reservoir Storage. Capacity in cubic kilometers, 1900–2017. Source: Peter H. Gleick, "China Dams," in *The World's Water*, vol. 7 (Washington, DC: Island Press, 2011).

New reservoirs also only help if there is water available to fill them. Reservoirs can allow a region to survive seasonal variations in precipitation and short droughts, but they can ultimately run dry during longer-term shortages. The Colorado River has suffered from dry conditions for most of this century. As a result, storage has been shrinking. By the middle of 2023, Lakes Mead and Powell held less than 30 percent of their designed capacities. Without reductions in water diversions (or increased precipitation), both reservoirs could reach "dead pool" levels where no water would flow out. The reservoirs have helped the Southwest weather two decades of drought, but reservoirs cannot create water where it does not already exist.[25]

A more fundamental problem with water imports and large reservoirs is that they are often environmentally unsustainable. As the world has diverted more and more water from rivers and lakes and dammed the rivers for reservoirs, the environment has gone to hell. Fish in a river are like canaries in a coal mine—declining fish numbers are a sure sign of an unhealthy waterway. The World Wildlife Fund (WWF) maintains a Living Planet Index (LPI) that measures the world's biological diversity in a variety of habitats. Globally, migratory freshwater fish have declined by over 75 percent in the last fifty years—a far more precipitous decline than for terrestrial and marine species (which have declined "only" about 40 percent). Looking at regional declines, over half of California's native fish species were stable in 1975; thirty-five years later, in 2010, only 17 percent were. The major change during this period in California? More diversions.[26]

GROUNDWATER DEPLETION

Many regions of the world have turned to groundwater to get around surface-water scarcity. Just as many areas are blessed with petroleum reservoirs created by the decay of ancient marine organisms over hundreds of thousands of years, many areas are blessed with underground reservoirs of water known as aquifers. As Figure 1.1 shows, groundwater aquifers contain far more freshwater than surface waterbodies like rivers and lakes. Groundwater, moreover, is available during dry seasons and drought. Most aquifers contain high percentages of "fossil water," which is water laid down from hundreds or thousands of years of historical precipitation and is available for use now no matter what the surface precipitation.

Groundwater, unlike petroleum, is also generally renewable. Every year, new surface precipitation will typically filter down into an aquifer and replenish its groundwater, with the renewal rate (what American law frequently refers to as the "safe yield") depending on the amount of surface precipitation and the local geography. Thirsty farmers and cities can thus treat groundwater aquifers like a bank account, pumping water in dry years and allowing aquifers to refill during wet years.

Pumping groundwater can be a sustainable strategy for meeting local water needs. So long as water users in the long run pump no more than the safe yield of an aquifer, that level of groundwater extraction can continue in perpetuity. As regions and economies grow, however, the temptation is to keep pumping until users at some point exceed the safe yield, leading to the "mining" or "overdraft" of the groundwater aquifer. And that is not sustainable.

Groundwater overdraft lowers the "water table" (defined as the upper limit of the saturated portion of the aquifer from which water can be pumped), requiring well owners to pump the groundwater a greater distance to the surface, which in turn requires more energy and costs more money. Ultimately, overdraft can dry up an aquifer entirely. Long before that point, however, groundwater users will stop using their wells because the cost of pumping the water will become prohibitively expensive. When that happens, a region that has become reliant on groundwater will suddenly find itself in trouble.

Happy, Texas, the "Town without a Frown," vividly illustrates this problem. Located in the Texas panhandle, Happy gets its name from Happy Draw, a local stream supported by local groundwater that made cowboys incredibly happy in the nineteenth century when they arrived there with a herd of thirsty cattle. For years, the local groundwater supported a robust agricultural economy, even though local precipitation was negligible. Happy, Texas, was home to Happy banks, Happy diners, and other Happy businesses. Happy farmers, however, overdrafted the local aquifer (which, because of an impermeable clay layer overlying the aquifer and low precipitation, has virtually no safe yield). When the groundwater grew too expensive to pump, local agriculture ran out of water. Today, many farmers eke out a living by dry farming.[27]

Dropping groundwater tables often have inequitable impacts on the local population. Pumpers who can afford deep wells continue to pump, while others suffer. In California's Central Valley, groundwater overdraft from agricultural overpumping has dried up the shallow wells of local households, most of which are poor and Hispanic. The problem is particularly acute during droughts when farmers further increase their pumping to offset the meager surface supplies. In the middle of a major drought in 2022, almost 1,400 residential wells went dry.[28]

Groundwater overdraft also can lead to compaction of an aquifer and subsidence of the overlying surface. Long-term overdraft in California's 20,000-square-mile Central Valley has led to a foot or more of subsidence in over half of the valley; some areas have fallen by as much as twenty-eight feet. Subsidence can damage overlying structures. Subsidence caused the crazy tilts that are visible in churches and other buildings of Mexico City, which overlies and depends on a massive aquifer. Subsidence in the Central Valley of California has damaged the overlying water canals, reducing the amount of surface water that can be delivered to local farmers. Subsidence also can increase flood risks. Because groundwater overdraft had lowered surface levels in Houston, Texas, Hurricane Harvey caused greater flood damage in 2017 than it otherwise would have. Even without surface subsidence, groundwater overdraft can lead to aquifer compaction and reduced storage capacity.[29]

Overdraft of coastal aquifers can lead to saltwater intrusion that precludes use of the groundwater by elevating its salinity to unacceptable levels. Coastal freshwater aquifers are typically perched next to saltwater. Overdraft can lower the pressure in the freshwater aquifer, allowing the saltwater to infiltrate the aquifer. Coastal groundwater pumpers throughout the United States have lost use of their wells because of saltwater intrusion. Many coastal regions have saved their groundwater aquifers only by injecting freshwater at the border between the freshwater aquifer and the intruding saltwater. In a phenomenon similar to saltwater intrusion, groundwater overdraft also can speed the spread of contaminants within an aquifer.[30]

Groundwater overdraft can even have an impact on surface water. Groundwater aquifers are frequently interconnected to surface waterways or groundwater-dependent ecosystems (GDEs) such as wetlands or springs. By lowering the groundwater table, overdraft can sever that connection and reduce the surface water. The reduced surface water, in turn, can harm both

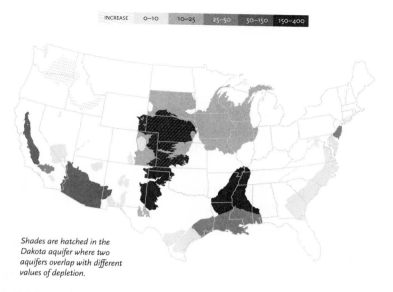

Shades are hatched in the
Dakota aquifer where two
aquifers overlap with different
values of depletion.

Figure 1.4 Groundwater Depletion in the United States. Depletion in cubic kilometers, 1900–2008, in 40 assessed aquifer systems or subareas. Source: Data from the US Geological Survey.

surface-water users and the environment. In extreme cases, overdraft can cause surface waters or GDEs to dry up entirely.[31]

Many aquifers around the world unfortunately suffer from overdraft. In the United States, the Ogallala Aquifer (which overlies eight states in the southcentral US), the Central Valley of California, and widespread areas of the Southeast, the Gulf Coast, parts of Arizona, and Las Vegas still suffer from sizable overdraft. Outside the United States, both the Indus River Plain Aquifer in India and the North China Plain Aquifer, two large aquifers of major importance, are subject to serious overdraft, with some areas of the Indus aquifer suffering groundwater declines of over thirty feet per year. Every continent except for Antarctica has major areas of significant over-draft, with attendant injuries to groundwater users, overlying landowners, surface-water users, and GDEs.[32] Indeed, overdraft seems to be inevitable when the water demands of a region grow larger than the safe yield of the local aquifer. The temptation to meet those demands by overdraft is simply too great to resist.

CLIMATE CHANGE

Climate change has bad news for water users virtually everywhere in the world. First, however, some good news: As temperatures increase, evaporation and surface drying rise, and the amount of water in the atmosphere grows. For each extra degree Celsius, atmospheric moisture increases by about 7 percent. More moisture would suggest more precipitation overall. Indeed, scientists expect that total global precipitation over the ocean will rise. But here's the first bit of bad news. Over land, other factors, such as shifting weather patterns and temperature, will dominate. Some land regions will see increased average precipitation, but others will see far less.[33]

Climate models unfortunately are not sufficiently nuanced and detailed to provide highly accurate predictions of future precipitation in much of the world. Some current climate models, for example, predict that California will be wetter, while others predict the opposite. But climate models do agree on a few things. Dry regions, for example, are likely to become drier, while humid regions are likely to become wetter. In short, climate change is likely to exaggerate current differences. Regions that are probably going to get drier include the Mediterranean, southern Africa (sorry, Cape Town), southwestern Australia, northern Chile, and the western coast of Mexico. Outside of these general predictions, however, current climate models provide little help in predicting future *average* precipitation.[34]

Climate models tell us more about precipitation *extremes*: there will be more of them. Droughts will become more common, but so will floods. Both droughts and floods will often be worse. Imagine the weather in your region as a normal bell curve, with droughts at one end and floods at the other. Climate change will squish that curve, with longer tails and with more years stuck in those tails. Cape Town's brush with Day Zero is a specific illustration of this phenomenon. What had been a once-a-century phenomenon has become a one-in-25-years risk. Regions will also become more susceptible to "weather whiplash": very dry years followed by super wet years, and vice versa. California has recently experienced this when it went from the worst drought that had been recorded in state history from 2012 to 2016, to the second wettest year on record and multiple floods in 2017, back to another drought period that culminated in the driest three years in California history from 2020 to 2022, followed by another exceptionally wet year in 2023.[35]

Rising temperatures also will contribute to the extremity of droughts. In California, for example, droughts and above-average temperatures were not historically correlated. About half of the drought years were warmer than average, but the other half were cooler. That has changed in this century. Droughts are now more likely to take place during years that, based on historic averages, are warmer than average. As climate change takes hold, the percentage of warm dry years will continue to increase, until it becomes almost a certainty that drought years will be historically warmer than average.[36]

Warmer temperatures, in turn, will turn a regular drought into a "hot drought" with even worse consequences for available water supplies. As temperatures rise, more water will evaporate from the soil and already dry rivers and streams, and plants will consume more of the water in each watershed because of higher transpiration rates. There also will be increasing snow "sublimation," in which snow and ice turn directly into water vapor rather than melting into liquid water. All these factors will reduce the amount of water that is available for human extraction and consumption.[37]

The Colorado River in the southwestern United States illustrates the problems of a hot drought. One of only two large rivers in the Southwest, the Colorado furnishes water to seven US states, Mexico, and dozens of Indian tribes. Representatives of the seven states met in 1922 to divide the waters of the Colorado and, due to unusually high river flows in the early twentieth century and a bit of wishful thinking, allocated more water to themselves than was typically available from the river. The Colorado has therefore always been a water management challenge. As noted earlier, however, the Colorado has suffered from a severe long-term drought in recent decades. From 2000 to 2014, Colorado River flows averaged about 20 percent less than the 1906–1999 average. While water storage in Lakes Mead and Powell helped the Southwest weather the drought for two decades, continued drought conditions will force the Colorado Basin states, their farmers, and some of their major cities, including Phoenix and Las Vegas, to reduce their water consumption from the river.[38]

About two-thirds of the reduced Colorado River flow has been the result of lower precipitation. The remaining third, however, has been the consequence of higher temperatures. In several recent years, runoff into the Colorado was below average even though precipitation was at or above normal.

Dry soil and thirsty plants consume more of the water, and more water evaporates. Continued warming in the region will further increase drought risk even if there is no precipitation decrease. Scientists estimate that with no change in average historical precipitation, the risk of a multi-decadal drought will increase to 90 percent by the end of the century; even with modest *increases* in precipitation, the risk is still 70 percent.[39]

Global warming is contributing to water shortages in other ways too. Many regions, including large parts of the western United States, depend on snowmelt for part of their water supply. Snowpack serves the West much like a giant natural reservoir; snow accumulates in the mountains throughout the winter season and then melts as temperatures rise, providing water in the spring and summer when farmers and cities need it. As temperatures have climbed over the last fifty years, however, snow and thus snowpack have declined at over 90 percent of monitoring sites in the West. Over the West as a whole, April 1 snowpack levels have declined 15 to 30 percent, a volume equivalent to or exceeding the capacity of Lake Mead.[40]

Snowmelt also is occurring earlier in the year as temperatures rise. Studies show that spring runoff has shifted one to three weeks earlier each year over the last half century. Scientists also estimate that in the face of continued global warming, runoff could advance another month by the end of this century. Where multipurpose reservoirs both store water and mitigate floods, storing the early snowmelt would use up flood capacity and risk flooding from later storms. By making the capture of snowmelt more difficult, early snowmelt again reduces available water supplies.[41]

Glacier melt is undergoing a similar phenomenon. Many major rivers depend in part on melting glaciers. The large international rivers in southern and Southeast Asia, for example, rely on glaciers in the Himalayan and Tibetan Plateaus. Indeed, over a fifth of the world's population depends on glacier melt for at least part of their water supply. For the last fifty years, however, most glaciers, including the Himalayan and Tibetan, have been melting under the stress of higher temperatures. With continued global warming, this trend will accelerate until the glaciers have entirely melted. In the short run, regions subject to glacier melt may see higher river flows (although, in some regions, lower precipitation has been offsetting the increased glacier melt); in some areas, melting glaciers may even cause floods. As the glaciers begin to disappear, however, these regions will increasingly suffer from water shortages.[42]

Higher temperatures also will increase demand for water at the same time that less water will be available. Transpiration of water from plants will increase, so farmers will need more water to grow their crops. Homeowners will similarly need additional water for their lawns and gardens. Reservoirs and canals will suffer greater evaporation loss.[43]

Climate change may even affect groundwater. Reduced surface precipitation as well as higher evapotranspiration rates may reduce the amount of water recharging groundwater aquifers, lowering their safe yields. Moreover, many coastal freshwater aquifers, as already noted, are located immediately next to salt water; as a result, groundwater overdraft can lead to salt-water intrusion. By raising ocean levels, climate change increases the pressure of the salt water on the coastal aquifers and thus can increase saltwater intrusion when overdraft occurs. Increases in demand also may lead to a higher risk of overdraft.[44]

DRINKING WATER ACCESS

For many impoverished residents of the world, including residents of South Africa's townships, the overriding water problem is not physical scarcity but lack of access. Even in areas where water is plentiful, many people do not enjoy access to running water. They often spend hours waiting in line at public taps and then lug water home. They may have to walk long distances to reach available water. Many societies relegate the task of fetching water to women, further undermining women's educational and work opportunities. Households without running water must make difficult choices about how best to use their limited water supplies; hygiene often suffers as a result. The water that the households collect is often contaminated, leading to disease and other illness. Over six thousand children die from waterborne diseases every day. While access to safe drinking water is an international human right, millions of people do not have it.[45]

In 2000, the international community adopted a set of bold development goals in the United Nations Millennium Declaration. At the time, only 40 percent of the world's population received piped water at their homes; a quarter got their water directly from rivers, springs, or other unimproved sources. In Millennium Development Goal (MDG) 7C, the world's nations promised to "halve, by 2015, the proportion of the population without sustainable access to safe drinking water" (as well as the percentage without basic sanitation facilities). Governments and nonprofits poured billions of dollars into meeting this goal. In 2011, the United Nations announced that it had achieved the MDG's promise of greater access to safe drinking water ahead of schedule.[46]

While important, this progress is not as meaningful as it first might sound. The United Nations measured progress toward MDG 7C by estimating the percentage of the world population without access to *improved* water sources. The world did cut this percentage by more than half, from 24 percent of the global population in 1990 to 11 percent in 2010, and even further to only 9 percent in 2015 (although much of this improvement resulted from people simply moving from rural to urban areas in China and India). An "improved" water source, however, is not the same as a *safe* source. One study of the users of improved water sources in India, for example, found that over 40 percent of New Delhi users and 60 percent of users in a poor rural village were consuming contaminated water.[47]

The safety of the source water is also only part of the global access problem. MDG 7C defined "access" as having improved water within a kilometer of one's home, so people who had access to an improved source of water still might need to carry the water a long way. And the process of collecting and transporting the water would still leave plenty of opportunity for someone or something to contaminate the water. By 2015, only about half of the world's population had water piped directly to their residences (up slightly from 2000). Over 20 percent had to leave their homes to obtain water; about a quarter of those who had to leave their homes had to walk over half an hour to find an improved water source. Rural areas suffered the worst access.[48]

In 2015, the UN member states assembled again to agree on a new set of Sustainable Development Goals (SDGs) to be achieved by 2030. SDG 6.1 seeks to "achieve universal and equitable access to safe and affordable drinking water for all." Embodying the principle of "no one left behind," SDG 6.1 promises that everyone will enjoy access to safe drinking water by 2030, finally fulfilling the human right to water. Under the SDG, water must be available to everyone on their premises (accessible) and free of fecal and priority chemical contamination (safe). Significant gaps in achieving that goal remain. According to the most recent joint survey by WHO and UNICEF, two billion people (most in sub-Saharan Africa and Central and South Asia) still lack access to safely managed drinking water services. Many regions do not even have accurate estimates of access.[49]

Access problems are not limited to the developing world. In the United States, approximately 1.6 million people lack access to at least one of the central features of indoor plumbing—running water, a flushable toilet, and a bathtub or shower. If you add the homeless, this figure exceeds 2.1 million (a population the size of Houston, Texas). Trends are not favorable. The number of people without complete indoor plumbing has recently increased in at least six states (Delaware, Idaho, Kansas, New Hampshire, Nevada, and South Dakota).[50]

Native American reservations face some of the most severe water access problems. About 6 percent of Native Americans lack running water in their homes—over twenty times the percentage of other Americans. Some reservations, particularly those in poor rural areas, suffer more than others. About a third of the residents of the Navajo Nation, for example, lack direct access to drinking water. Most must haul water from remote locations, some as far as forty miles away.[51]

Even where water is available in the United States, it is not always affordable. Water rates, which have been rising in recent years, are stretching the incomes of a growing percentage of the urban population. The affordability challenge, moreover, is growing. In 2017, US low-income households spent an average of 10.9 percent of their income on water. Two years later, that percentage had risen to 12.4 percent. Affordability became a highly visible issue during the early days of the coronavirus pandemic, when millions of Americans were unable to pay their water bills and cities and states throughout the nation adopted moratoria to protect their water from being disconnected. Given the critical role of hygiene in fighting the pandemic, the loss of water could have had a devastating health effect. The threatened loss of water, however, also emphasized the extent and importance of the affordability problem that existed even before the pandemic.[52]

Drinking water quality is also a problem in the United States. In 2019, over thirty million Americans (or almost a tenth of the population) lived in areas that failed to meet standards set by the federal government under the Safe Drinking Water Act, which became law in 1974. Another 14 percent of the American public supplied their own drinking water, typically from groundwater wells. A federal study in 2010 showed that a quarter of such wells contained unhealthy levels of at least one regulated contaminant. Many homes, moreover, use old water pipes made of lead or copper that can leach into the water, leading to the type of health crisis experienced by the residents of Flint, Michigan.[53]

WATER POLLUTION

Covered by oil slicks and other flammable pollution, the Cuyahoga River of Cleveland, Ohio, caught fire on the morning of Sunday, June 22, 1969. It was not the first time that the Cuyahoga had caught fire, and the fire lasted only thirty minutes, but the fire caught the public's attention and led to passage of the US Clean Water Act in 1972. While the Cuyahoga no longer catches fire, other waterways around the world still do. Between 2015 and 2018, Bellandur Lake in Bengaluru, India, caught fire four times; the final time, the lake burned for thirty hours, spewing ash as far as six miles away. Once famed as the City of Lakes, Bengaluru is now known as the City of Burning Lakes.[54]

Water quality is a critical health, ecological, and economic issue. Many contaminants are harmful to human health, and humans come into contact with those contaminants through multiple vectors: by drinking contaminated water without adequate treatment, by consuming contaminated fish, by eating agricultural products irrigated with contaminated water, and by using polluted water for recreation. Childhood exposure to nitrates (a major risk in California's Central Valley) can cause both blue baby syndrome (in which an infant's body is starved of oxygen) and significant stunting of growth (which can lead in turn to a decline in future earning potential). Contaminated water can also harm fish, birds, and other species that rely on the water for habitat. A World Bank study has found that water pollution can even reduce local GDP. According to the study, GDP drops by up to a third in regions that encounter severe reductions in biological oxygen demand in their principal waterway.[55]

Water quality and water quantity are two sides of the same coin, intimately linked to one another. Because of the importance of clean water, water pollution can effectively prevent consumptive uses of the contaminated water, reducing water availability and increasing water scarcity. Water withdrawals themselves can contaminate water, depriving others of its use. The growing global problem of water salinity is an example. As already discussed, overdraft of coastal aquifers can lead to saltwater intrusion. Significant withdrawals of water from coastal rivers can similarly lead saline water to move upstream from the ocean. Agricultural return flow also can frequently carry added salt into rivers, streams, or lakes. Without treatment, however, highly saline water is unusable for many purposes. The increase in salinity in the world's waterways over the last several decades has suppressed agricultural production; economists estimate that the lost agricultural yield could have fed 170 million people per year (a population the size of Bangladesh).[56]

Water pollution remains a significant problem around the world. A 2016 assessment of waterways in Asia, Africa, and Latin America found that a third suffered from severe pathogenic pollution, a seventh from severe organic pollution, and a tenth from moderate or severe salinity. Globally, the most common water pollution problem, caused by the accumulation of excess nitrogen and other nutrients, is eutrophication, which leads to harmful algal blooms, dead zones, and fish kills. Pharmaceuticals and other micropollutants have become a more recent concern because of their toxicity even at low concentrations. Both rich and poor countries suffer from water pollution, and richer countries are subject to an even greater variety of contaminants.[57]

There are multiple sources of water pollution. Point sources, such as wastewater treatment facilities and factories, discharge waste directly into rivers and other waterways. Few cities around the world treat or recycle their wastewater, which is loaded with fecal matter and all the other wastes and detritus of modern urban communities. Globally, 80 percent of wastewater remains untreated; in some undeveloped countries, the percentage is closer to 95 percent.[58]

Agriculture, a non-point source of pollution, is the major cause of water pollution in many parts of the world. Because contaminants run off fields into waterways or aquifers in a diffuse pattern, control can be difficult. Nutrients such as nitrogen and phosphorous and a brew of pesticides are the major agricultural contaminants. Increased agricultural production in response to the world's growing population is expected to create greater agricultural pollution in coming decades.[59]

Even though the US Clean Water Act in 1972 promised to eliminate all water pollution in the country by 1985, water pollution is still a severe problem in the United States. The United States Environmental Protection Agency last issued a comprehensive report on the status of the nation's waterways in 2017. Almost 60 percent of the nation's rivers and streams, by mileage, failed to meet the prescribed water quality standards. Forty-six percent were in poor biological condition. Lakes also were in poor shape, with over 20 percent being hypereutrophic. As in the world at large, nitrogen and phosphorous, primarily from agriculture, were the major culprits. While the Cuyahoga River is no longer flammable, the United States has a long way to go to ensure that its waterways are fishable and swimmable.[60]

AGING WATER INFRASTRUCTURE

Water infrastructure in the United States and the world also increasingly faces a multi-pronged crisis. Water infrastructure is aging and, in many cities and regions, either is approaching or has exceeded its expected lifespan. This is particularly true in developed countries where infrastructure development took place earlier in time. The United States, for example, built much of its water infrastructure—its 2.2 million miles of drinking water pipelines and 91,000 dams, water treatment plants, and other facilities—in the decades immediately following World War II. This infrastructure is now in its eighth decade of use. Some of the nation's infrastructure is over a century old. The useful lifespan for drinking water distribution systems averages 60 to 95 years; for dams, the average useful life is 50 to 80 years; for wastewater treatment plants, it is only 50 years.[61]

As the infrastructure ages, it also deteriorates. The American Society of Civil Engineers (ASCE) currently gives water infrastructure in the United States a barely passing grade. In its most recent assessment of the nation's infrastructure, ASCE awarded a C– to US drinking water infrastructure, a D+ to the nation's wastewater infrastructure, and a D to both its dams and stormwater systems. As a result of its aging drinking water systems, the nation currently experiences over three hundred thousand water main breaks per year, an average of one every two minutes. Drinking water systems lose more than six billion gallons every day from leaks and breaks in their distribution systems—enough water to service twenty million households. Over 15,000 dams present a "high hazard" risk, which includes loss of life; of these, 2,300 do not have an approved emergency action plan. Another 11,000 dams present a risk of significant economic damage but, thankfully, not loss of life.[62]

Deteriorating infrastructure also poses a health risk. Failures in water mains, for example, can depressurize water distribution systems and draw in contamination. This polluted water can endanger the health of anyone who consumes it, uses it for hygiene, or is otherwise exposed to it. While the total outbreaks of waterborne diseases in the United States declined between 1971 and 2002, the percentage of outbreaks resulting from deficiencies in the nation's distribution system increased. As already noted, many communities still use lead or copper pipes that pose serious health risks. Indeed, the EPA estimates that six to ten million lead service lines remain in use.[63]

At the same time that cities face the problems of aging infrastructure, they also confront multiple new infrastructure challenges. Health experts are increasingly worried about the health risks of so-called "contaminants of emerging concern" such as per- and polyfluoroalkyl substances (PFAS). Addressing such contaminants, for which existing treatment plants were not designed, will demand the construction of more advanced treatment facilities. Climate change also poses a new challenge for the nation's water infrastructure. Many of the nation's wastewater plants, for example, are in low-lying areas that will be particularly prone to flooding as sea levels rise and storms intensify. Major storms can also overwhelm combined sewage-stormwater systems, leading to serious sewage spills. Large storms will test the safety of existing dams.[64]

Many water suppliers unfortunately are not keeping up with their increasing infrastructure needs. In 2019, for example, US water suppliers spent $48 billion on new water infrastructure, but total needs were $129 billion, almost three times the level of expenditures. The ASCE estimates that the annual gap between expenditures and need will continue to grow until it reaches $136 billion in 2039. By that time, the cumulative deficit in infrastructure spending will exceed $2 trillion.[65]

This chapter has highlighted some of the major water challenges facing the United States and the world: water scarcity, unsustainable water practices like groundwater overdraft, degradation of freshwater ecosystems, climate change, lack of adequate access to safe drinking water, water pollution, and the growing infrastructure gap. The United States and the world at large also face other challenges that later chapters will cover. Much of the world's water is wasted, for example, despite its importance as both a human right and an economic necessity. Governing institutions are often fragmented, inefficient, and poorly managed. The global challenges facing effective water management, in summary, are large and numerous. The remainder of this book looks at potential solutions and the role of the private sector in supplying them.

TWO

Why Businesses Care About Water

Water scarcity and other freshwater challenges pose a growing risk to business, particularly to those sectors such as agriculture, energy, mining, and beverages that are highly reliant on water. These same challenges, however, also provide opportunities for businesses interested in trying to solve them. Beer provides an illustration of both the risk and the opportunity.

Beer is 90 to 95 percent water. And the water found in a bottle of beer is just the start of beer's water footprint. To produce a liter of beer, a brewery normally needs another seven to ten liters of water. The brewery uses most of this water, about three to eight liters, to clean its bottles and equipment. Beer's total water footprint also includes the water needed to grow hops, barley, and other ingredients. A joint study by the World Wildlife Fund and SABMiller estimated that one liter of beer typically requires 60 to 180 liters of water in total. A UK consulting firm calculated that the true number is more like 300 liters of water.[1]

The source of the water that goes into the beer itself also can make a difference to the beer's formula and taste. Ireland is known for darker beers, like Guinness, because the water in the Dublin region contains high amounts of bicarbonate and therefore has a high pH level, which prevents yeast from working effectively. To reduce the pH level, brewers historically added extra barley, which yielded a darker beer. The waters of the River Trent, from which pale ale was originally brewed, are ridiculously hard and particularly high in calcium sulfate, leading to the unique bitterness of pale ale, along with its slight sulfur smell. Pilsner Urquell tastes clean and refreshing because the local water in Pilsen, Czechoslovakia, is low in minerals.

Although brewers today can alter water to produce a particular beer by filtering or adding minerals, many beer manufacturers prize and tout the local waters with which they brew their beers. Coors will always be associated with the Rockies (even if Coors is now brewed around the world). Coors Banquet Beer advertises that it uses water from the Clean Creek Watershed in Colorado, where "snow covering the Rockies naturally melts and gathers minerals as it makes its way down the mountain." As Coors says, "water matters." Or to quote the Olympia Beer slogan, "It's the Water."[2]

Water from the Russian River in Sonoma County, California, produces great craft beers, at least judging from the success of the many breweries that have sprung up in the area around it. One of the first Russian River breweries was the Lagunitas Brewing Company, started in 1993 by Tony Magee when the printing company for which he was working folded. Magee set up a small brewing operation near the town of Lagunitas and quickly found himself presiding over one of the fastest-growing craft breweries in the nation. Attracted by the immense popularity of Lagunitas beer, Heineken bought Magee out in 2017, ending Lagunitas's status as a craft beer but further increasing its growth trajectory. Another popular local brewery is the Russian River Brewing Company (initially started by Korbel Champagne Cellars in 1997 and then sold to its master brewer in 2002). Beer aficionados line up around the block virtually every day to grab a pint of Pliny the Elder or one of its other uniquely crafted beers. Rounding out the local breweries are other names well known among craft beer aficionados, such as Bear Republic and the Stumptown Brewery.

The region's freshwater supply, however, is limited and shrinks significantly during California's periodic droughts. California is the eleventh-driest state in the nation, even though it supports both the largest population and the largest agricultural economy (measured by gross receipts). The Russian River region blessedly receives more rainfall than most parts of California. The Russian River is the largest river in Sonoma County and the second-largest river in the greater San Francisco Bay region; only the Sacramento River is larger. The Russian River, however, is still puny compared to most rivers in the United States. And the Russian River watershed, like California as a whole, is also subject to severe drought. From 2012 to 2015, precipitation dropped 58 percent in the watershed, plunging the region into its worst three-year drought in recorded history. Reservoir levels shrank, local ranchers suffered a 54 percent revenue loss, wine growers lost almost $15 million, and salmon populations were battered.[3]

The drought sent chills down the spines of Russian River brewers. The breweries rely on the high-quality water they receive from the Russian River to produce their highly regarded craft beers. Lagunitas feared having to turn to local well water, which was heavy in minerals compared to the "unique, signature, clean Russian River water" for which its beers are known. Bear Republic initially tried to avoid any drought impact by paying its home-town, Cloverdale, California, $500,000 to drill two new groundwater wells to free up the Russian River water that the brewery needed. This effort, how-ever, proved insufficient as the drought worsened. When the state of Cali-fornia placed the town on a list of communities in danger of running out of water entirely, Bear Republic had to reduce its water use by 25 percent and shelve a plan to expand its local brewing operation. Throughout California, craft breweries contemplated moving their operations to regions with more reliable water supplies. As Bear Republic's master brewer noted, the brewer-ies learned an invaluable lesson not to take the water for granted.[4]

Brewers throughout the Russian River area began looking for ways to reduce their water use and reduce the risk from future droughts. Most turned for help to Cambrian Innovation, a pioneering technology firm started in 2006 by Matt Silver, a PhD student at MIT, while he was still completing his dissertation. Cambrian Innovation specializes in distributed water reuse systems that allow companies to treat and recycle their own wastewater. Because breweries use immense amounts of water for cleaning, they can reduce their water needs significantly by recycling that water.

Historically, however, recycling has required substantial energy and thus has been prohibitively expensive, particularly when done onsite without the economies of scale possible in large, centralized facilities. Silver developed a new recycling technology, EcoVolt, that solves these problems. EcoVolt takes advantage of the energy potential embedded in wastewater to produce both recycled water and energy. Electrically active bacteria scrub the brew-eries' wastewater of up to 90 percent of pollutants and produce methane that EcoVolt converts into both heat and electricity. EcoVolt's modules are also perfect for small manufacturing operations. EcoVolt can reduce a brewery's water use by 20 to 40 percent at a cost 30 to 60 percent less than traditional recycling. By saving water while producing energy, Lagunitas's EcoVolt system reportedly can save the average craft brewery more than $20 million over the technology's lifetime.[5]

Many craft breweries, however, have neither the capital available to invest in an EcoVolt system nor the expertise to run it. Borrowing a lesson from distributed solar, Cambrian Innovation therefore developed a program by which companies do not have to pay anything to install and use EcoVolt. Under Cambrian's Water Energy Purchase Agreement (WEPA), Cambrian will finance, install, and operate an EcoVolt system for a brewery without any upfront cost. The brewery incurs no capital outlay or operating risk. Cambrian makes a profit by selling back the clean energy and water that it produces on a take-or-pay model. Cambrian successfully turned to private investment firms for the capital needed to finance WEPA. One of those companies, Boston-based Spring Lane Capital, specializes in providing funds that small companies need for sustainable water and energy projects.[6]

By reducing their water use, breweries in the Russian River watershed and elsewhere are not simply protecting themselves from drought and shrinking their water and wastewater bills. The brewing companies are also increasing the brand value of their beer by demonstrating their commitment to sustainability. And they are maintaining the "social license"—the social acceptability of their business activities—needed to operate in local water-scarce communities. All the major Russian River breweries tout their water stewardship. Bear Republic's "Sustainability" webpage emphasizes the brewery's success in halving the amount of water that it uses to produce each liter of beer. Recognizing the importance of "pure water" to a beer's image, the breweries' sustainability commitment also extends to water quality. Both Bear Republic and Lagunitas, for example, have joined the Natural Resource Defense Council's "Brewers for Clean Water" pledge to protect the quality of their source water and reduce the impact of their own wastewater on downstream communities.[7]

Heineken, which owns Lagunitas Brewing, has an extensive sustainability strategy employed by all its breweries around the world. The strategy's headline program is "Every Drop," which seeks to both reduce water consumption and improve water quality. Heineken has reduced its consumptive water use by over a third and now treats almost 100 percent of its wastewater before discharge. In 2019, Heineken further committed to replace every liter of water from the water-stressed watersheds that it uses to produce its beer.[8]

Breweries that fail to practice sustainable water practices can lose their social license to operate in a community. The mere perception of profligate water use can undermine a community's willingness to host a brewery. While no one in the Russian River area has yet argued for the closure of the local craft breweries, water concerns have sometimes led other communities to oppose larger breweries. In 2020, for example, giant Constellation Brands sought to build a brewery in Mexicali, Mexico, to produce its Corona, Modelo, and Pacifico lines of beer. Local citizens feared that Constellation would use more water than all the other industrial facilities in Mexicali combined. Rumors spread that the brewery's peak water use could equal 25 percent of the city's average water reserves. When the brewery was put to a local plebiscite, over 76 percent of the citizens of the water-impoverished city voted against the brewery. How much of an actual water risk the Constellation facility would have posed to Mexicali is uncertain, but voters were unwilling to take the chance. Many breweries in the dry region of northern Mexico have attracted local protests, particularly during droughts, leading Mexican president Andres Manuel Lopez Obrador to announce in 2022 that he would end beer production in the region.[9]

This story of Russian River breweries illustrates several important lessons about the importance of water to business. To an ever-increasing degree, companies throughout the world are encountering water shortages, both in the short term and the long term, that threaten their operational continuity. In response, they are looking for new ways to conserve water and, as we will see, access new sources of water. Companies are also finding that their customers, employees, investors, and local communities are demanding greater water stewardship. To help meet the water challenges that these businesses face, technology companies are providing innovative approaches not only to conserve water but also to purify water and expand water sources. And private finance companies are supplying the capital to install the technology and ensure the water infrastructure that everyone, including businesses, will need in the future.

The private sector, in short, is increasingly concerned about water availability but, more importantly, is also playing an increasing role in solving global water problems. From a business perspective, water not only poses growing risks but also presents new opportunities.

BUSINESS RISKS

Start with the risks. All businesses need water to at least some degree, but some businesses are critically dependent. Among business sectors in the United States, agriculture and energy vie for the dubious distinction of being the most reliant on water. Which sector wins the distinction depends on whether you measure water use by withdrawals (the amount of water that the sector withdraws from surface waterways or groundwater aquifers) or consumption (the amount of withdrawn water that the sector actually consumes). Most water users consume only a portion of the water they withdraw, with the unconsumed water often returning to waterways or seeping down into aquifers, where it is available for withdrawal by others. As shown in Figure 2.1, the energy industry currently withdraws the most water in the United States by a slight margin, but it consumes only a small portion of that water; most of the water goes to relatively nonconsumptive uses like the cooling of power plants. By contrast, agriculture consumes a high percentage of the water it withdraws and consumes, by far, the most water of any sector in the nation. Globally, agriculture uses the most water whether you measure use by consumption or withdrawals.

Agriculture currently accounts for over 70 percent of the global freshwater that humans use, dwarfing the use of every other sector. Farmers

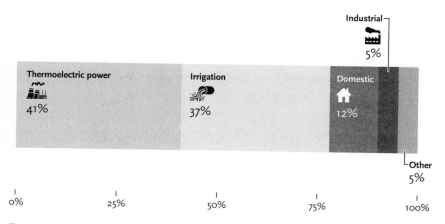

Figure 2.1 Water Withdrawals by Use. Source: Cheryl A. Dieter et al., "Estimated Use of Water in the United States in 2015," US Geological Survey, Circular 1441 (2018).

need a lot of water to grow the crops and raise the livestock that feed the world's eight billion people. They will need even more water as the global population continues to grow and as global affluence rises, increasing both per-capita food consumption and intake of meat (which has a particularly large water footprint).[10]

Agricultural freshwater consumption varies among regions depending on the extent of irrigation. Agriculture, for example, constitutes 80 to 90 percent of water consumption in the arid American West where irrigation is typically essential. Agriculture makes up only 30 percent of water consumption, by contrast, in the humid South and less than 5 percent in the rainy East. Even in wet regions, however, irrigation can increase agricultural yield and is thus increasingly used. In many areas of the world, irrigated acreage can be two to three times as productive as non-irrigated land. Only 20 percent of global agricultural land is currently irrigated, yet it produces almost 40 percent of the world's food. To meet the needs of the world's growing population with the world's limited arable lands, farmers will need to irrigate even more land in the future, increasing agriculture's global water consumption over the next three decades by an additional 10 percent.[11]

Water shortages, not surprisingly, can be devastating for farmers and agricultural economies. Farmers must leave fields fallow and watch their planted crops wither; those farmers also buy fewer supplies, spreading the economic loss to other businesses. California's agricultural sector lost $3.8 billion during the state's severe drought from 2014 to 2016. A regional drought in the western United States between 1988 and 1989 caused $15 billion in crop losses alone. Global grain production could drop 30 percent this century because of climate-induced reductions in water supplies. The *Farmers' Almanac* includes precipitation forecasts for good reason: water availability can spell bounty or famine, wealth or bankruptcy.[12]

The energy sector, as noted, withdraws more water than any other sector in the United States, but it consumes only a fraction of that water. Energy returns most of the water to surface streams or waterways where it can be reused by others. Hydropower plants, for example, typically use virtually all of a river's flow at the site of the facility but consume virtually none of that water. Instead the water flows through the facility's turbines and is then available for downstream use by others (including other hydroelectric facilities).

Hydropower is completely dependent on water to produce energy. Indeed, hydroelectric energy production is proportional to water flow (as well as the height that the water drops). Halve the flow, and you halve the energy. Droughts, upstream water diversions, and long-term climate change can all reduce hydroelectric energy by reducing water flows. In the first year of California's 2014–2016 drought, hydroelectric power fell by almost half, from 18 percent of the state's total power production to only 10 percent. In the second year, it dropped to only 6 percent.[13]

Such declines have multiple economic impacts. They obviously reduce revenues from hydroelectric facilities. California's 2014–2016 drought cost Pacific Gas & Electric, Southern California Edison, and the state's other energy utilities about $5.5 billion in lost revenues. Production declines also can threaten the economy of regions that are dependent on hydropower. Hydroelectric facilities furnish 15 percent of global electricity. In some regions, the contribution of hydropower is much higher; in Washington, hydropower accounts for almost 70 percent of net power generation; in Brazil, the figure is over 70 percent. In these areas, hydropower reductions can force industrial shutdowns and raise local energy prices. Brazil's 2015 drought cost General Motors $2.1 million in water disruptions, but the company's electricity bill rose by almost $6 million because of the drought's impact on the country's energy supply.[14]

Other segments of the energy industry are also highly dependent on freshwater. Both thermoelectric and nuclear generating facilities rely on immense quantities of water for cooling, which is why they are often located on a riverside or coast. Once again, the facilities withdraw far more water than they consume, with most of the cooling water returning to rivers, lakes, or estuaries after use. Thermoelectric energy plants account for over 40 percent of freshwater withdrawals in the United States, more than the total withdrawals for all of US agriculture, but the plants consume only about 3 percent of the water that they withdraw. In Europe, where agriculture requires less water for irrigation, the electricity sector as a whole is responsible for 55 percent of water withdrawals.

Droughts and other water shortages around the world have often curtailed or shuttered power plants that are unable to get the cooling water that they need. In 2007, for example, a serious drought in the southeastern United States forced the curtailment or closure of multiple power plants. In 2015, a drought in India shut down the Parli Thermal Power Station for 226 days. Unfortunately, about half of the world's thermal power capacity comes from regions experiencing water stress. A recent climate change study found that future droughts are likely to have devastating impacts on power plants, particularly on older plants with less efficient cooling systems.[15]

Water is also essential to mine and process fossil fuels. Coal has the greatest water footprint, followed by oil. Indeed, mining of all natural resources is highly water-dependent. And over three-quarters of mining, by value, takes place in regions suffering from moderate to extreme water scarcity, leaving the industry at significant risk from droughts and often pitting the mining industry against other water users. New mining projects frequently incite conflicts with residents concerned about the impact of mines on water availability and quality. These conflicts have given rise both to lawsuits and to stricter, costlier water regulations. Partly as a result, water stress has contributed to a slump in global hard-rock production and profits over the past decade. In a 2012 survey of thirty-six major mining companies, 64 percent reported that they had recently experienced "detrimental water-related business impacts," with water stress the most common cause.[16]

Water worries are not limited to agriculture, energy, and mining. All industrial facilities require water. Some products, however, require more water than others. Not surprisingly, manufacturers of all beverages, not just beer, use vast quantities of water—particularly when you include the water needed to grow the ingredients. One of my favorite kitchen aprons reads, "Save water, drink wine!" but of course this has it backwards. While production of a liter of beer can require 300 liters of water, a liter of wine can take as much as 800 liters. A liter of Coca-Cola requires about 3.8 liters of water (including the water needed to grow the sugar beet, which is the primary ingredient of Coca-Cola). Even a liter of bottled water requires about 1.3 liters of water. None of these figures includes the water needed to manufacture the bottles or cans that contain the beverages, which can take six or seven times the amount of liquid found in the bottle.[17]

Not surprisingly, beverage companies have faced significant water challenges in recent years. Local water users and environmental groups have repeatedly sued to block Nestlé, the largest purveyor of bottled water, from building new plants in their water basins. As discussed in Chapter 10, Coca-Cola shut down its bottling plant in Kerala, India, after residents blamed Coke for depleting local groundwater supplies. In the face of a 2017 drought, the government of India restricted groundwater withdrawals by PepsiCo. Residents of Mexicali, Mexico, as noted earlier, killed the construction of a new Constellation brewery in their city because of water fears.[18]

Take virtually any product, and if you look closely enough at the overall production process, including supply chains, you will find a sizable need for water. Consider for example that pair of jeans in your closet. Creating those jeans probably used 10,000 to 20,000 liters of water—enough water to produce more than 2,500 bottles of beer. The farmer who grows the cotton for your jeans accounts for about 90 percent of the jeans' water footprint. Almost three-quarters of global cotton is irrigated, and cotton farming is the sixth-largest agricultural water user (exceeded only by such thirsty crops as paddy rice, sugar cane, and soybeans). The jeans manufacturer then adds another 10 percent to the jeans' water footprint by dyeing the jeans, "slashing" the jeans with a starchy coating to stiffen them, and (because you like the look) prewashing or stonewashing them. (In the event that you are horrified at how much water is needed to produce your pair of jeans, you use even more water washing them over their lifetime.) Reduced water availability in California, which produces most Pima cotton, has many manufacturers worried about their supply chain.[19]

Or consider the computer industry. Each silicon chip in your computer or smartphone requires up to thirty liters of water. That's not a lot of water compared to a pair of jeans, but the average chip plant makes a lot of computer chips. Because chip manufacturing requires ultra-pure water, many plants also put local water through a purification process that requires even more water. The average semiconductor factory consumes as much water each year as a 50,000-person town. Many data centers also consume enormous quantities of water to cool their computers. For example, the National Security Administration's data center in Bluffdale, Utah, uses more water than the town's population of 12,000 people does. Computer companies therefore increasingly consider water availability when deciding where to locate new chip factories and data centers—and sometimes buy independent water supplies so that they are not reliant on limited public supplies. The water demands of chip manufacturers and data centers also have led to lawsuits and new regulatory measures and incentives. California, for example, offers financial incentives to data centers that use waterless cooling systems.[20]

Despite businesses' immense reliance on water, most companies historically did not worry about water supplies. Water was sufficiently ample in major business regions to meet local needs most of the time. During droughts, local water suppliers typically made sure that commerce had the water that it needed, even if residential users had to cut back. Governments around the world also spent billions of dollars building massive water projects—dams, reservoirs, aqueducts, pumping plants—to store water when available and move it scores or hundreds of miles to arid regions without sufficient water of their own. The United States, for example, made its western deserts bloom—and its farmers more water-secure—by building almost 200 federal reclamation projects, comprising over 600 reservoirs and 16,000 miles of canals and aqueducts. Today, the federal reclamation program supplies water for about 10 million acres of farmland, producing 60 percent of the nation's vegetables and a quarter of its fresh fruit and nuts.[21]

Those carefree days of seemingly plentiful water are over. Economic growth and population increases have more than tripled global water demand since the 1950s. As a result, most nations around the world are suffering increasing levels of water stress. Forty-four countries, home to over a third of the world's population and spread over five continents, now suffer from "high" levels of water stress. Scientists estimate that by 2050 at least half of the global population will live in water-stressed regions. Environmental regulations, reduced governmental budgets, and already-stressed water supplies limit the opportunity to meet new water demand by building more water projects. Aging infrastructure and rising environmental demands are also threatening water deliveries from existing water projects. And climate change will bring more frequent and extreme droughts at the exact same time as it raises agricultural water demand through higher evapotranspiration. The United Nations predicts that future water shortages in some parts of the world will actually decrease GDP.[22]

Not surprisingly, an increasing number of companies throughout the world see water as a significant business risk. In 2014, the World Economic Forum ranked water scarcity among the top three global systemic risks, based on its survey of leaders from business, government, academia, and nongovernmental and international organizations. In a 2019 survey of almost 2,500 global companies, over 45 percent reported "inherent water-related risks with the potential to have substantive financial or strategic impact" on their businesses. The companies expected that 40 percent of those risks would arise in the next one to three years. Over 70 percent of the companies in fossil fuels, power generation, and mineral extraction reported risks; 55 percent of the companies in the food, beverage, and agricultural sector did the same. The total business value at risk for the approximately 500 companies reporting a dollar figure was large—over $400 billion.[23]

Water scarcity is a multidimensional problem for businesses, both big and small. Short-term droughts can force businesses to shut down temporarily or reduce production. Permanent shortages can force businesses to relocate. Even when a company enjoys sufficient water for its own operations, physical limits elsewhere in the world can impact its supply chain by either reducing supplies or increasing prices. The global character of today's supply chains puts businesses at often far-flung geographic risk from droughts or other water shortages. Exports now consume a fifth of the world's water supplies.[24]

Direct water rationing is not the only concern. Regions with scarce water supplies may impose costly conservation requirements on local businesses, raise local water prices to reduce demand, or refuse to license new business operations. Other water users in a region may sue to prevent a business from using water that they believe will negatively affect their rights. Finally, businesses may face reputational risks if they utilize substantial amounts of water in water-scarce regions.

Water pollution is also a growing problem for companies throughout the world. Businesses and cities historically have treated rivers, lakes, and other waterways as a common dumping ground for their waste. Even today, over half a century after pollution fires on Lake Erie ignited popular outrage over unregulated discharges in North America, 80 percent of the wastes dumped into the world's waterways are untreated. Increasing public concern in much of the world, however, is leading to greater regulation and a growing number of clean-up efforts, even in regions with already strong pollution control laws. Companies in some regions have had to cease operations while they addressed discharges. Other companies have faced reputational risks. Fossil fuel companies, power generators, and mineral extractors face the greatest risks. But the threat does not stop with these industries: in early 2021, California adopted new wastewater rules for the wine industry, threatening the economic viability of many smaller wineries.[25]

Pollution is a business risk not just for polluters. As already noted, some businesses, such as breweries and silicon chip manufacturers, require exceptionally clean water for their operations. For them, unregulated pollution is a major problem. As a result, many environmental groups and businesses are becoming allies in the effort to reduce water pollution. Over one hundred brewing companies have joined forces with the Natural Resources Defense Council in the previously mentioned "Brewers for Clean Water" pledge to lobby the federal Environmental Protection Agency to adopt stricter water-pollution standards. As one brewer wrote to the EPA, "our product is made with water, and beer can only be as good as the water it is made with."[26]

Businesses, of course, must address and manage all of their environmental, economic, and social impacts. Businesses must reduce not only their water footprint but also their carbon footprint and ecological footprint. Water, however, is a growing concern for virtually all businesses, and to be sustainable, businesses must carefully manage their water use.[27]

PRIVATE SECTOR OPPORTUNITIES

The water problems that businesses face are not the primary focus of this book. Instead, this book examines whether and how the private sector can help solve the multiple water challenges described in Chapter 1 and elsewhere in this book. Opportunities, not risks, are the driving force for the growing involvement of the private sector in freshwater management.

The private organizations involved in water can be usefully divided into at least eight different sectors, each of which is the focus of later parts of the book. Table 2.1 identifies each of these sectors and provides a thumbnail summary of what the sector does, the opportunity it offers for improved water management, and a list of several illustrative organizations working in the sector.

The growing water technology sector illustrates the emerging promise of the private sector to improve water management. For decades, advances in water technology languished compared to technological advances in energy and telecommunications. *Innovative* was not a word that historically came to mind when describing the water field. Most of the world's water managers were trying to solve twenty-first-century problems with early-twentieth-century technology (and nineteenth-century laws). That is finally changing. The water technology sector is now a $65 billion industry. Startups are quickly multiplying. Over 60 percent of the companies in the digital water sector are less than two decades old. The market for many cutting-edge technologies is also growing at a rapid pace. The market for smart water meters, which are wireless and provide detailed data that can optimize water management, is increasing by over 12 percent per year.[28]

Table 2.1 Major Private Water Sectors.

Sector	Description	Illustrative Companies
Technology	Develop and commercialize new water technologies. *Potential Opportunity: Create new water supplies, achieve lower cost and improve performance.*	Cambrian Innovation; DeSaH; Evoqua Water Technologies; Xylem
Water Markets	Create and facilitate water trades. *Potential Opportunity: Promote water conservation and lower economic losses from shortages.*	Kilter Water Fund; Water Asset Management; Waterfind Water Management Specialists
Large Water Consumers	Agricultural companies, beverage companies, and industrial firms. *Potential Opportunity: Improve water sustainability on a large scale.*	AB InBev; Marathon Oil; Rio Tinto; Driscoll's
Water Suppliers	Investor-owned water utilities. *Potential Opportunity: Bring scale advantages and expertise to small and fragmented water systems.*	American Water; Aqua; Veolia; Thames Water
Engineering and Consulting Firms	Provide advice and other services to water agencies. *Potential Opportunity: Disseminate best practices and technologies.*	AECOM; Jacobs Solutions; Montgomery & Associates; Tetra Tech
Infrastructure and Finance	Fund water infrastructure and other needs. *Potential Opportunity: Fill global funding gaps and meet growing infrastructure needs.*	Poseidon Water; Carlyle Group; KKR & Co.; XPV Water Partners
Social Enterprises and Impact Funds	Help address social challenges such as safe drinking water and the environment. *Potential Opportunity: Bring new approaches/funds to social goals.*	Murray-Darling Basin Balanced Water Fund; Sustainable Water Impact Fund; Water Access Acceleration Fund; WaterEquity
Non-Profit Organizations and Foundations	Help address social challenges such as safe drinking water and the environment. *Potential Opportunity: Bring new approaches/funds to social goals.*	Charity Water; The Freshwater Trust; The Nature Conservancy; The Water Foundation; Water.org

Source: author created.

New water technologies are focusing on four major needs. Information is the first. Data has long been in short supply in the water sector, robbing water managers of the information needed to maximize performance. Satellite imagery, remote sensors, smart sensors, and artificial intelligence, however, are now offering water managers a massive stream of new information that they can use to do everything from locating leaks in underground water mains to measuring water use in agricultural fields. A second set of technologies is driving improvements in water use efficiency, led by smart irrigation systems (such as the irrigation controller for my house that uses local weather reports to determine the amount of water each portion of my yard needs). Third, engineers are developing a new generation of water purification technology that produces higher-quality water at a lower total cost and more flexible scales. The EcoVolt system installed by the Russian River breweries is an example. These systems promise expanded recycling of wastewater, increased desalination of saltwater and brackish groundwater, and improved water quality. Finally, some emerging companies are developing technologies to supplement local water supplies by, for example, extracting water from humid ambient air or by capturing and safely storing flood waters.

A second set of companies is supporting water markets in which water users can buy and sell water and water rights. In much of the world, water is inefficiently allocated. Farmers in one region may use tremendous quantities of water to grow a low-value crop such as alfalfa, while farmers in a neighboring region lack sufficient water to support a higher-value crop such as oranges and as neighboring industrial facilities are forced to reduce production due to insufficient water. A small but growing number of countries allow water trading, enabling scarce water resources to find their most valuable economic use. Water markets also encourage water conservation because water users who can save water can sell that water for a profit. Where water trading is allowed, private companies have helped support the markets by creating trading platforms, providing needed market information, crafting new market derivatives such as water futures, brokering trades, and directly buying and selling water assets.

Many private companies that consume water or dispose of wastewater have also begun to view water as an asset rather than just an input or waste product. Large agricultural companies, for example, have recognized that conservation can pay since they can sell the excess water they do not use. Some large farms also have begun to store unused water, often in the groundwater aquifers under their land, for later use or sale. Petroleum companies that for years have spent large sums to get rid of the water that they produce as a by-product of their drilling operations, often by deep underground injection, are instead studying the opportunity to reclaim and sell that water to other water users near their well fields. If these companies had a motto, it would be "No drop left behind."

A growing number of companies with large water appetites are also investing in water stewardship programs. These companies are decreasing their water use and working with the communities in which they operate to help improve local water management and solve local water challenges. Reduced water use lowers the companies' costs and risks. Helping public agencies to better manage local water supplies also reduces risks. And by demonstrating the companies' commitment to sustainable water use and management, water stewardship programs can facilitate permitting of new facilities, avoid costly new regulations, and attract new customers, employees, and investors. Heineken's "Every Drop" program, described earlier, is an example of these emerging water stewardship programs. Heineken and over two hundred other companies from around the globe have already joined the United Nations' CEO Water Mandate that commits the companies to make continuous progress on water sustainability. Companies pledge, among other things, to contribute their expertise, capacities, and resources to multi-stakeholder collaborations, encourage the development and use of helpful new technologies, and support the development of adequate water infrastructure. Investors and large corporate buyers are promoting such practices by including water stewardship in their decisions to an increasing degree.

Another set of private companies, currently dominated by the French giant Veolia Water, has long supplied water to cities and communities around the world and disposed of their wastewater. Private water suppliers play a major global role and currently supply water to almost a billion people. Their relative importance to countries and regions of the world varies tremendously. Public water suppliers have long dominated in the United States, where investor-owned utilities serve only about 15 percent of all domestic customers. Private companies supply 100 percent of urban water users, however, in England, as well as over 50 percent in Chile, the Czech Republic, France, and Malaysia. Yet other countries, such as Canada and Japan, have no private water suppliers at all.[29]

Even in those countries dominated by public water suppliers, a vast array of engineering and consulting firms supports the public sector by advising them and by designing, building, and operating needed infrastructure. Traditionally these companies were the heart of the "water industry," and they still constitute one of the largest private water sectors. When in the depths of the Great Depression the United States built Hoover Dam, the tallest dam in the world at the time, it hired a private consortium known as the Six Companies that included the Bechtel Corporation and the Henry J. Kaiser Company to construct it. Similar public-private partnerships continue today at all scales. Private companies continue to design, engineer, and build large water infrastructure. More importantly, private engineering and consulting firms play a major and often invisible role in advising public water agencies on everything from what technologies to acquire to how to plan for future water conditions, how to price and allocate water, and how to meet regulatory standards. While decisions might be public, they often reflect significant private input.[30]

The private sector also helps to finance the water infrastructure needed to store, transport, clean, and deliver water. Institutional and individual investors have long purchased the public bonds used to finance water infrastructure. More recently, private companies have begun to finance new water infrastructure through public-private partnerships in which they also construct and sometimes operate the infrastructure. Growing infrastructure needs, paired with limited public funding, will make private financing even more important going forward. As described in Chapter 1, much of the world's current infrastructure is aging and must be replaced. Growing water demand, stricter environmental and health regulations, and climate change will also generate the need for additional infrastructure. Yet governmental funding is not keeping up.[31]

Impact investing offers an opportunity to bring private capital to bear on the immense social and environmental challenges involving water. Recognizing the over eight hundred million people who lack basic access to water, the United Nations' 2015 Sustainable Development Goals, as discussed in Chapter 1, call for concerted efforts to provide "universal and equitable access to safe and affordable drinking water for all." The UN goals also urge the world community to "protect and restore water-related ecosystems," including rivers and wetlands, and to improve water quality. A growing number of investment funds and for-profit social enterprises are seeking to bring private funding to these humanitarian and environmental efforts. Some of the funds and companies support startups developing innovative approaches to expanded water access. Others invest in nature-based conservation projects that reduce water use while improving the environment. In all cases, investors seek both a financial and philanthropic return.[32]

Nonprofit organizations and private foundations also are pursuing philanthropic water goals and often take business approaches to achieve their goals. Water.org, for example, extends access to safe drinking water in developing nations by offering small affordable loans that families and communities can use to acquire needed infrastructure and services. A growing number of "water trusts" in the western United States are leasing or buying water rights and then dedicating the water to instream flow or other environmental uses. The Nature Conservancy has established dozens of "water funds" in South America and elsewhere that raise money from local water users to protect the watersheds from which they receive their water.

All these corporations, firms, funds, and organizations make up what can be called the "Business of Water." The exact global size of the Business of Water is uncertain because no one measures it as a comprehensive economic sector. But it almost certainly borders on a trillion dollars a year. Frost & Sullivan tracks what it labels the "global water and wastewater industry," which includes engineering and technology firms, but is both over-inclusive (it includes bottled water) and under-inclusive (it does not include water markets, financing, and several other important sub-sectors). In 2020, Frost & Sullivan estimated the value of the water and wastewater industry at $805 billion.[33]

The remainder of this book looks in greater detail at the varied ways in which the private sector can help meet the water challenges in the United States and the world (and in many cases is already improving water management) as well as the risks that this involvement poses to important public values and the policies that governments can adopt to ensure appropriate private involvement.

PART II
COMMODIFICATION DEBATES

Private involvement in water management is more controversial in some contexts than in others. The private provision of drinking water (what is frequently called "water privatization") and the use of markets to trade water are among the most contentious types of private involvement. Critics worry that both privatization and markets inappropriately commodify water resources. This criticism has multiple layers. At a very practical level, critics legitimately ask whether private businesses and markets, driven by profit-making motivations and demands for efficiency, will undermine the human right to water, environmental water needs, and other public interests grounded in equity and rights-based justice. Critics more broadly argue that the provision and allocation of water, given its immense public importance, should be under democratic, not private, control. And at the rhetorical and sociological levels, critics fear that allowing private entities to trade and manage water will, by treating water as a "commodity," lead policymakers and the public to think of water as merely another economic good rather than a resource suffused with public concerns and sensitivities.

This part looks in detail at both privatization and water markets. Chapter 3 examines private water suppliers, the oldest private involvement in water management as well as the largest, constituting about half of global and US revenue from water businesses. Whether private companies are able to improve the provision of domestic water is context-specific. While privatization can be beneficial in some settings (e.g., by improving drinking water quality), it can backfire in others. Privatization has generated fierce opposition in recent years, particularly from advocates of the human right to water and of environmental justice.

Chapters 4 through 6 turn to water markets. Compared to privatization, water markets are a relatively recent phenomenon that so far have been limited geographically to the western United States, Australia, Chile, China, and scattered other regions. Water markets can provide enormous value in the face of water scarcity. Yet markets have proven no less controversial than privatization, with opposition focused on the use of market prices to allocate water resources and the ability of investors to earn a profit from a public resource.

Chapter 4 explores the rise of water markets, their documented benefits, and the concerns they generate. Chapter 5 looks at how nonprofit environmental groups, including the new class of "water trusts," are using water markets to increase and improve instream flows. Chapter 5 also looks at the rise of impact investment funds that seek to protect and improve the environment while making money for their investors. Chapter 6 examines the ways in which water markets and other economic incentives are leading water users to search for innovative ways to conserve, reuse, and store water or, more generally, to treat water as an "asset."

THREE

Private Suppliers of Drinking Water

Public water suppliers provide most of the drinking water in the United States. While many do an excellent job, others are failing. This latter group is neglecting aging infrastructure, violating safe drinking-water standards, and ignoring climate change. In 2022, the United States imposed an outside manager on Jackson, Mississippi, after its deteriorating water system left residents without safe drinking water. Many private companies believe that they can help by either privatizing failing systems or contracting to assist the public owners to manage them better. According to the National Association of Water Companies, private water providers "offer a vast network of experienced water utility management professionals with a singular focus on ensuring safe and reliable water service to the communities they serve." Proposals to privatize water systems, however, increasingly attract strong opposition. Food and Water Watch, a nonprofit that advocates for government and corporate responsibility, argues that privatization "often backfires, leaving communities with higher water bills, worse service, job losses, and little control to fix these problems." The water system of Pittsburgh, Pennsylvania, provides an illustration of both the reasons that cities sometimes reach out to private companies for help and the controversy that privatization increasingly generates.[1]

For decades after the founding of Pittsburgh, the town's residents pulled water directly from the Allegheny River. The development of a formal supply system proceeded haphazardly. In 1813, the father of American composer Stephen Foster announced that he would start a private company to furnish domestic water, but he never pursued his idea. Private companies developed water systems for many neighboring regions. Pittsburgh ultimately built its own municipal water system, which, as it grew, absorbed some of the adjacent private suppliers. In 1995, the city water department morphed into the Pittsburgh Water and Sewer Authority (PWSA).[2]

Politics, cronyism, corruption, and just plan incompetence plagued the PWSA's early years, supporting the belief of many free-market advocates that public management is inherently inferior. One external review of the authority found "excess turnover among top managers" (the PWSA went through five executive directors from 1995 to 2001) and a "lack of accountability at all levels." The PWSA often hired people with political connections but no knowledge or experience relevant to their job. Highly qualified job candidates were not willing to work for the low pay that the PWSA offered. Customers complained about poor service and unfair fees. Most importantly, the PWSA was not investing in deferred maintenance and necessary infrastructure, allowing the water system to deteriorate. City hall did not want increases in water rates or taxes. The available funds went to other city priorities, not to fix the existing water system.[3]

As with many cities at the turn of the twenty-first century, the PWSA board decided to seek expertise and help from the private sector. In 2001, the PWSA hired US Water LLC to review and audit its operations and to develop a strategic and tactical business plan. US Water was a subsidiary of United Water (a former US supplier of water to over eleven million people), which in turn was a subsidiary of Suez (a former French transnational company that at the time supplied water to over 120 million people in thirty different countries). It thus brought significant experience and expertise to its review.[4]

The PWSA continued to decline, however, after US Water completed its review, in part because the PWSA did not implement many of US Water's ideas and in part because the PWSA still neglected major issues. The PWSA still underinvested in needed infrastructure, leading to a large break in a downtown main in 2005. The PWSA also inadvisably engaged in interest-rate swaps, a highly risky financial practice popular with municipalities in the early 2000s, to try to reduce its capital costs. When the economy plummeted into recession in 2008, the PWSA lost more than $100 million, adding new debt to the PWSA's already struggling balance sheet. By 2010, the PWSA was facing more than $720 million in debt.[5]

In July 2012, Pittsburgh again turned to the private sector to try to cure the PWSA's problems. The city's new mayor wanted an experienced and professional group to help the PWSA. He also wanted to cure the PWSA's financial problems without raising rates, which meant cutting costs and finding other sources of revenue. Following a national competition, the city entered a year-to-year contract with Veolia, an experienced French-based multinational giant, under Veolia's Peer Performance Solutions program (PPS). In PPS, public agencies retained control of their water system, but Veolia looked for cost savings and performance improvements based on its experience with the 8,500 other systems that it managed throughout the world. Under its contract with Veolia, the PWSA's board continued to wield ultimate authority and the current staff stayed in place, but Veolia provided an interim executive team and managed daily operations. Veolia also identified ways to improve service, looked for efficiencies and other cost savings, and brought the promise of both expertise and skill to its interim management. Veolia pledged to find budgetary cuts of at least a million dollars each year. To give Veolia an incentive, the PWSA provided in the contract that Veolia could keep 50 percent of any savings that it produced in the first year and 40 percent of any savings after that.[6]

The incentive worked. Veolia cut costs dramatically. In just the first two years, Veolia saved the PWSA $3 million annually in operating costs and another $2 million in debt refinancing. Veolia also found $2.5 million in supplementary yearly revenue and instituted financial controls to limit future spending and increase financial accountability. In 2014, the National Council for Public-Private Partnerships gave Veolia an award for reducing the PWSA's costs and increasing its revenues. In addition to these financial achievements, Veolia cut service response time and implemented other management improvements. Most importantly, Veolia launched a needed stormwater program and a long-term plan to address the PWSA's failing infrastructure.[7]

Despite these improvements, the PWSA continued to misfire while Veolia's interim executive team was in place—and in publicly visible ways. The PWSA introduced new automated water meters to eliminate the need for meter readers to travel home to home as a way to save money. The meters, however, were incompatible with the PWSA's billing software, resulting in inaccurate bills and very unhappy customers. When the PWSA proved unable to cure the problem, some customers stopped paying their bills. After three and a half years, the PWSA board let the Veolia contract lapse.[8]

Worse was still to come. In June 2016, tests for lead in the PWSA's drinking water registered 22 parts per billion (ppb), far higher than EPA's action level of 15 ppb and the PWSA's earlier lead readings. As Flint, Michigan, would make famous, high lead levels can cause anemia, damage people's kidneys and brains, and slow children's growth and development. The PWSA and local politicians blamed the high lead levels on Veolia, which had laid off water-quality staff in cost-saving moves. The PWSA sued Veolia for $12.5 million, charging that the company "grossly mismanaged the PWSA's operations, abused its position of special trust and confidence, and misled and deceived the PWSA." Veolia denied the charges and countersued for defamation.[9]

The PWSA's rates also rose during the time that Veolia's contract was in effect. Politicians hate rate increases, and the PWSA's water rates had remained low for years, leading to the deteriorating infrastructure that Veolia inherited in 2012. City hall, as noted, hoped that it could continue to avoid rate increases by bringing Veolia on board. Yet a year after Veolia took over, the PWSA board approved a four-year, 20-percent rate increase. The year after Veolia left, the PWSA's rates were triple the average water price in the Midwest.[10]

Veolia's degree of responsibility for these issues is uncertain. According to Veolia, the PWSA called the shots: "Veolia's role was confined to providing a small group of management-level professionals to work alongside more than 200 PWSA staff, all of whom remained PWSA employees." The PWSA, not Veolia, chose to upgrade its meters, selected the meter technology, and sent bills to customers. The lead problem predated Veolia's contract. The PWSA's poor testing protocols had likely hidden the seriousness of the problem for years. A decision to switch the chemicals used to reduce pipe corrosion during Veolia's tenure probably contributed to higher lead levels. But Veolia claims that, here again, the PWSA, not Veolia, made the change and did not even inform Veolia for two years. Finally, the PWSA set the water rate, which needed to be aggressive to meet rising infrastructure needs. According to Veolia, its cost savings avoided even higher rates.[11]

Veolia, however, bore at least some responsibility for the failures during its watch. As noted earlier, its management team provided "day-to-day leadership." Yet Veolia failed to identify or fix the problems that arose. The accumulation of problems left the multinational corporation with a black eye and required it to launch a substantial public relations defense. Veolia abandoned its PPS program when it found it difficult to sign up other cities.[12]

Whatever Veolia's exact responsibility for the PWSA's failures, its departure did not immediately improve the PWSA's performance. The water authority's problems predated Veolia and continued after. The PWSA still could not send out accurate bills. Lead levels remained high. And infrastructure continued to deteriorate. The question remained how to fix the PWSA.[13]

Private help was again a leading option, despite Pittsburgh's experience with Veolia. Over twenty private companies expressed interest in helping to turn the PWSA around. Peoples Natural Gas Company, a local investor-owned utility, was one. It had successful experience billing customers and operating a major utility. Managing both water and gas also presented possible economies of scale. Since gas and water pipelines are typically adjacent, Peoples speculated that it might be able to replace both at the same time, avoiding the need to dig up streets twice. Peoples therefore pitched the idea of taking over the PWSA. Peoples also proposed building a new regional water treatment facility, which garnered interest from other water suppliers in the area. The Allegheny Conference on Community Development and state Republicans advocated strongly for such private involvement.[14]

Neighboring communities had enjoyed good experiences with other private water companies, suggesting that a different company might succeed where Veolia had failed. South Hills, an affluent Pittsburgh suburb, had long received water from Pennsylvania American Water, a subsidiary of American Water, the largest private water supplier in the United States. Pennsylvania American Water had a reputation for good management. It had invested in needed infrastructure over time and received awards for high water quality. Pennsylvania American Water also expressed potential interest in acquiring the PWSA.[15]

This time, however, talk of private management or ownership attracted strong opposition from local activists. Environmental, labor, civil rights, women's health, and community organizations had already come together in "Our Water Campaign" to protest the high lead level. When Peoples began to talk about taking over the PWSA, Our Water Campaign switched its focus to fight private involvement. Our Water Campaign and other opponents believed that privatization of the PWSA would inevitably result in poor service, higher rates, and neglect of lower-income customers. The coalition also believed that private control of domestic water supplies was fundamentally wrong. In the coalition's view, water systems should be under democratic control.[16]

To galvanize public opinion, Our Water Campaign chose to pillorize Veolia's tenure and make it, and its association with the PWSA's lead problem, the poster child of the inherent evils of private involvement. When the lead debacle led Pennsylvania's attorney general to bring 161 charges against the PWSA, the coalition demanded an investigation of Veolia too. The coalition held a "Not Another Flint" town hall to call attention to the lead failures and Veolia's alleged role. Our Water Campaign also protested outside the Peoples headquarters and put political pressure on the mayor and city council to oppose privatization. In response, the mayor signed a pledge not to sell the PWSA to a private company, and the city council refused to even hear Peoples' proposal.[17]

Our Water Campaign built on a growing global campaign by environmental justice groups to stop the privatization of domestic water systems. In shaping its arguments, the coalition worked actively with Corporate Accountability, a US nonprofit organization that works for public control of water systems around the world. Members of Our Water Campaign also attended a water summit in Abuja, Nigeria, focused on the threat of privatization to the human right to water. And the coalition drew from campaigns against Veolia in other parts of the world. Our Water Campaign's fight against the PWSA's privatization focused first and foremost on equity, transparency, and democratic responsibility.[18]

Because the coalition opposed private management as a matter of principle rather than pragmatism, its campaign did not lend itself to discussion or distinctions. Peoples' CEO, Morgan O'Brien, tried to engage coalition members in a discussion of his company's proposal but reportedly found them uninterested in dialogue. Our Water Campaign saw no difference between a local investor-owned utility like Peoples and a multinational like Veolia. The mayor also failed to convince privatization opponents that there was a meaningful distinction between full privatization, where a private company acquires and runs a water system, and the various forms of long-term management contracts, where a private company might design and build a new facility and then manage it for forty years before turning it over to the city. According to Our Water Campaign, all forms of "privatization" are bad.[19]

The PWSA today remains a public agency and seems finally to be succeeding. It has fixed its billing problems. It has replaced almost 59 miles of lead service lines. Most importantly, it is finally investing in new infrastructure. Remedying the PWSA's infrastructure problems, however, will not be cheap. In its 2021 rate proceeding, the PWSA sought a 15 percent rate increase over two years from the Pennsylvania Public Utility Commission (which helps oversee the PWSA), plus a new stormwater fee. The Pennsylvania Public Utility Commission ultimately cut the rate increase to 9 percent. Some experts project that the PWSA's monthly bill by 2040 will be 150 to 250 percent higher than it was when Veolia's contract ended. To help poorer customers, however, the PWSA has begun a financial assistance program.[20]

As this chapter will explore, private companies can provide valuable water-supply services, including expertise and insight for struggling public water systems. Both US Water and Veolia recommended changes that improved the PWSA's performance in important areas of operation, and Veolia helped improve the PWSA's financial position. But as the PWSA's story shows, private water companies are not a panacea.

Private water companies also are facing increasing headwinds in many cities, no matter what value they might bring to water supply systems. Some opponents worry that, motivated by profits, private water suppliers will cut corners on service, focus on wealthier customers, and dramatically increase rates. Other opponents worry that private operation and management will reduce water suppliers' accountability to the public. The acknowledgment that water is a human right strengthens both sets of concern. Opposition to private involvement is transforming from pragmatic, localized debates over the best way to supply water to local communities into a global movement focused on broader issues of equity and social justice.[21]

A HISTORY OF PRIVATE WATER COMPANIES

Studies disagree on the number of privatized water systems globally and in the United States. Data is poor for many parts of the world, and studies use different definitions of privatization. Globally, however, about 1.1 billion

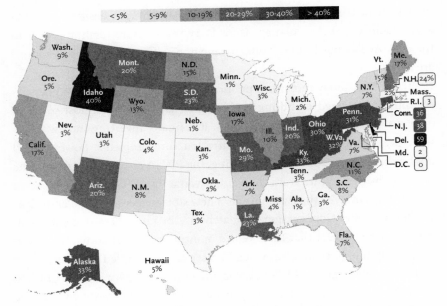

Figure 3.1 Population Served by Private Water Systems (excludes federal and tribal ownership). As of June 2017. Sources: Data from the US Environmental Protection Agency, Safe Drinking Water Information System; Elizabeth Douglass, "Towns Sell their Public Water System—And Often Regret It," Inquire-First and McGraw Center for Business Journalism, 2017; Danielle Cervantes, InquireFirst.

people (or 14 percent of the world population) receive water from a supply system that is either managed or owned by a private company. The extent of privatization varies widely from country to country: private companies supply all domestic water in England and Wales, but little or none in most countries.[22]

In the United States, private companies supply at least 12 percent, and perhaps as much as 18 percent, of domestic water. As is the case internationally, the percentage of the population served by private companies varies significantly from state to state. Private companies, which are often small, make up a much higher percentage of water suppliers than of water supplies. Nineteen states have more private than public water suppliers, but private companies provide water for a majority of the population in only one state.[23]

These numbers look vastly different from those of other utility sectors, where large private companies dominate over smaller public entities. In electricity, for example, a relatively small number of investor-owned utilities supply 72 percent of the US population. In natural gas, municipal suppliers far outnumber other providers but meet less than 3 percent of national needs. Private companies also dominate telephone service and control virtually the entire broadband market. The dominance of public water suppliers is thus an outlier and calls for a brief history lesson.[24]

Private involvement in the supply of domestic drinking water has waxed and waned over time. Prior to the eighteenth century, most US residents were rural and obtained their water from local rivers, shallow domestic wells, or cisterns in which they captured rainwater. Cities often constructed public wells from which their denizens could obtain water, but the water was typically contaminated and residents had to carry the water from the wells to their homes. Richer urban residents sometimes purchased cleaner water from landowners outside town who marketed water from the springs or wells on their properties. Other private entrepreneurs collected and delivered this water directly to urban residents for a charge.[25]

As cities grew in number and size in the late eighteenth century, private water companies sprang up to meet the need. In the United States, water companies constituted 10 percent of all corporations formed in the 1790s. In 1799, Aaron Burr and Alexander Hamilton briefly joined forces to create the Manhattan Company (now JPMorgan Chase & Co.) to furnish "pure and wholesome water sufficient for the use of all citizens dwelling" in New York City. While the city could have built its own water works, Burr and Hamilton argued that their private company would have better capital access and allow the city to use its limited revenues on other important matters. Supported by similar arguments, private water suppliers proliferated and expanded late into the nineteenth century in both the United States and Europe. By 1850, private companies ran 50 of the 83 water supply systems in the United States. In Europe, the Compagnie Générale des Eaux (now Veolia) formed in 1853 to furnish water to Lyon, France; by the end of the century it was providing water to Constantinople, Paris, and Venice.[26]

While the number and size of private companies continued to grow, a new set of concerns led a growing set of cities to create their own water systems or to "municipalize" privately run systems. As doctors learned more about the linkage between contaminated water and diseases such as typhoid, some cities grew worried that private companies might not ensure adequate water quality. As one local reformer argued, municipal governments should generally own and operate water supplies for the same reason that police and fire protection are public. "We will entrust our light, heat and transportation, but not our life, to the mercies of money-making concerns."[27]

Cities also began to question whether private companies might subvert the broader public interest. Private companies had an incentive to maximize profit and reduce costs. Because water was a natural monopoly, many companies could raise their rates without fear of losing customers. Private water companies could also increase their profits by focusing on the wealthier parts of a town and by underinvesting in system growth. Private companies also had an incentive to cut corners, reducing the quality of service. The Manhattan Company had proven an unfortunate illustration of private companies' self-interest. Rather than transporting water from distant rivers, the company drew primarily from polluted local wells, and it resisted laying more than the bare minimum of pipes.[28]

Rapidly expanding cities with dreams of further growth also wanted massive new import projects that would ensure sufficient water for their future citizens. Denver wanted to tap water from the other side of the Continental Divide; Los Angeles set its eyes on water in the eastern Sierra mountains; New York initially turned to the Croton. Few private businesses, however, were willing to risk their capital on expensive water projects for which future customers might not materialize. Many of the projects that cities contemplated also would require far more capital than most private companies could raise. Cities therefore often decided to build and run their own water systems using public bonds. Courts in the West gave public systems a further boost by ruling that cities, under a "growing cities" doctrine, could appropriate water before they had an actual need for it. Private appropriators, by contrast, had to wait until they had a current need.[29]

Municipalization of drinking water also had a political side. Progressive politicians at the turn of the twentieth century argued that democratic ownership would rid water systems of the type of corruption and monopoly behavior that plagued railroads, oil production, and other major industries at the time. "Municipal socialists" believed that the supply and distribution of basic human needs such as water should always be in the hands of the people.[30]

For all these reasons, most cities were running their own municipal water systems by the middle of the twentieth century. Many had publicly run their own systems for decades. In the 1870s, the number of publicly owned systems in the United States surpassed the number of privately run systems for the first time. By 1930, private companies owned only around 30 percent of piped water systems, and these systems on average served fewer customers than public systems. The City of Baltimore purchased the Baltimore Water Company in 1854; Los Angeles took over the Los Angeles City Water Company in 1902; San Francisco replaced the Spring Valley Water Company in 1930.[31]

The pendulum seemed ready to swing back toward private ownership and management in the late twentieth century. The rise of neoliberal economics in the 1970s and 1980s renewed calls for the private management of public services, including water. Public entities, like Pittsburgh's water agency, were often not providing the quality of water and service that municipalization had promised. Many economists attributed the deficiency to governmental mismanagement. In their view, governments were inherently less efficient and less interested in ultimate consumer satisfaction than private businesses were. Politicians sought to advance powerful constituencies, such as labor unions, and were readily subject to bribery and corruption. Private companies, by contrast, competed through performance. Even natural monopolies like private investor–owned water utilities needed to perform well if they were interested in expanding to new regions.[32]

This neoliberal view found a foothold with the two main international financial institutions, the World Bank and International Monetary Fund. These institutions had previously lent money to local public corporations and other parastatal units for large urban water and sanitation projects. Many of these projects ended up as failures. While multiple factors undermined success, corruption and inefficiencies were frequent contributors. Beginning in the 1990s, international financial institutions therefore began to encourage governments that were seeking funds for new or expanded water systems to privatize those systems.[33]

The privatization movement achieved its greatest degree of success in England and Wales. England's water supply system was largely public and highly fragmented at the end of World War II; in 1945, 1,186 systems, virtually all public, supplied the nation's water. To promote efficiency in 1973, the Conservative government reduced the number of suppliers to ten large governmental water authorities. Fifteen years later, Prime Minister Margaret Thatcher privatized the water authorities, culminating an era in which Thatcher privatized British Telecom, British Airways, and almost forty other government-owned businesses. The governmental water authorities faced both funding constraints and water quality problems, which Thatcher argued private enterprise could better address. England and Wales are still fully private today. Under a 2014 Conservative reform, the private water companies can now market water outside their traditional territories to non-household water consumers, allowing those consumers to choose among the providers.[34]

TYPES OF PRIVATE INVOLVEMENT

Although frequently lumped together under the simple label of privatization, private involvement has taken on a variety of different forms, as shown in Figure 3.2. In the purest, most complete form of privatization, municipalities sell or lease their water supply systems to private companies, which then furnish water to the local population either as an investor-owned public utility or under municipal contract. In the 1990s, for example, the American Water Works Company purchased the water system of Howell Township, New Jersey, which services 16,000 customers, for $35 million, while the

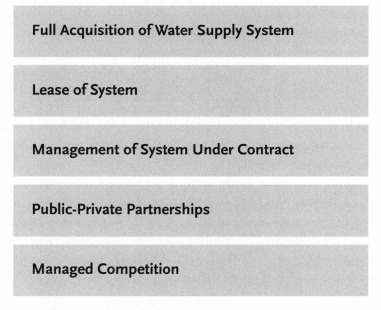

Figure 3.2 Types of Water Privatization. Source: author.

California Water Service Company agreed to a fifteen-year lease of the water system of Hawthorne, California, serving 74,000 customers, for $100,000 in annual lease payments and a $6.5 million upfront bonus. Both companies continue to operate the systems today with general customer satisfaction.[35]

Far more common than acquisitions or leases, even in the late-twentieth-century heyday of privatization, are management contracts in which a private company agrees to operate, manage, and maintain a city's water supply system for a fixed period, typically ranging up to twenty years. Under an operations and management (O&M) contract, the city continues to own the system but turns management over to a private company. In the most prominent private takeover of a public water system in the 1990s, United Water Services (now part of Veolia) contracted to operate the entire water supply system of Atlanta, Georgia, for an annual fee of $21.4 million. The Atlanta O&M contract was the largest US agreement ever and at the time was highly touted as a model by which cities could save money. The Atlanta contract lasted less than five years, with Atlanta terminating the agreement over dissatisfaction with both service and savings. Other cities, such as Buffalo, New York, and Jersey City, New Jersey, entered more successful O&M contracts that they have subsequently renewed.[36]

In more limited public-private partnerships (PPPs), private companies contract to manage only parts of a city's water system or to design, build, operate, and/or finance new infrastructure. United Water, for example, contracted to manage the Southeast Water Purification Plant for Houston, Texas, which continues to contract with a variety of private businesses for the management of individual parts of its water system. US Filter (now also part of Veolia) agreed to design, build, finance, and operate a large water reclamation plant for Honolulu, Hawaii, along with a fifteen-mile distribution system, which continues to be the biggest water recycling facility in Hawaii. Because cities often use PPPs to access private financing for new infrastructure, Chapter 8 will examine them in more detail.[37]

Interest in these forms of privatization skyrocketed in the 1990s and early 2000s. In one survey in the late 1990s of the largest one hundred metropolitan governments in the United States, almost a third reported they were considering enlisting private companies to help manage some or all of their water supply infrastructure and services. These large cities were overwhelmingly interested in management contracts or PPPs. Only three

(Stockton, Minneapolis–St. Paul, and San Diego) expressed an interest in selling or leasing their systems. None ultimately did.[38]

A few cities also experimented with "managed competition" in which private companies competed directly with public agencies to manage and operate the city's water system. The public agencies, which enjoyed tax exemptions and other public benefits and did not have to return a profit, often won, but the competition helped drive the public agencies to look for new efficiencies. The management department of Charlotte, North Carolina, for example, beat out several private companies for the right to operate and manage the city's wastewater and water-supply systems in a competition the city predicted would save ratepayers $4.2 million.[39]

Governmental and public attitudes toward private ownership and management appear to be pivoting again in recent years. Cities throughout the world continue to bring in private companies to help manage their water supplies and occasionally take over their systems. Interest in privatization, however, peaked nationally in the early 2000s. A growing number of cities are instead looking at municipalizing or, where the system was previously public, "remunicipalizing" their water systems. In the first two decades of this century, over 250 cities in almost forty nations municipalized their water systems; in total, about a million customers were involved in these switches from private to public suppliers. Interest in municipalization has been strongest in the United States and France. Over sixty US cities municipalized their water systems from 2000 to 2020, although the overall percentage of the American public served by private companies appears to have remained relatively stable since the 1990s.[40]

REASONS FOR PRIVATIZATION

A major question in privatization and municipalization debates has been, "What, if anything, do private companies bring to the table?" At first glance, drinking water systems are not an obvious focus for private companies. After all, public agencies start with several cost advantages over businesses. Public entities do not need to earn a profit for their shareholders. They do not need to pay property taxes. They can issue tax-exempt bonds at lower interest rates (although bonds issued by investor-owned utilities are typically exempt from taxes too). Municipal management also reduces transaction costs. Cities that wish to pursue privatization must solicit and evaluate private bids and negotiate an acceptable contract. They then must police the performance of the private company. Any advantages that a private business brings to the table must outweigh the benefits of full municipal control.[41]

Proponents of private ownership and management often claim that businesses, driven by the rigor of the market, provide greater cost efficiency. Dozens of studies over the last two decades have undermined this claim. Some studies have found public entities more efficient, some that private companies are more efficient, but the majority have concluded that there is no material difference in managerial efficiency between municipal and private water suppliers. Legal rules and regulations that restrict public managers may sometimes give private companies a cost edge. Private companies, for example, may be able to hire non-union labor, fire unproductive employees, avoid highly regimented purchase regimes, or otherwise ignore costly public requirements. This advantage, however, has a flip side. Opponents often criticize private businesses because they hire non-union labor and lay off employees. Whether the ability to escape governmental restrictions is good or bad depends on what one thinks of the restriction.[42]

Businesses can also provide access to private capital. As the Pittsburgh case study illustrates, many cities need substantial amounts of capital to meet their water systems' growing infrastructure needs. As described in Chapter 1, water infrastructure is aging and needs replacement, while ever more rigorous standards under the US Clean Water Act and Safe Drinking Water Act require the installation of new infrastructure. Driven by public demand for low water rates, however, a significant percentage of cities have failed to set aside the funds needed to maintain and replace their water infrastructure. And until Congress passed the 2021 Bipartisan Infrastructure Law, available state and federal funding for water infrastructure had been declining.[43]

The only long-term solution to the increasing infrastructure needs is to raise water rates or taxes. Water managers must pay to replace and maintain needed infrastructure, and either customers or taxpayers must pay for that cost. Private businesses, however, can provide municipal water systems with the immediate financing they need to clear their backlog. In many cases, cities can raise the needed capital themselves by issuing tax-free municipal bonds. In other cases, however, cities may face municipal debt limitations or poor credit ratings that prevent them from turning to municipal bonds.

Where this is the case, private companies can provide private funding that municipalities would be unable otherwise to tap.[44]

Cities also have sometimes turned to privatization as a means of funding other municipal needs such as education or health care. Water supply systems are valuable assets, and cities can raise immediate cash by selling them to investor-owned utilities. Private companies are also often willing to pay upfront bonuses, or make periodic payments, to cities for leases or long-term management agreements. Not surprisingly, cities with significant unmet financial needs have often found such payments irresistible. But such payments almost always come at an ultimate cost to the water system or ratepayers.[45]

Business can also help cities overcome problems that stem from the excessive fragmentation in US domestic water systems. As discussed in the introduction, there are over 150,000 separate water systems in the United States, more than the combined total of public elementary, middle, secondary, and postsecondary schools. Over 80 percent of these systems serve fewer than 500 people; an additional 15 percent serve between 501 and 3,300 customers (see Figure I, 1 at page 10 of the introduction). These systems often cannot buy or contract for supplies and services at an economically efficient scale and do not enjoy the expertise on their staff needed to use increasingly sophisticated technology or meet progressively more rigorous and detailed environmental and other regulatory standards.[46]

Private businesses can help mitigate these problems. By running or managing multiple water systems in a region, private companies can achieve economies of scale unattainable by the individual systems. Large private water companies also can provide the expertise needed to manage smaller water systems and identify new innovations that can help improve service. Several studies have found that private utilities suffer fewer violations of the Safe Drinking Water Act than public agencies do. While cities once municipalized water systems out of health concerns, similar concerns may lead them today to turn to private companies for the companies' needed water-quality expertise. Because the lead disaster in Flint, Michigan, increased attention to water quality standards, it also at least temporarily heightened interest in privatization.[47]

Small municipal water systems often have other options for addressing the problems of fragmentation. As discussed in Chapter 9, such systems can turn to consultants for needed expertise. In many parts of the country, local water systems have also formed consortiums to jointly negotiate contracts and buy in bulk. Other states and regions have developed cooperative purchasing agreements in which small water systems can piggyback on larger systems' purchasing contracts. Small, fragmented water systems also can consolidate into a single, larger system or create an umbrella water agency to address regional needs. In many cases, however, private ownership or management can provide the simplest, least expensive, and most effective solution to fragmentation.[48]

Finally, private businesses can offer municipalities a means to transfer and spread risk. Municipal water systems bear multiple financial risks such as cost overruns, new regulatory requirements, and emergencies. Private water contractors may be willing to assume those risks, albeit for a financial premium—acting as an insurer. Large private companies also can sometimes spread such risks across multiple water systems. By accepting and spreading financial risks, private companies can enable more stable and predictable water rates. As discussed in Chapter 8, municipal water systems also may be able to transfer infrastructure risks to the private sector through various financing mechanisms.[49]

OPPOSITION TO PRIVATE SUPPLIERS

Market fears and a belief in direct democratic control of water have fed increasing political opposition to private ownership and management. There is empirical reason, as noted, to be skeptical of some of the arguments for market superiority such as greater managerial efficiency. As discussed below, privatization also appears to lead in many cases to higher water rates. Concern has also grown in recent years about public accountability. Civil rights and environmental justice groups have often led recent fights against privatization and in favor of municipalization. Bred on social justice issues, these groups are inherently skeptical of corporations, market incentives, and any claim that markets can help solve social issues. Opponents of greater private involvement see corporations and markets as the cause of social injustices, not part of the solution.[50]

Virtually all private water companies are for-profit corporations. A few are mutual companies in which the customers are the shareholders. None to date is a nonprofit or a B Corporation (a for-profit corporation certified for its social and environmental performance and focused on benefiting the social good—hence the B in the name). Private for-profit water companies have a fiduciary duty to their shareholders to return a profit and promote the long-term value of the corporation. This does not mean, as some have argued, that the companies must or will ignore the interests of non-shareholders. Indeed, private water companies will be unsuccessful if they ultimately do not meet the needs of their customers. To remain in business, private companies also must carefully consider the interests of their employees and suppliers—and even the broader community and environment in which they operate.[51]

Private water companies, as already noted, start at a financial disadvantage to public water suppliers. Unlike most public suppliers, for example, private companies do not enjoy tax exemptions and cannot use property taxes to subsidize their water rates. Private companies also must return a profit to their shareholders. Unless private companies are significantly more efficient than public suppliers, private water rates are therefore likely to be higher. And, in fact, recent studies of the water rates of investor-owned utilities and public water suppliers in the United States have found that private water suppliers on average charge higher rates (previous studies of water-rate differentials were more ambiguous). Higher water rates, in turn, can affect the affordability of water within a supplier's service area (although suppliers can address affordability through their rate structures or by adopting affordability programs).[52]

Because investor-owned water utilities are natural monopolies, public utility commissions (PUCs) regulate their rates in all but five states. PUCs, however, vary in their rate policies and in the rigor with which they investigate and control rates. While PUCs in some states, like California, are relatively strict, PUCs in other states, like New Jersey and Pennsylvania, are more supportive of the rate requests of private water suppliers. The water rate differential between private and public suppliers follows suit, with private water rates closer to public rates in states like California. Indeed, one recent study found that PUC rules in New Jersey and Pennsylvania resulted in an almost $90 higher annual average water bill.[53]

Privatization critics also worry that a private company's profit motivation will lead them to reduce service, inappropriately cut costs, or find other ways to maximize profit at the expense of the customers. PUCs again generally oversee private water suppliers' operating decisions. Any deficiency in a privately managed water system, however, is likely to confirm the market fears of privatization opponents, even if the private manager is not directly responsible for the problem. Unsurprisingly, cities typically municipalize water systems or terminate private management when problems arise that attract the public's attention. As stories of failed private involvement have spread in recent years, private water managers are often kept on an increasingly short leash.[54]

Opponents of private involvement also prefer governmental water suppliers because of the greater democratic control that public management offers. Customers who dislike the current performance of a public water supplier can apply direct democratic pressure to the board of directors, if the supplier has an elected board, or to the mayor or council members, if the supplier is a city or county unit. If necessary, residents can vote out incumbents and replace them with officials who promise to correct the problems. Social justice groups also have experience leading successful campaigns to change public policy but have found campaigns for corporate change both more costly and less successful, particularly where it is impossible, as with water, to boycott the company's product. The importance of direct democratic control is particularly important to social justice groups given that the human right to water is potentially at stake.[55]

Governments have mechanisms to control the behavior of private water companies. Where cities enter management contracts with private companies, they can structure the contract to both require and incentivize the companies to pursue particular social goals. When contractors prove unsatisfactory, cities can look for a replacement. As already noted, PUCs regulate the rates, investments, and policies of investor-owned water utilities in virtually every state. To opponents of private involvement, however, these mechanisms are not substitutes for direct democratic control. While customers and other stakeholders can try to influence contract terms, contract renegotiations, and PUC oversight, their influence is less direct and immediate than the democratic control they believe they can exercise over municipal managers.[56]

The increasing focus on issues of democracy and human rights has transformed protests over privatization from local disputes over the practical implications of private versus public management to a global social movement. While campaigns to defeat privatization proposals still sometimes focus on specific local issues, such as poor current service or strong opposition to rate increases, they are more likely to rely on broad political arguments and examples of unsuccessful privatizations elsewhere in the world. As in Pittsburgh, opposition increasingly involves coalitions of social groups and labor unions. National and international groups also frequently help shape local arguments. The emphasis on rights and democracy makes it harder for privatization proponents to counter the arguments of opponents or for the opponents to find room for compromise.[57]

THE PRIVATE WATER SECTOR

While increasing opposition to private water suppliers may be slowing the growth of private ownership and management, the business sector continues to expand. While exact data is scarce, the total number of private systems and management contracts have continued to increase in this century. O&M contracts appear to be growing the fastest, at a rate of slightly over 6 percent per annum. Cities also do not appear to be rushing to cancel private management agreements; indeed, the annual renewal rate for contracts is currently close to 100 percent.[58]

Investors also remain interested in private water suppliers, whose stock has proven a reliable if not exciting asset. Seemingly unconcerned by the growing global campaigns against water privatization and by periodic municipalizations, investment advisors predict that the market for safe and dependable drinking water will continue to grow with the world's population and that the revenue of private water suppliers will likely grow with it. The MSCI ACWI water utilities index, which tracks stock prices for large and mid-cap water utilities in twenty-three developed markets and twenty-five emerging markets, increased about 13 percent per annum from 1994 to April 2023 (significantly outperforming MSCI's overall global stock index, which rose only 7.61 percent per annum).[59]

Recent years have seen several global trends in private water suppliers. First, the private water supply sector is growing increasingly concentrated, although many private suppliers remain small. Both globally and domestically, increasing constraints on new privatization have made acquisitions and mergers critical to growth. Large multi-state and international companies are also better able to enter local markets if they have acquired and operate as locally established water providers. Expertise in new water technologies and services, including advanced water recycling, is also an increasingly important calling card for private water suppliers, encouraging the suppliers to acquire companies with emerging technological capabilities. Finally, the expanding social campaign against privatization gives an advantage to large companies with the political resources needed to respond to the attacks and lobby for supportive laws.[60]

Globally, the top ten water companies control about half of the private water market (with the top five controlling about 35 percent). Two French companies, Suez and Veolia (formerly Vivendi and Compagnie Générale des Eaux), dominated the global market for over a century. In 2021, a partial merger of the two companies further increased market concentration at the top. Not surprisingly, this increasing concentration has worried privatization opponents. According to one opponent, the Veolia-Suez merger sets "the stage for the monopolization of the water sector" and provides "more resources to influence governments."[61]

Second, water suppliers have become increasingly international, with China developing into a major player. By merging, Veolia and Suez hoped to better compete against the growing Chinese water sector. Prior to 1992, all water suppliers in China were state-owned enterprises. China subsequently opened its market to private companies backed by domestic and foreign investors. The resulting Chinese companies have grown rapidly in response to Chinese urbanization and are now expanding into both new Chinese regions and African and other foreign markets. In 2021, Chinese companies constituted three of the top five water companies in the world and thirteen of the top twenty. No American company placed in the top twenty, which also included companies from Brazil, India, the Philippines, and Spain, all of which have aggressively pursued privatization.[62]

In the United States, fourteen publicly traded corporations service customers in thirty-three states. Two are foreign (Suez and the Canadian Algonquin Power & Utilities Corporation). Consolidation is also on the rise domestically, as the major players acquire smaller companies and their water systems. From 2010 to 2020, twelve of the corporations acquired 353 smaller water utilities for approximately $5.8 billion. The merger of water, natural gas, and energy companies has also become a trend in recent years. Peoples Natural Gas, after failing to privatize the Pittsburgh Water and Sewage Authority, still fulfilled its vision of combining water and gas operations when Agua America acquired it in 2020 and merged its water and gas operations as Essential Utilities. Two of the largest private water utilities in the US also supply natural gas; four supply electricity.[63]

A NEED FOR ENHANCED BUSINESS BEHAVIOR

Private water suppliers will continue to play an important role in water management, both globally and in the United States, despite increased opposition to privatization. As explained earlier, private suppliers offer expertise and economies of scale to smaller communities, additional financing to communities with funding constraints, and risk reduction to systems seeking greater financial stability. To many cities, moreover, private suppliers may provide the easiest means to rectify a failing public system. While private companies are not inherently more efficient than governmental agencies, replacing public with private management often improves performance. Such pragmatic attractions are unlikely to fade.[64]

Opposition to the private ownership and management of water, however, reflects legitimate concerns over private companies' commitment and responsiveness to human and environmental rights. Private water suppliers can and must do more to address these concerns. As Chapter 11 will discuss, the responsibility to achieve and promote human and environmental rights in water rests with everyone involved in water management, not just governments. In some nations, rights violations may carry legal penalties. Even when they do not, corporations have a responsibility to avoid negatively impacting human rights and to cure adverse impacts related to their operations. Corporations also have a practical reason to ensure that their operations promote human and environmental rights. Unless corporations act, opposition to private involvement is likely to continue to grow and may pose significant obstacles to private water suppliers in the future.

Many private water suppliers have already announced an increased commitment to human and environmental rights. Several suppliers, for example, have explicitly recognized and endorsed the human right to water (which puts them ahead of most public water suppliers, as well as most states, the United States, and the many other nations that abstained from the U.N. vote to acknowledge the right). Many companies have adopted formal policies on social and environmental issues. Larger companies have adopted formal environmental, social, and governance (ESG) standards and policies and are tracking their performance through quantifiable measures. To obtain local public input, many companies also have created community advisory panels for each of their supply systems. Some companies also have created specific programs to advance human rights or environmental goals. A growing set of companies has established financial assistance programs for customers who cannot pay their water bills. Some have adopted programs to assist in ecological restoration of waterways in their communities.[65]

Private water suppliers, however, can and should do even more to enhance their ESG practices, including promotion of the human right to water. Only a few companies currently employ best practices. Even the formal ESG programs that exist often appear to be more showcases than an integrated part of the company's culture. ESG programs, for example, are often under the supervision of the company's communications or investor-relations officers, with little if any operational linkage. Only a few companies utilize outside advisory panels to help guide, nudge, and critique their ESG practices. Policy statements often reflect a conservative, uncreative view of how companies can help promote social and environmental goals through their operations.[66]

Private water suppliers should also consider how they might bring stronger advantages to water management in the future. As privatization and municipalization debates continue, cities are more likely to ask whether private companies bring sufficient added benefits to the table. Technological expertise and innovation could be one of those benefits. As explained in Chapter 7, integration of new technologies (from low-cost recycling to the use of artificial intelligence to diagnose and solve problems) will be increasingly valuable to the management of water supply systems. While many of the large international water businesses such as Veolia have long combined service and technology divisions (and the emerging Chinese companies are increasingly doing so), most American water suppliers have remained narrowly focused on service. By pursuing and integrating new technological advances into their businesses, American companies can better demonstrate their value. The trend toward greater consolidation, both geographically and across utilities, could also bolster the benefits that private companies bring to water supply systems by further improving their economies of scale and expertise.[67]

PUBLIC POLICY

Governmental policy can play several important roles in determining the role of private companies in the supply of domestic water. First, it can ensure that cities choose whether to privatize with their eyes wide open. In the

United States, most states subject privatization decisions to the same processes required for other major financial decisions: cities must engage in
transparent and competitive bidding processes and hold public hearings
before deciding to pursue full privatization or a management contract. Reflecting the greater implications of full privatization, a growing number of
states have imposed additional processes, substantive requirements, or other
constraints on sales and leases. New Jersey, for example, does not permit a
city to lease or sell its water system except where the public system suffers
from material deficiencies. Several states require that voters approve a lease
or sale if enough ratepayers request an election. Some states also require
public utility commissions or other state agencies to review and approve
a lease or sale. A handful of states regulate the terms of management contracts. State policies should ensure that governments carefully and openly
review privatization options without imposing unnecessary hurdles.[68]

Second, governmental policies also can influence how readily a city can
retake control of its water system. Management contracts generally dictate
when and how they can be terminated. Condemnation policies, however,
are critical when a city is considering municipalization of a private system.
When a private utility does not want to sell its system (and few utilities do),
the government's only option is typically to condemn the utility's system for
its fair market value. This ensures that cities can municipalize when they
believe that it is in the best interest of their residents, while protecting the
financial interest of the utility. In a handful of states, however, governments
cannot use their condemnation authority to municipalize a water system. In
other states, utilities can fight the condemnation in court on the ground that
it does not promote the public interest. State policies should again ensure
that decisions to municipalize are prudent and transparent but should avoid
imposing additional hurdles that are not required to protect the private
suppliers' investment. Even straightforward condemnation proceedings, although necessary to protect investment, can be difficult for cities to pursue
because of the time and administrative expense involved.[69]

Third, government policies can influence the economics of privatization
or municipalization. When a city is considering the sale of its water system,
the amount that an investor-owned utility can pay for the system is obviously a major consideration for both the city and utility. Water suppliers will
typically not pay more than a public utility commission will permit them
to include in their rate base. A commission's valuation rules are therefore

critically important, particularly where, as is often the case with older water systems, the book value of a system (its original cost minus depreciation) is significantly less than its replacement value. In most states, utilities must use the book value, reducing the financial viability of complete privatization. A handful of states, by contrast, have passed "fair market value" statutes that permit utilities to value the systems at the higher cost needed to replace the infrastructure. Not surprisingly, states that permit higher valuations have seen greater levels of privatization. When a city is considering whether to municipalize a system, how a court determines the value of a utility in a condemnation proceeding can similarly affect the city's decision.[70]

Finally, and perhaps most importantly, state public utility commissions can use their regulatory authority to enhance the performance of investor-owned utilities. As already noted, PUCs regulate utilities' rates and policies, reducing the risk that water utilities will abuse their natural monopolies by charging excessive water rates or pursuing actions that are contrary to the public interest. PUCs also can serve as a forum for bringing together private utilities and customers to discuss and negotiate areas of disagreement. They can encourage or require investor-owned utilities to adopt programs or policies that address public concerns such as affordability. PUCs, in short, can and should ensure that private water suppliers perform as well as, if not better than, public agencies. The case for complete privatization crucially depends on the performance of state PUCs.[71]

Effective PUC regulation may actually provide private companies with advantages over public suppliers. Public agencies work at a potential disadvantage: they must respond directly to the short-term interests of voters, even if that is inconsistent with the longer-term interest of a sustainable water system. As Pittsburgh's experience illustrates, voters often demand low rates, even if those rates are inadequate to maintain, replace, and upgrade important infrastructure. In this regard, the very democratic responsiveness that privatization opponents seek to promote can undermine sustainability and reliable service. Public utility commissions provide a level of insulation between voters and utilities that PUCs and private utilities can use to provide for less shortsighted and more sustainable water management that is still in the public interest. Partly for this reason, states have occasionally extended PUC oversight to the rates and policies of public agencies.[72]

In California, the PUC has allowed private water utilities to collect rates that have enabled them to stay ahead of deteriorating infrastructure, while protecting consumers against unjustified rates. For many years, the California PUC also required private water utilities to decouple their rates from consumption levels—a major step in encouraging utilities to promote conservation, but one seldom taken by public agencies. (When the PUC recently voted to abandon this program, the California legislature required them to reconsider.) The PUC has required water utilities to adopt inclining block rate structures under which low-income consumers pay less for their water and large consumers pay increasing rates the more water they use—another important conservation measure that California constitutional law has blocked many state agencies from pursuing. And the PUC actively considers affordability in its rate proceedings, leading private water utilities to develop innovative affordability programs.[73]

PUC policies and procedures, in short, are a critical determinant of the success or failure of privatization. If PUCs are insufficiently protective of the public interest, privatization can lead to excessive rates and poor service. On the flip side, however, PUCs can affirmatively strengthen the practices of private utilities and ensure that private water companies promote the public interest in the communities they serve.[74]

FOUR

Water Markets

Growing water scarcity will make water markets increasingly important. In most US states and most parts of the world, water is not tradable. In a small but growing number of regions, however, individuals and organizations can buy and sell water. If cities, farmers, or other water users do not have enough water, they can buy water from someone else. Water markets encourage conservation because water users can sell the conserved water. Markets also allow water allocations to adjust to changing economic and hydrological conditions. Studies have repeatedly found that water markets reduce the economic cost of droughts and other water shortages. Like privatization, however, water markets have attracted both suspicion and opposition. As illustrated by efforts to buy water from farmers in California's Imperial Valley, trading water also can be challenging.[1]

The Imperial Valley of California was once known as the Valley of the Dead. Nestled near the Colorado River in the state's southeastern corner, the Valley was a desert wasteland before the twentieth century. Imperial gets less than three inches of rain a year (a fifth of what Los Angeles receives and a small fraction of the 38-inch national average). In the summer, when temperatures exceed 100 degrees Fahrenheit, it never rains. The Valley is a natural habitat for desert tortoises, bighorn sheep, and flat-tail horned lizards—not most

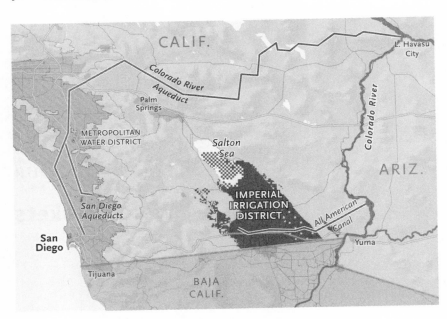

Figure 4.1 Southern California Water Agencies. Source: author.

humans. While several indigenous groups long survived and even thrived in the Valley, American and European settlers largely bypassed it until the late nineteenth century.[2]

Water from the Colorado River changed that. In 1901, a private company, the California Development Company, began to divert water from the Colorado River and import it into the Valley for agriculture. The California Development Company quickly went bankrupt, but in 1911, the newly formed Imperial Irrigation District (IID), a local public agency, took over. Today, the IID imports over 2.5 million acre-feet of water each year into the Valley, making it the largest water user in the Colorado River Basin. Ninety-eight percent of this water goes to irrigate about five hundred thousand acres of farmland that grow over $2 billion in crops.[3]

Some call this a success story of how the Imperial Valley has overcome its natural aridity. Others, however, see the Valley's use of so much water as inordinately wasteful. Agricultural and urban areas throughout Southern California, including major cities like Los Angeles and San Diego, receive Colorado River water. But the IID holds senior rights to about two-thirds of California's total entitlement of 4.4 million acre-feet of Colorado River water. Yet the Valley constitutes less than 8 percent of the land mass of Southern California and has a population of fewer than two hundred thousand people. Farmers use five to six acre-feet of water for every acre they plant, compared to an average agricultural water use in the western United States of about two acre-feet per acre. Much of the acreage grows low-value crops like alfalfa and other grasses, which pencil out financially for growers only because the IID charges farmers about $20 per acre-foot, dramatically less than water costs in many neighboring regions.[4]

Los Angeles, San Diego, and other major cities line the Southern California coast. And in the early 1980s, they faced a looming water shortage. Earlier in the century, they had formed a giant public agency, the Metropolitan Water District of Southern California (MWD), to help meet their water needs by importing water from two sources: Northern California and the Colorado River. The MWD's right to Colorado River water is junior to the rights of the IID and other neighboring agricultural districts; as a result, the MWD is the first to lose its water when Colorado River supplies drop. For years, the MWD had been able to take as much Colorado River water as it wanted because upstream states like Arizona were not taking all the water to which they were entitled. But in the early 1980s, an increase in upstream diversions placed the MWD's Colorado River water supplies in jeopardy. In response, the MWD began looking for ways to import more water from Northern California rather than the Colorado River. Such imports, however, threatened to harm salmon and other native fish species that inhabit the northern waterways. Shrinking Colorado River supplies, in short, led the MWD to look north—to the horror of environmental groups.[5]

One of those groups, the Environmental Defense Fund (EDF), proposed a novel market alternative. Rather than importing more water from the north, why didn't the MWD pay the IID for a share of its Colorado River rights? The IID and its farmers could use the money to conserve the water that the Southern California cities needed. Everyone would benefit—IID farmers, Southern California cities, and the environment. EDF estimated that the IID could save almost 450,000 acre-feet per year of Colorado River water through conservation without impairing the local agricultural economy. To EDF, markets provided a "win-win model" that could "make everyone better off."[6]

The idea went nowhere. Because the IID, not its farmers, owns the Valley's Colorado River rights, the IID had to approve any transfer. Even if the IID's farmers were happy to conserve water for a profit, they could not sell that water without the IID's permission. And the IID board, which Valley residents popularly elect, opposed a transfer. According to the board, the water belonged to the Valley and should remain in the Valley. Water should not just go to the highest bidder. Water markets were a bad idea, particularly if they led water to flow from rural regions like the Imperial Valley to big cities like Los Angeles and San Diego.[7]

Deprived of the opportunity to market their water, farmers in the Imperial Valley continued to use it in enormous volumes. Indeed, they used so much water that the wastewater began to flood other farmers' land. Agricultural wastewater in the Imperial Valley drains into a shallow and highly saline 300-square-mile lake known as the Salton Sea. For hundreds of years prior to agriculture's advent in the Imperial Valley, the Salton Sea was a dry salt bed. In 1905, Colorado River waters breached the head gate of the canal that brought river water into the Imperial Valley and began flooding into the Valley, creating the Salton Sea. The lake would have evaporated once the flooding stopped but for the agricultural wastewater that continued to feed the Salton Sea. At times, the lake even grew, threatening the land that bordered it.[8]

John Elmore owned some of that land. In 1980, Elmore took the unusual step of filing a complaint with the California State Water Resources Control Board, which regulates California water rights. Elmore claimed that the IID was wasting water to his detriment. The Board agreed. In a 1984 decision it ordered the IID to reduce its water use through conservation. In California and throughout the West, waste is illegal, and the state can order it curtailed. The IID appealed the Board's decision, threatening a long and contentious legal battle.[9]

The Board's decision revived EDF's idea of a voluntary water sale between the MWD and the IID. Buoyed by the Board's decision, the MWD offered to pay the IID $10 million in return for 100,000 acre-feet of Colorado River water each year for thirty-five years. The MWD's offer looked generous, particularly since the Board had ordered the IID to save that much water without any compensation. In 1985, however, the IID's board, by a 3–2 vote, rejected MWD's proposal. The IID ultimately agreed to the offer only after additional haggling over deal terms, a 1987 decision of the California Court of Appeal rejecting the IID's legal challenge to the Board's 1984 conservation order, and a new order by the Board requiring IID to conserve at least 100,000 acre-feet of water per year.[10]

Even with the conservation that came with the MWD-IID deal, IID farmers continued to use a lot of water for relatively low-value agriculture, attracting investors who spotted a potential arbitrage opportunity. In the early 1990s, Ed and Lee Bass, two members of a Texas family that had made billions of dollars in the oil industry, purchased thirty thousand acres in the Imperial Valley, making them the region's second-largest landowner. The brothers, who continued to farm the land under the moniker of Western Farms, saw an opportunity to meet the growing demand of Southern California coastal cities by conserving and selling water for a profit to the coastal region. They found a willing buyer in San Diego, which wanted to firm up and diversify its water supply and was willing to pay over $400 per acre-foot to lease up to 200,000 acre-feet of water (significantly more than Valley farmers paid for their water).[11]

To many economists, this proposed transaction demonstrated the market's ability to efficiently reallocate a scarce resource in a way that benefits all parties. Farmers would voluntarily conserve water currently used for relatively low-value crops and make a profit. Cities would receive the water needed to meet their growth. Water, in short, would move from a low-value use to a higher-value use, and all the market players would be better off. Yet multiple lawsuits and political controversy stood in the path of the transfer, which would take a decade to accomplish.[12]

Reaction in the Valley to a San Diego transfer was wildly mixed. While many farmers thought it was a good idea, other Valley residents feared that it would spell the Valley's doom. The Valley is highly reliant on agriculture, and some feared that farmers would sell their water and stop farming, drying up the land and the local economy. According to a local county supervisor, if you "tinker with water," you risk "losing it all." Or as one local resident put it, water transfers might leave "nothing left in this valley except a gas station and a Circle K near the freeway." Even some farmers were opposed to any further water transfers. In the words of one prominent farmer and market critic, water markets threatened the community's ability to "control our own destiny." As before, the IID had to approve any transfer, and IID board support remained uncertain.[13]

Other Colorado River users questioned whether the IID had the right to transfer conserved water to San Diego even if its board approved. Water rights are often far less clear than rights to a piece of land. The IID at the time did not own a specific quantity of Colorado River water but shared a right to 3.85 million acre-feet with two water agencies that serviced neighboring farm regions. When the IID started talking about transferring water to San Diego, one of those agencies claimed that any unused water belonged to it, not the IID. As noted earlier, moreover, no one has a right to "waste" water. To the MWD, the proposed transfer showed that the IID could get by with less water and therefore must have been wasting the water it now planned to conserve. Under western water law, any wasted water goes to other appropriators who need water. And MWD needed more water. According to the MWD's general manager, farmers in the IID should not "profit from reducing the amount of water they waste." Once Imperial farmers made clear that they could get by with less water, in short, other claimants to the unused water came out of the woodwork.[14]

Another problem was how to get the Colorado River water to San Diego. The Laguna Mountains separate the Valley from San Diego and made it difficult and expensive to build and operate a pipeline between buyer and seller. The Colorado River Aqueduct, however, already carried water from upstream on the Colorado River to the MWD's service area, where the MWD could easily transport the water to San Diego. Unfortunately, the MWD, which owned the Aqueduct, opposed the transfer. As just noted, the MWD believed that it was the rightful owner of any unused water. San Diego was also a MWD customer and would buy less water from the MWD if it could buy water from the IID. California had a "wheeling statute" that required aqueduct owners to allow water marketers to use any available capacity, but the MWD demanded a high price for the use of its aqueduct. San Diego challenged the MWD's rate in court and, after multiple rulings and help from the state, the parties finally settled on a price that kept the deal alive.[15]

The Salton Sea loomed as another issue. Recall that the Salton Sea today consists of runoff from Imperial farm fields. Less agricultural water in the Valley therefore means less inflow to the Sea. Deprived of runoff, the Sea will shrink, threatening both the environment and people. The Sea has become an important habitat for migrating birds. The soil underneath the Sea, moreover, is laced with selenium and other hazardous substances. If the Sea shrinks, winds could pick up the dried soil and blow it into residential areas, threatening human health. California law prohibits water transfers that will unreasonably harm the environment.[16]

The federal and state governments ultimately needed to step in to solve these various challenges and push the IID–San Diego transfer over the finish line. The federal government, which manages water deliveries in the lower Colorado River, convened all the local water agencies and negotiated a Quantification Settlement Agreement (QSA) in which the agencies resolved their competing claims to Colorado River water and agreed to the transfer. As part of the QSA, California also offered to develop and largely fund a solution to a shrinking Salton Sea. When the IID board still wavered on whether to sign the QSA, the federal government threatened to unilaterally reduce the IID's Colorado River deliveries on the ground that the IID was still wasting water. After all parties approved the QSA, multiple parties, including the Imperial County Board of Supervisors, sued to invalidate it, delaying the transfer by yet another two years.[17]

San Diego today imports 200,000 acre-feet of water from the IID, which conserves the water through a combination of improvements to district infrastructure and a fund that pays local farmers to conserve water on their lands. The Imperial Valley's local agricultural economy is still thriving on irrigated alfalfa and other crops, despite the earlier concerns about the transfer's impact. In 1997, long before the QSA signing, the Bass brothers sold their land for a profit to US Filter Corporation (later absorbed into Siemens). The IID bought the same land to fallow as part of the San Diego water transfer but ultimately sold off all but 18,000 acres. California unfortunately is still figuring out exactly what to do about the Salton Sea. The current plan is to develop a complex of smaller lakes that will provide bird habitat and mitigate health risks. California has estimated that just Phase 1 of the restoration project will cost over $400 million.[18]

The Imperial Valley meanwhile is back in the news again for its sizable water holdings. Even after the water transfer to San Diego, the IID still provides over 2.5 million acre-feet of water annually to its farmers. Because of a multi-decade drought in the southwest US, however, there is not enough water in the Colorado River in most years to meet all needs in the region. As explained in Chapter 1, Colorado River users have therefore been drawing down water previously stored in the Colorado River's major reservoirs, Lakes Mead and Powell. Both reservoirs are now at less than 30 percent capacity. To balance supply and demand, the federal government in 2022 announced that water users together must reduce their annual withdrawals of Colorado River water by two to four million acre-feet. Many water officials, particularly from outside California, see the IID as an obvious place to cut water use. Paying Imperial farmers to reduce their water use would be an effective strategy, just as it was in making water available for San Diego.[19]

The National Research Council once said that transferring water out of the IID was "an 'easy' case" for water markets, perhaps proving that water transfers are anything but easy. As the IID-San Diego transfer illustrates, water transfers often confront multiple hurdles—even when the government permits water markets and, as California does, encourages them. To transfer water rights, the holder typically must obtain multiple authorizations, each of which raises risks, takes time, costs money, and invites lawsuits. In many cases, water transfers can also impact local communities or the environment, generating political opposition. Water markets also often need conveyance facilities to transport water from buyer to seller, but the holders of these facilities, if the facilities even exist, may not want others to use them or may demand monopolistic prices. As a result, large transfers can often resemble complex international negotiations more than simple buyer-seller trades.[20]

THE CONDITIONS NEEDED FOR WATER MARKETS

Formal water markets exist in only a few regions and countries. Australia, Chile, China, South Africa, the western United States, and limited parts of Europe (England, Italy, and Spain) have formal water markets. Informal markets, in which water users trade water outside of formal governmental frameworks, exist in a larger set of countries, including parts of both India and Pakistan, but are still limited geographically. Governments also sometimes create temporary trading programs in response to droughts or other extraordinary water shortages but do not allow longer-term trading.[21]

Several factors determine the viability of formal water markets in a region. To begin, markets make sense only in areas with high water demand and limited availability. If water is plentiful, water users do not need markets because they can simply take whatever they need. And in areas of low demand, markets may not justify their administrative cost. Formal water markets therefore exist primarily in regions of the world with significant agricultural demand and Mediterranean climates that suffer from low summer precipitation and frequent droughts. There are no water markets in the Amazon, nor in the UAE.[22]

Figure 4.2 Water Rights Doctrines in the United States. Source: author.

Where water is scarce, regions may still prefer for policy reasons to allocate water rights by administrative or judicial fiat rather than by markets. The eastern United States, for example, has frequently eschewed water markets even in the face of increasing scarcity. The explanation why requires a bit of water-law history.

As shown in Figure 4.2, states allocate surface water by either the "riparian doctrine" or the "prior appropriation doctrine." Eastern states follow the riparian doctrine, which historically allocated water only to those who own land through which a river flows ("riparians") and divided water among riparians based on how much water each riparian "reasonably" needed. Western states instead follow the prior appropriation doctrine, which allows anyone to divert water from a river and awards rights based on priority of diversion—a "first-come, first-served" system.

Water markets were impossible under the riparian doctrine that eastern states originally adopted because no one had a right to a fixed quantity of water, so there was nothing to trade. If water were insufficient to meet all needs, riparians went to court, where a judge decided how much water each should reasonably receive. If conditions changed, the amount of water to which each riparian was entitled could also change. This approach to allocating water was expensive and inefficient, and it provided riparians with little predictability or security. But judicially administered riparianism worked reasonably well so long as water was abundant and conflicts over water were therefore unusual.[23]

As water has become scarcer in the East in recent decades, most eastern states have moved to permit systems, known as "regulated riparianism," in which riparians receive long-term water permits to a fixed amount of water based on an administrative agency's determination of how much they "reasonably" need (providing greater security and reducing expense); in some cases, non-riparians also can receive water permits (increasing efficiency). Trading could further improve these systems' efficiency. A permit holder who needed more water could buy water from another permit holder. Yet eastern states such as Florida and Georgia have rejected water markets, convinced that the government, not markets, should decide how much each person uses based on the riparian doctrine's concept of reasonableness.[24]

Formal water markets also require private water rights that are secure, certain, and enforceable. Under the prior appropriation doctrine, most water users receive enforceable permits to fixed quantities of water, enabling market trade. Some eastern states permit water trading at least on paper, but the inherent uncertainty and insecurity of riparian rights, even under regulated riparianism, has undercut the development of markets. Many countries do not recognize private water rights at all but allocate water instead by governmental fiat. Even where private water rights exist, countries often do not carefully monitor diversions, so farmers or others needing extra water simply steal it. In these settings, formal water markets are neither feasible nor effective.[25]

Conveyance availability also can make a difference to the viability of water markets. As the IID–San Diego transfer illustrates, transfers require a way to get water from seller to buyer. California, which has the largest water market in the United States, benefits from multiple aqueducts and canals that crisscross the state. By contrast, there is not much of a market for water in the northern Rockies because, while water is relatively inexpensive, moving it to major metropolitan or agricultural areas with water shortages would be costly and difficult. You could transport the water by truck, but that would be prohibitively expensive. Water is heavy.[26]

Opportunities exist to develop water markets in new regions. Dozens of countries that suffer from water scarcity have laws in place that could support water trading, yet do not have formal markets of any magnitude—including western Canada, India, Mexico, and Peru. Building markets in new regions will often require revisions to water laws and institutions. Water rights must be clear and secure, oversight and approval processes must be streamlined, and conveyance facilities freed for use. As scarcity increases, however, the pressure for such reforms will grow, and new markets are likely to arise.

THE BENEFITS OF WATER MARKETS

Water markets are invaluable when the enabling conditions exist. Markets help ensure that water is put to its highest economic use, maximizing water's value to the economy. The western United States, as noted, allocates water under a "prior appropriation" system of first come, first served. The first person to start diverting water from a stream gets the best right; latecomers may get nothing. The first farm to the stream, however, does not always have the most productive use for the water. And even if a farm had the highest economic use for water in 1870, that farm probably does not have the most productive use today. Conditions change, and water allocations should change in response. In the western United States, water markets allow newcomers with more valuable economic uses to purchase appropriative water rights from existing users. A study of New Mexico's Rio Grande Valley showed that water markets created significant economic value for the local economy by allowing water to flow from lower-value to higher-value crops.[27]

In the same manner, water markets help reduce the societal cost of new or sudden shortages. Imagine that a drought hits Colorado. Under the prior appropriation doctrine, senior appropriators will get their water before juniors. The most senior users may get 100 percent of their rights, while juniors get nothing. But the juniors may need water to ensure that their new fruit trees survive, while the seniors may not need all their water to irrigate their tomatoes. Markets allow the juniors to buy water from the seniors, minimizing the economic loss of the drought. One recent study calculated that water markets can potentially reduce the impact of droughts on the farm economy of California's Central Valley by almost 4.5 percent—or over $360 million per year.[28]

For this reason, water markets often emerge when water supplies shrink. Parts of the West, for example, have begun to protect groundwater aquifers against overdraft by limiting total water withdrawals. To minimize the economic disruption of the new restrictions, many regions couple the pumping reductions with groundwater markets that can help make sure that the limited groundwater goes to the economically most valuable uses. Indeed, farmland can be even more valuable when groundwater use is regulated and coupled with markets than when groundwater pumping is unrestricted.[29]

As the Imperial Valley case study illustrates, water markets also can encourage water conservation. As water grows scarcer, conservation becomes increasingly important. While some water users will voluntarily conserve because of the societal benefits, economic incentives are far more powerful. If farmers know that they can sell the water that they save, they are far more likely to conserve. Many water users also cannot afford to voluntarily invest in the infrastructure, like drip irrigation or smart irrigation controllers, or other improvements, such as field leveling, needed to reduce their water use. Markets can provide such users with the funding needed to invest in conservation.[30]

Water markets also can help the environment by reducing pressure on the water remaining in a region's streams and lakes. EDF urged the MWD to purchase water from the Imperial Valley with exactly this benefit in mind. Rather than exporting more water from Northern California's streams and placing increased stress on native fish species, the MWD could encourage conservation in the Imperial Valley and purchase the resulting water.[31]

MARKET OPPOSITION

Despite these benefits, water markets have long been controversial. Elwood Mead was one of the most consequential water engineers of the nineteenth century. Mead designed Wyoming's prior appropriation system, headed the US Bureau of Reclamation, helped shape Australia's water supply scheme, and even assisted Zionists in developing irrigation plans for Palestine. He also rabidly opposed water markets. Mead began with a very practical concern. If people can market water rights, they have an incentive to appropriate or claim as much as possible so they can later sell the water they do not need. And a century ago, water administrators could not readily police such speculatively large appropriations. Mead also worried that someone might try to monopolize local water supplies. According to Mead, the "growth and danger of monopolies in oil, copper, coal, and iron afford a warning of the greater danger of permitting monopolies in water."[32]

In Mead's view, water was free to appropriators in the West because water, like air and sunshine, are "gifts from God." Mead did not believe that appropriators should be able to turn around and sell that water for a profit. "If water is to be . . . bartered and sold then the public should not give streams away," Mead wrote. "Instead, the government itself should auction them off to the highest bidder." To Mead, moreover, water was not a commodity. Water resources "belong to the people, and ought forever to be kept as public property for the benefit of all who use them, and for them alone, such use to be under public supervision and control."[33]

Mead's views convinced Wyoming to severely limit water markets. Wyoming allowed appropriators to sell their water rights, but if you transferred your right, it lost all seniority—reducing water transfers to the equivalent of a new appropriation and depriving transfers of virtually all value. Other early western legislatures were similarly hostile to water markets. Early in the twentieth century, most western states either banned or severely restricted water transfers. Only a few, like California and Colorado, permitted them.[34]

Water users' need for flexibility slowly eroded western opposition to water markets. Today, all western states permit some form of water marketing. As Figure 4.3 illustrates, substantial water markets have arisen throughout much of the West. Markets, not surprisingly, tend to be larger and more active in those areas with the greatest imbalance between supply and demand, such as the Central Valley of California and the front range of Colorado. California trades the highest volume of water, while Colorado has the highest number of trades per year.[35]

Mead's concerns, however, continue to haunt water markets. Worried that water markets might attract speculators who will hoard or monopolize water rights, all western states require appropriators to have reasonable and beneficial uses for the water that they acquire. Under what the Colorado Supreme Court has labeled the "anti-speculation doctrine," no one can appropriate water purely for investment. You must have a use for the water. Any other rule, according to the courts, "would encourage those with vast monetary resources to monopolize, for personal profit rather than for beneficial use, whatever unappropriated water remains." The anti-speculation doctrine does not prevent someone from investing in water, but it typically requires that they acquire both water and the land on which to use the water—increasing the cost and complexity of water investments.[36]

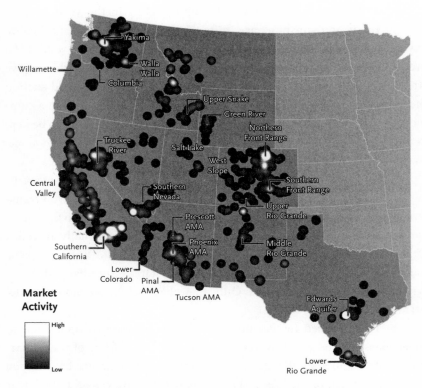

Figure 4.3 Water Market Activity. Source: WaterlitixTM Water Right Transactions Database (2022), owned and maintained by WestWater Research LLC.

The western United States is unique among major marketing regions in tying water to land in this fashion. To promote more robust water markets, Australia unbundled water and land in 1994; investors can now own water rights separately from any land or beneficial use. The result is an active water market where water investors with no related land holdings consummate 15 percent or more of all trades. Studies have discovered no evidence of hoarding or other problems under this approach. In 2021, the Australian Competition and Consumer Commission, after studying the Australian market's performance, rejected calls by some market critics to recouple water and land. Chile similarly permits investors to own water independently of any land (although, under recent changes in Chile's water law, anyone who does not put their water to use risks losing their right).[37]

The anti-speculation doctrine is not only of questionable value but can also thwart creative solutions to water challenges. In the 1980s, a private development company called Delta Wetlands Properties had an ingenious idea. Two major water conveyance projects, the California State Water Project and the Central Valley Project, run through a region of California known as the Delta. The Delta was once wetlands, but over a century ago, farmers "reclaimed" the land by building levees around plots of highly fertile land, forming what the farmers call "islands." Over time, the islands have subsided from compaction and are now below water level; protected by the levees from inundation, the islands have become giant bowls.[38]

Delta Wetlands Properties realized that the islands could serve as natural reservoirs for the two water projects, storing water at a fraction of the cost of building a new reservoir. Delta Wetlands bought four islands and announced a project to appropriate and store excess water in two of the islands and dedicate the other two islands to wildlife habitat. Delta Wetlands planned to sell the stored water to needy users in the future. No one had any doubt that the water would ultimately be needed, and California administrators okayed the appropriation. California courts, however, ruled that because Delta Wetlands did not have an actual, current beneficial use for the water, the anti-speculation doctrine barred the project. While the Delta project also faced technical issues and other legal challenges, the anti-speculation doctrine killed it. Zurich Insurance subsequently bought Delta Wetlands and tried to resuscitate the storage project but ultimately gave up and sold the land to the giant Metropolitan Water District of Southern California.[39]

Cities, interestingly, are partially exempt from the anti-speculation doctrine. Virtually every western state allows cities to appropriate water in anticipation of potential future needs under the "growing cities" doctrine. Private water investors must demonstrate an immediate use; growing cities do not. Western water law often provides special advantages or exceptions, such as the growing cities doctrine, to public water agencies, to the comparative disadvantage of the private sector.[40]

MARKET DESIGN AND OVERSIGHT

Governments must carefully design and oversee water markets, just like all other markets. Markets need sufficient transparency and regulation to provide confidence to those who use them. Water users, for example, must have sufficient information to feel comfortable buying and selling water. They also must trust the brokers and other market intermediaries who assist them in trades.[41]

Governments also must ensure that water transfers do not injure third parties. Water uses are interrelated. A portion of the water used upstream on a river, for example, typically flows back to the river and is used again downstream. Changes to where and how a water right is used can therefore affect other water uses. Western states protect those uses through a "no injury" rule that prohibits transfers that would injure other water rights holders. For over a century, for example, a canal system known as Swadley Ditch has provided water from Clear Creek to farms near Boulder, Colorado. Just upstream of Swadley Ditch is the Gold Rush–era town of Golden. As Golden grew in the twentieth century, it sought to buy rights in Swadley Ditch for municipal use. However, because cities can consume a higher fraction of the water they divert, Golden's acquisition of the Swadley rights could have reduced return flow and thus the water available to downstream users on Clear Creek. Under the "no injury" rule, a Colorado court required Golden to protect the downstream appropriators by limiting how much of the purchased water it used.[42]

Water transfers also can threaten the environment if not carefully policed. San Diego's purchase of IID water threatened to dry up the Salton Sea, impacting the health of both the local population and migrating birds. Governments can address such threats in several ways. In an extension of the "no injury" rule, many western states like California prohibit transfers that will unreasonably harm the environment. South Africa starts by allocating a share of every river to a "reserve" for environmental protection (and human rights) that markets cannot affect.[43]

Many observers also believe that governments should ban transfers that might reduce local economic activity in areas from which water is being exported. If farmers fallow their fields and sell their water to a distant city, local farm unemployment might rise, and demand for seed, farm equipment, and farm services might fall. Tax revenues might also drop, placing financial pressure on public schools, hospitals, and other governmental services. Reduced employment and public amenities may lead people to move away, unravelling communities.[44]

Call this the Owens Valley Syndrome. In the early twentieth century, a growing Los Angeles turned for water to the Owens Valley, an agricultural region two hundred miles northeast of L.A. in the eastern Sierra Nevada. By hook and by crook, L.A. purchased or otherwise acquired most of the Valley's water, destroying the local agricultural economy and reducing the Valley to a sleepy, largely undeveloped borderland. The Owens Valley saga inspired the movie *Chinatown*. While L.A.'s behavior was extreme and perhaps illegal (new scholarship discounts the degree of chicanery), even well-managed markets can negatively affect agricultural communities that are making low-value uses of water. A recent governmental study found that the Australian water market, by reducing economic activity in exporting regions, can leave "some communities feeling like the collateral damage of improved outcomes in another region."[45]

A critical policy question is whether and when the law should prohibit or limit water transfers out of rural communities. Cities can suffer economic losses and population declines when businesses or industries close or move because of labor costs or declining demand, but the United States generally does not force the businesses or industries to continue operating. Instead, society typically views such impacts as the unfortunate cost of a free economy and changing market conditions, what economists call a "pecuniary externality." Should water be different? Governments need to find better ways to ease economic transitions, but such transitions are no worse when they result from changing water values than when they result from changing labor costs or consumer taste. Economists also have concluded that communities are unlikely to suffer material harm so long as water transfers are temporary, involve less than about 20 percent of a region's water supply, or free up water through conservation rather than fallowing.[46]

Community concerns, however, have led most western states to constrain water markets that might injure communities. Some states, like California, have statutes or policies on their books that prohibit transfers that would "unreasonably" affect the local economy. In Oklahoma and Wyoming, the state considers local economic impacts in deciding whether to approve transfers. Nevada imposes a tax on inter-county transfers that it uses to help pay for economic development, health care, and education in the exporting county. Even without governmental restrictions, community fears can undermine water trading by mobilizing political opposition. Community opposition to the transfer of water from the San Luis Valley in southern Colorado to the Denver suburbs killed transfer efforts twice in the late twentieth century and again in 2022.[47]

In the United States, governmental water districts like the IID also pose a constraint on water exports. Irrigation districts supply water to many farms in California and other western states. In most cases, the districts own the water that their farms use and must approve any sale or lease of water out of the district. Historically, these districts frequently opposed exports and blocked transfers between otherwise willing water users. Districts acted because of local community concerns, resistance from local farmers who wanted to save any excess water for themselves, and administrative challenges. Some districts have grown more receptive to water markets in recent years, recognizing the potential benefit of broader water markets to their farmers. Other districts, like the IID, remain hostile.[48]

Unfortunately, many of these protections unnecessarily undermine the viability of water transfers. In the United States, water transfers of varying length and size can face months of hearings before state agencies and courts designed to determine their potential impact on other appropriators, the environment, and local communities. (A participant in a Colorado conference noted that one dispute over a proposed transfer involved a potential impact on other appropriators of less than a cup of water.) Hearings can generate sizable legal and expert bills. Market proponents have pushed for reforms designed to reduce review costs or provide less burdensome processes for short-term or small transfers. In contrast to the United States, other countries, like Australia, avoid the need for special oversight by separately protecting the environment and other public interests and defining water rights to minimize third-party impacts.[49]

PRIVATE INVOLVEMENT IN WATER MARKETS

Public agencies were long the most active participants in US water markets. Because public agencies owned and distributed much of the water in the West, they were typically both buyer and seller in market transactions. In a typical deal, large municipal water suppliers like the Metropolitan Water District of Southern California purchased water from governmental irrigation districts like the Palo Verde Irrigation District. If private entities played a role, they were typically sellers, not buyers. Cities like Aurora, Denver, and Phoenix acquired water from farmers, ranchers, canal companies, and mutual water companies. Private entities seldom purchased water.[50]

Public dominance of US water markets persists but is declining. Private investors are increasingly buying water rights, attracted by the large arbitrage opportunities between rural and municipal water prices and by the growing scarcity of water stemming from growth, environmental restrictions, and climate change. Because of the anti-speculation rule, private water investments in the United States typically take the form of land purchases to which valuable water rights are attached. Large farms that have invested in permanent or high-value crops and need water to protect their investments are also increasingly important buyers and sometimes even outbid municipal purchasers.[51]

While small investment groups have long acquired water rights in the western United States, the 1990s saw an upsurge of private water acquisitions as investors recognized the large disconnect between water prices in many rural and urban areas. During this period, the Bass brothers purchased IID land, T. Boone Pickens bought groundwater rights in Texas, Enron created a water-investment wing known as Azurix (shortly before declaring bankruptcy), and a new group called Vidler Water acquired water rights and a conveyance tunnel in Colorado. Most of these early investors focused on assembling large blocks of water that they could buy low and sell high. They were arbitrage traders at heart and frequently held at least some Texas connection. Few, except for Vidler, are still large water investors today.[52]

A new breed of investment companies, epitomized by groups such as the Renewable Resources Group (RRG) and Water Asset Management (WAM), have arisen in recent years. Unlike earlier investors, these companies are long-term players in water trading. They typically buy and manage agricultural land both to increase the land's economic returns and to find ways to free up water for sale. In the process, they often benefit both water markets and society. First, they invest in water conservation and switch to crops with higher returns per unit of water consumption, increasing the economic productivity of the water they are using. Second, they increase the societal value of their unneeded water by selling it to cities or other farmers with a high need for the water. Third, because they are constantly searching for market opportunities, they reduce the search costs of both buyers and sellers in the water market—a critical function in markets that historically have been localized and thin. Fourth, they serve as aggregators, putting together portfolios of water at scales helpful to large buyers such as cities. Finally, they bring expertise to the market process, reducing the administrative cost of transfers and increasing market liquidity.[53]

The companies frequently generate needed capital by raising money from outside investors. WAM, for example, has created two major water investment funds so far, with the second raising over $100 million in assets and offering a projected return of 17–22 percent per year. Investors historically found it difficult to invest directly in US water rights. The financial investment firm Morningstar tracks over sixty open-end "water funds" in the United States. Most of these funds invest in the stock of investor-owned water utilities, water-service firms, or water technology companies; as of 2022, none invested in water rights. The only way an investor historically could buy water rights was to buy land with water rights attached. WAM and other water investment groups now make it possible for large, sophisticated investors to invest in a portfolio of water rights and accompanying land. Vidler Water, which is traded on NASDAQ, enables equity investments in water holdings.[54]

Australia's unbundling of water and land in 1994 has created an even more fertile market for private water investments. Australia's Murray-Darling Basin covers one-seventh of the country and includes all but one of its seven longest rivers. Anyone can buy and trade water in the basin. Over $80 billion in water entitlements is available for acquisition and trade. About a tenth of this water changes hands each year, and institutional investors account for about 15–20 percent of the trade volume. The Canadian Public Sector Pension Investment Board holds about 2 percent, the largest share of water rights held by a single entity, but it is not alone. Large wealth management firms like Argyle Capital Partners, as well as property investment groups like Kilter Rural, have created water funds. Australia even hosts the first public water fund—Duxton Water—with water assets of over $300 million and an average annual rate of return of over 10 percent since the fund's launch in 2016.[55]

The rise of water markets has attracted not only private investors but a cottage industry of companies helping to meet the needs of buyers, sellers, and regulators. Mammoth Water, a subsidiary of ERA Economics, helps water agencies and others to build water markets. Water markets require structure. A groundwater management agency wishing to develop an efficient local market, for example, must have a structure for recording and tracking groundwater rights, must ensure that transfers from one part of the aquifer to another do not harm other pumpers or the environment, and must minimize search and trading costs. Mammoth consults on market design, develops software for tracking groundwater rights and transfers, and monitors and analyzes market performance. Nonprofits like EDF and The Nature Conservancy also have expert teams helping governmental agencies design effective water markets.[56]

A large assortment of water brokers helps match buyers and sellers and provides transactional advice in both Australia and the western United States. In Australia, where water rights are highly homogeneous, H_2OX and Water Exchange run exchanges designed to provide prices and trading information transparently and efficiently. In the United States, where trading information is far less transparent, WestWater Research has built a water consulting business around its tracking of water transactions. In 2019, NASDAQ, Veles Water, and WestWater Research created a California Water Index (HQH2O) that tracks the price of water right leases and sales in California's five largest and most active water markets.[57]

Such private intermediaries may not be sufficient by themselves to create effective markets. In some cases, the government may need to step in too. While intermediaries have improved markets by providing their customers with information and expertise, the exclusive nature of that information and expertise has raised equity issues and sometimes undermined water users' confidence in the fairness of markets. Although not calling for the abolition of private intermediaries, the Australian Competition and Consumer Commission has called for the development of governmental water exchanges and price data to ensure that all market participants have the basic information needed for confidence in the nation's water markets. Private companies can provide such information (think Redfin or Zillow in the American real estate market), but governments may need to provide such basic information in the early development of water markets.[58]

Private companies, in summary, are investing in water rights, bringing needed liquidity to water markets, and providing critical expertise to the design and operation of markets that are efficient and transparent. Without private businesses, water markets would be far smaller and less effective in delivering benefits to water users and society. Private businesses, however, cannot alone provide the transparency, trust, and confidence needed to assure all market participants. Government still has a role.

TYPES OF MARKET TRANSACTIONS

As water markets have expanded, so have the types of market transactions and products available to participants. Interested water purchasers can buy water entitlements outright or purchase the water through multi-year leases or for shorter terms through spot markets. Some states and regions in the United States have created water banks that buy and sell water, often at a preset price, in place of individually negotiated transactions. Rather than formally buying water, which requires state approval, users in the United States can pay upstream appropriators simply not to use their water under "forbearance agreements."[59]

Users also enjoy several ways to anticipate future needs. Dry-year options, in which users acquire the option to receive water during dry years, are common in the West. In 2020, NASDAQ and the CME Group created a cash-settled futures contract allowing water users to hedge against the risk of future increases in water prices. Farmers can purchase a futures contract based on the current expectation of future prices; at maturity, the contract pays the farmer the price of water at that time. Australian users often employ forward contracts in which sellers agree to supply water in the future for a fixed price, providing buyers with both supply and price certainty without any upfront outlay.[60]

FEAR OF SPECULATORS

The rise of large private investors in Australia and the western United States has recently triggered a new wave of concern over "water speculators." Like Elwood Mead a century ago, critics object that investing in water for profit is antithetical to the public nature of water. Popular articles and books, as well as politicians, raise varied concerns that echo the long-term debate over water markets. In the United States, critics worry that private investors will harm both rural communities (by selling agricultural water to cities) and cities (by charging more than farmers for the water). In Australia, critics fret that smart investors, who have computer systems and market experience, will get the better of farmers who must spend time farming and, according to one critic, "struggle even to use a smartphone." Australian critics also worry about the paucity of regulatory rules in Australia's open water market, creating the risk, in their view, of undisclosed conflicts of interest, insider trading, market manipulation, and information disparities. Many agricultural users also protest that "speculators" and "hoarders" have increased the price of water in recent years, making it more expensive to farm.[61]

Political leaders have found it difficult to ignore the growing chorus of concerns, despite the absence of any compelling evidence that private investment has been problematic. In response to complaints and higher water prices, the treasurer of Australia instructed the Competition and Consumer Commission in 2019 to review the nation's water markets and the role and practices of market participants, including water brokers, water exchanges, investment funds, and other large traders. In the United States, the Colorado legislature created a diverse twenty-two-member work group in 2020 to explore what changes the legislature should make to "strengthen current water anti-speculation law." In 2022, two California state legislators wrote to the US attorney general demanding an antitrust investigation into "hedge funds and other monopolistic entities" that, according to the legislators, trade water at the expense of the public. A year later, the California legislature considered a bill to prohibit investment funds from selling water for a profit.[62]

The Australian Competition and Consumer Commission issued its report in March 2020. After extensive research, the Commission found no evidence that private investors had "exercised market power or manipulated markets" or that their involvement in the market had increased water prices. A growing number of academic studies support the Commission's finding. In the most comprehensive study of the Australian market to date, economists found no evidence of hoarding or other market manipulation. Even the largest investors do not have sufficient market power to influence water prices. While water prices rose in Australia in the late 2010s, economists have concluded that drought, not market manipulation, was the cause.[63]

The Commission found that, far from undermining markets, private investors are providing public value. Investors, for example, have brought new capital to Australia's water markets and increased liquidity. Investors also have provided market products that help meet user needs; investors, for example, have leased water to farmers on a long-term basis, relieving farmers of the need to invest their own capital in permanent entitlements. Academic analyses agree that private investment has promoted more efficient markets and benefited agricultural water users.[64]

The Commission, however, recommended changes to the structure of the Australian market. Some proposed reforms focused on better monitoring and reporting of market activities. While there was no evidence of market manipulation, the Commission found that the lack of transparency and effective oversight has given rise to the "perception of misconduct," undermining public confidence in the market.[65]

Other reforms focused on regulating the behavior of private players in the Australian market. To ensure public confidence and avoid the risk of wrongdoing, the Commission recommended that Australia adopt behavioral standards like those applicable to security markets. Insider trading, for example, should be illegal; brokers should be subject to fiduciary obligations. While private companies often follow a private code of conduct, the Commission concluded that the Australia market needs clear and enforceable rules and obligations.[66]

The Colorado Work Group tasked with investigating private water speculation ended in disagreement. While all members of the Work Group concluded that water speculation was bad, they could not agree on what constitutes speculation. Members, for example, could not agree on why it was bad for an outside investor, but not a farmer, to sell water for profit—other than, as one participant suggested, the latter wears boots, but the former does not. The Work Group also could not agree on how to regulate improper speculation, whatever it might be. Most of the legislative reforms that the Work Group recommended for further study dealt with other market concerns, such as out-of-state transfers and transfers from rural to urban communities—not with speculation. A few proposed to ban, regulate, or tax "Investment Water Speculation"—but did not attempt to define it.[67]

Water markets will be increasingly important as climate change, growth, and governmental regulation shrink the amount of water available for consumptive use in a region. As noted earlier, droughts have consistently increased market activity. State efforts to reduce groundwater use to sustainable levels have also often led to the creation of local groundwater markets. The spontaneous development of markets in response to shortages is perhaps the best proof of their value to water users and the economy. Economic studies showing the substantial benefit to regional and state economies simply confirm what most water users already know.[68]

Water markets, however, can risk harm to other water users and the environment if not carefully designed and regulated. Governments must continue to oversee water markets to avoid such externalities. As water markets increasingly attract private investors, they also are likely to generate concerns about "speculation" similar to those already raised in Australia, California, and Colorado. The most valuable step that governments can take in response is to ensure that water markets are transparent and employ rules that protect against abuse and provide everyone with an equal opportunity to participate.

FIVE

Environmental Water Investors

Environmental organizations actively use water markets to improve aquatic environments. They buy water from farmers and other consumptive users, for example, and then return that water to rivers and streams, increasing instream flow. In the process, they help to remedy environmental problems that governments created by failing to protect the environment when the governments first issued water rights. As the next story illustrates, private companies and environmental groups are now going a step further and creating investment funds designed to attract private dollars that can be used to buy water for the environment.

The world has lost about 90 percent of its wetlands since 1700. In the nineteenth century, the United States rewarded people who drained wetlands by giving them the land under the Swamp Lands Acts of 1849, 1850, and 1860. The pace of loss has sped up since 1900, with one study estimating that the world has lost 64 to 71 percent of its wetlands in just the last 120 years. In 1971, the international community responded with the Ramsar Convention on Wetlands that encourages countries to protect wetlands and provides for the designation of "Wetlands of International Significance." To date, the 172 countries that have joined the Ramsar Convention have designated almost 2,500 Wetlands of International Importance. Australia was one of the first

Figure 5.1 The Murray-Darling Basin. Source: author.

countries to join the Ramsar Convention and has designated sixty-six Wetlands of International Importance, the fourth-most of any country. (The United Kingdom has designated the most, followed by Mexico and Spain.)[1]

Sixteen of Australia's Ramsar wetlands are in the Murray-Darling Basin. The Murray Darling is one of the largest river basins in the world, covering over four hundred thousand square miles, or 14 percent of Australia. It is home to over thirty thousand wetlands, including lakes, floodplain billa-bongs, small spring soaks, alpine bogs, and shallow freshwater depressions. The basin also supports a highly productive agricultural economy. The region's rich soil and abundant water have attracted ranchers and farmers since the nineteenth century. The basin now produces a third of Australia's food supply, worth almost $20 billion in annual revenue.[2]

Environmental and agricultural needs in the Murray-Darling Basin have frequently collided. Agricultural water extractions, along with stream modifications and land conversions, have decimated many of the local wetlands. Recent drought conditions, likely caused by climate change, have further damaged the wetlands. As a result, many local wetland-dependent species, from the freckled duck to swamp wallaby grass, are imperiled. In 2012, a government study of ecosystem health in the Murray-Darling rated over 80 percent of the basin's river valleys to be in "poor" or "very poor" health.[3]

The Yambuna Wetlands Complex sits in the ecologically rich lower floodplain of the Goulburn River, a major river in the Murray-Darling Basin's southeast corner. Like the rest of the Murray-Darling, the Goulburn basin is home to both major wetlands (200,000 acres' worth) and agriculture (half a million acres of ranchland, dairy farms, orchards, vineyards, and row crops). The Yambuna Complex consists of four connected wetlands. Three of the wetlands are part of an Australian national park. The fourth, Greier's Lagoon, is less than thirty acres in size and sits almost entirely on private land.[4]

Greier's Lagoon might be small, but it is ecologically important. It supports two depleted vegetation types (Bushy Riverine Swamp and Riverine Swamp Forest), two threatened plant species, and scar trees of significance to local Indigenous people. It also provides an important link between the Goulburn River and the rest of the Yambuna Complex. Unfortunately, Greier's Lagoon and the rest of the wetland complex have suffered in recent years from insufficient water. Jamie McMaster, the rancher on whose land Greier's Lagoon lies, strongly supports restoring the lagoon, but there is not much he or anyone else can do to restore a wetland without water.[5]

In September 2017, Grier's Lagoon received an infusion of about one hundred acre-feet of water from an unlikely source—a private impact investment fund known as the Murray-Darling Basin Balanced Water Fund. The infusion raised the water level in the Yambuna Wetlands Complex by a meter and attracted local and migrating bird species, including the eastern great egret, the royal spoonbill, the white-bellied sea eagle, and the azure kingfisher—all listed as threatened or endangered under Australia's Endangered Species Act.[6]

The Nature Conservancy, the Murray-Darling Wetlands Working Group (a local nonprofit dedicated to rehabilitating degraded wetlands), and Kilter Rural (an Australian investment firm specializing in farmland and water) created the Murray-Darling Basin Balanced Water Fund in 2015. A major goal of the Balanced Water Fund is to provide water needed for degraded wetlands in the Murray-Darling Basin, protecting both the wetlands and the dozens of imperiled birds and other species reliant on the wetlands.[7]

By furnishing water to needy wetlands, the Balanced Water Fund helps reduce the conflict between agriculture and the environment. But the Fund is not a charity. The Fund also provides water to farmers and makes money for its investors. The Murray-Darling Basin, as Chapter 4 explained, is home to perhaps the most robust water market in the world. The Balanced Water Fund raises money from private investors and uses it to buy Basin water. The Fund then exploits the fact that wetlands and farmers in the Murray-Darling Basin most need water at separate times. Wetlands have the greatest water need in wet conditions, while farmers' demand soars in dry conditions. In wet and very wet years, the Fund therefore contributes 40 percent of its water to wetlands, adding to natural flows and increasing the amount of inundated land. The Fund sells the rest of its water in wet years to farmers, providing a small financial return to its investors. In dry years, by contrast, the Fund's donations of water to wetlands shrink to 10 percent or less of its water portfolio, and the Fund makes a high rate of return by selling the remaining 90 percent of its water to farmers.[8]

The Balanced Water Fund has been successful both environmentally and financially. In its first four years, the Fund furnished over five thousand acre-feet of water to twenty-four wetlands in the Murray-Darling Basin. Its water donations have helped improve the condition of multiple imperiled species, including the return of a locally extinct fish known as the Murray hardyhead. Wetland inundations have also increased local bird diversity by over 200 percent, bird abundance by almost 300 percent, and aquatic plant species in the wetland areas almost tenfold.[9]

The Balanced Water Fund has also done well for its investors. The Fund offers a diversified investment as well as significant risk mitigation, because the returns are uncorrelated to traditional asset classes. The Fund originally promised a targeted return of 9 to 12 percent per annum but, as of March 2020, had delivered an 18.83 percent return per annum.[10]

The Balanced Water Fund will not singlehandedly solve the water challenges of the Murray-Darling Basin. The Fund is relatively small (only $66.8 million as of March 31, 2020). Governmental agencies, such as the Victorian Environmental Water Holder, own a much larger share of water rights in the Murray-Darling Basin and provide most of the water needed for wetlands restoration. The Fund, however, fills critical gaps by furnishing water for those wetlands that the governmental agencies do not help (such as privately owned wetlands) and by "topping off" the water that the governmental agencies do provide to wetlands (furnishing that extra kick of water that can be essential to successful restoration).[11]

The Balanced Water Fund is an example of a partnership between an investment company and two nonprofits making an innovative use of water markets to improve wetlands and, in the process, contribute to the more sustainable management of water resources. It also shows how markets can sometimes be used to reduce conflict between agriculture and the environment. The Fund's key importance, according to Jamie McMaster, the cow farmer on whose land Greiner's Lagoon sits, is that it helps show the farming community that "environmental flow isn't [necessarily] in conflict to farming priorities." The Fund is also another illustration of how the private sector is helping to better manage water resources in many parts of the world.[12]

THE FAILURE TO PROTECT FRESHWATER ECOSYSTEMS

The Murray-Darling Basin is not the only freshwater ecosystem in the world struggling for water. For decades, most governments ignored environmental needs in allocating freshwater to consumptive users. In the western United States, for example, most states initially set no limits on how much water could be diverted from rivers, streams, and lakes or from underground aquifers (which support groundwater-dependent wetlands and streams). Anyone interested in appropriating water for instream flow, moreover, was out of luck. A key requirement for an appropriative right was diversion of water from the waterway, which automatically precluded instream appropriations. Water rights were for offstream use, not instream protection, and water right owners who failed to consumptively use their water lost those rights. States also did not consider the environment to be a beneficial use of water. As a result of these policies, over the past century and a half many rivers and wetlands throughout the American West have dried up or dramatically shrunk.[13]

The failure to protect instream flows in the American West has been catastrophic to freshwater ecosystems and the species that rely upon them. Even 10 percent reductions in instream flows can seriously impair a freshwater ecosystem. Diversions, however, rob most western rivers of more than 50 percent of their flows in summer months; a quarter of western rivers lose more than 75 percent of their summer flows. Flow reductions, in turn, are the leading cause of freshwater fish impairment and are partially responsible for 75 percent of all the listings of freshwater fish species under the US Endangered Species Act. Depletions have contributed to the imperilment of two-thirds of the native fish species in the Colorado River basin, over 80 percent of native fish species in California, and more than 360 water-dependent plant and animal species throughout the West.[14]

Unconstrained freshwater consumption has also led to major losses in the freshwater ecosystems relied upon by migratory bird species. As a result of water diversions and climate change, wetlands along flyway gradients in parts of the American West declined by almost 50 percent from 1984 to 2018. In California, wetlands have shrunk since statehood (1850) by over 90 percent because of diversions, dams, and land conversion.[15]

Over the past sixty years, governments have begun to protect critical instream flows from new water diversions. Various western states, for example, have protected specific rivers under "wild and scenic river" laws, required applicants for new appropriations to show that their diversions will not injure the environment, imposed minimum streamflow requirements on new appropriations, and authorized state agencies to appropriate water for instream flows. These protections, however, have often been too late to adequately protect instream flows, coming only after many rivers were already fully appropriated or even over-appropriated.[16]

Governments have been slow to reduce existing diversions. Current water users strongly oppose reductions, politically dooming most efforts to restore instream flows. In the United States, water rights are also constitutionally protected property. Water users therefore challenge new laws that reduce their diversions without compensation as an unconstitutional expropriation of their property. While governments have argued in response that harmful diversions do not satisfy the requirement that appropriations be "reasonable and beneficial" and therefore are not legal, courts have some-times still awarded compensation for reductions in water rights.

The US Endangered Species Act (which prohibits diversions that injure or kill an endangered species) and water-quality laws (which proscribe diversions that lower water quality) have sometimes forced water users to reduce their diversions. The legislatures that passed such laws, however, never realized that the laws would affect water diversions, or they probably would never have passed them. Strong political opposition and the threat of lawsuits deter administrative agencies from pushing such laws very far. Consequently, there is little chance now of a complete regulatory fix to the inadequate instream flows that are still impacting the ecology of many surface waterways in the West and elsewhere in the world. While progress has been made to protect remaining instream flows and wetlands, regulatory programs are failing at restoration of what has been lost.[17]

ENVIRONMENTAL WATER TRUSTS

An alternative strategy to increase instream flows in both the American West and Australia is to buy existing water rights from farmers and others and then return the water to rivers, streams, lakes, and wetlands. Historically, the law in the American West would not have permitted this. As noted, failure to divert the water would have resulted in abandonment or forfeiture of the water right, and the law did not consider instream uses to be "beneficial." Beginning with Oregon in 1987, however, every western state changed its laws to recognize instream flow as a beneficial use and to permit the conversion of diversionary rights to instream rights. As part of a major reform of Australia's water laws at the turn of the century, Australia purchased about 2 million acre-feet of water rights from farmers and other consumptive water users for some $2.3 billion, returned that water to the rivers, and authorized environmental organizations to acquire additional water rights of their own.[18]

Established conservation organizations like The Nature Conservancy and a new set of "water trusts" have quickly taken advantage of this legal opportunity. These nonprofit organizations are building on the land conservation model that TNC and other land trusts have successfully employed to protect terrestrial ecosystems over the last half century: purchase environmentally important lands and then hold and manage them for conservation.

Just as TNC once purchased and preserved the "last great places," it and other nonprofits now acquire the water needed to protect the last great waterways and wetlands.[19]

Six years after Oregon became the first US state to authorize the acquisition of water rights for instream flow, the head of a large land company, the manager of a major irrigation district, and two environmental representatives met in 1993 to form the first freshwater trust, the Oregon Water Trust. Explicitly adopting the land trust model, the Oregon Water Trust sought to test the value of "market environmentalism" for instream flows. Now known as The Freshwater Trust, the organization has undertaken more than two hundred flow restoration projects over the last three decades, involving over 650 freshwater transactions in eight different Oregon basins. The Trust has made a significant difference to the health of Oregon's rivers. In the Lostine River basin, for example, the Trust's investment of $7.5 million in water leases and irrigation upgrades has helped increase the number of Chinook salmon in the river from less than fifty adults in the early 1990s to about 2,000 today.[20]

The Oregon Water Trust was a harbinger of a growing water trust movement. The Trust quickly spawned a variety of other state and local water trusts, including the Colorado Water Trust (formed in 2001), Deschutes River Conservancy (1996), Friends of the Tejon River (2001), Scott River Water Trust (2009), and Washington Water Trust (1998). A handful of existing land trusts, such as the Arizona Open Land Trust and TNC, also expanded their work to include the acquisition of water rights. So did river advocacy groups like the Clark Fork Coalition and Trout Unlimited. Australia's water reforms led to the creation of similar water trusts in Australia, including the Murray-Darling Wetlands Working Group.[21]

Water trusts and other environmental nonprofits use various techniques to return water to streams. Virtually all buy or lease existing water rights and then either hold them for instream use themselves or transfer them to state or federal agencies for such use. Both purchases and leases have grown over the last fifteen years, with leases growing far faster. Leases are more common for multiple reasons: they are less expensive, instream needs change from year to year and month to month, current owners of water rights are often more willing to lease their rights than to give them up forever, and administrative review standards for leases are often simpler. Where instream or wetland needs are tied to droughts or other temporary conditions, some water trusts also enter into option agreements that allow them to purchase water when needed.[22]

Water trusts also have pioneered innovative approaches to restoring instream flows and wetlands. In the western United States, water trusts have sometimes sought to avoid formal acquisitions of water rights because of the expensive, lengthy, and often complicated regulatory approvals required. Water trusts, for example, sometimes pay consumptive users to voluntarily forebear using their water right for a set period of time, allowing the water to remain in the river without a formal transfer. While this can lead to loss of the water right under the "use it or lose it" principle, a growing set of states have enacted new laws removing that disincentive.

Increasingly, water trusts are also looking for creative transactions that can better benefit everyone. Water trusts sometimes pay the holder of a water right to increase the flow in a critical segment of a river without reducing water use. The water user, for example, might move its point of diversion downstream or switch to a different, less vulnerable water source. In other cases, water trusts pay to modernize irrigation infrastructure to reduce water use, saving water users money and freeing up water for instream flows. The Colorado Water Trust has created a program where private companies lease water for a hydroelectric facility that, after using the water to produce energy, returns the water to the river to increase instream flow.[23]

TNC's BirdReturns program is an example of the market ingenuity that the private nonprofit sector has brought to the provision of environmental water. BirdReturns seeks to provide critical wetlands in California for migrating bird species. While less than 10 percent of California's historical wetlands remain, inundated rice fields can provide a valuable substitute. The problem is that rice farmers frequently drain their fields before the time each year when birds need the local habitat. TNC combines real-time data from birders with historical migration data to predict where migratory birds will need habitat when they arrive. It then runs a reverse auction in which rice farmers in those regions bid to keep water on their property for the birds, and TNC accepts the lowest bids. The result is a cost-effective program that, in its first year of operation, protected more than 220,000 birds and achieved bird densities much higher than found off the flooded land.[24]

Efforts to use private philanthropic funds to restore instream flows have also spilled over national borders into regions without historical water markets. The Colorado River flows through seven thirsty western states before crossing into Mexico. While the river once created a biologically rich estuary in Baja California before discharging into the Sea of Cortez, the river has not naturally made its way to the ocean since the 1980s. Diverted by water users in both the United States and Mexico, the river effectively ends at the Morales Dam just south of the border. As a result, the former Colorado River estuary is far saltier than before, harming the many species that call it home.

A group of nonprofit organizations in both the United States and Mexico, coming together under the banner of "Raise the River," created the Colorado River Delta Water Trust to buy water from local farmers and return it to Mexican parts of the river and the estuary. Two international agreements in 2012 and 2017 authorized the purchases and provided additional water. Several of the nonprofits also paid for the creation of artificial wetlands in Baja California that simultaneously filter and clean wastewater for the city of Mexicali, provide bird habitat, and supply more water to the estuary. Water trusts in the United States similarly look for ways to achieve multiple benefits, not just fish protection, with their water acquisitions.[25]

Water trusts are not saving freshwater ecosystems by themselves (no more than land trusts are saving terrestrial ecosystems all on their own). Government action remains critical. Regulatory programs such as the US Endangered Species Act create much of the demand and funding for environmental water transactions. Governments are also the largest purchaser of water rights for the environment. In Australia, as noted, the Commonwealth has purchased over two million acre-feet of water for the environment. In the United States, the federal government leased almost 3.7 million acre-feet of water in the western United States to help meet regulatory requirements between 2008 and 2018, and western states added another 570,000 acre-feet. Nonprofit organizations leased about 530,000 acre-feet (almost as much as the states acquired but still only about 10 percent of the total amount leased). Finally, governmental tax policies, which allow deductions for contributions to nonprofit organizations, encourage monetary donations that support the water trusts and their acquisitions as well as direct donations of water rights themselves. Saving instream flows, in short, is a public-private partnership.[26]

The role of private water trusts and similar nonprofits is nonetheless critically important. Governmental regulations, purchases, and leases do not fully meet freshwater ecological needs. While governmental transactions are significant in some basins, they are not in others. Nonprofits often focus on those basins that are not the subject of major governmental efforts but still suffer from inadequate flows. Nonprofits also provide important supplemental flows for those rivers and streams with active government programs. Water trusts, moreover, often acquire water on behalf of governmental programs. Because nonprofits are more flexible than governmental agencies, have strong business acumen, and enjoy the trust of landowners, they often can acquire water that governments are unable to buy, acquire it more quickly, and acquire it for less money.[27]

Water trusts face a variety of obstacles in their work. Water trusts continue to face regulatory hurdles despite the liberalization of western water law over the last several decades. Freshwater instream flow acquisitions, for example, typically must go through lengthy and expensive state approval proceedings. While some states authorize simplified processes for short-term leases, others do not, making some short-term leases either prohibitively expensive or infeasible given time constraints. Some states also allow only governmental agencies to hold instream flows, forcing water trusts to take the circuitous and administratively more complicated step of purchasing rights and then transferring them to the government. In other states, farmers who increase instream flow simply by reducing their water use risk losing that water under the "use it or lose it" principle, limiting the ability of water trusts to increase instream flows without engaging in a formal transfer of water rights to instream use. Some state laws also allow state agencies to reduce instream flow rights during water shortages. Finally, only a few states explicitly provide that instream acquisitions are additive to regulatory requirements. In states without such a provision, consumptive users can argue that instream acquisitions count toward regulatory standards and cannot be "stacked" to increase total instream flow.[28]

Environmental water transactions also continue to confront political opposition. To many consumptive water users, environmental acquisitions of senior water rights are a potential threat to their water use during periods of drought. Environmental water transactions, moreover, violate the traditional view of many consumptive water users that the government, not markets, should decide how water is allocated and that agricultural use deserves primacy. In response to these concerns, legislators frequently propose to repeal environmental water authorizations. The need to obtain state approval of environmental water purchases or sales provides water consumers with another opportunity to challenge the underlying water right or the size of the instream right. Some environmental organizations also oppose voluntary market transactions. In their view, environmental water acquisitions will never be large enough to make a difference and can take political attention away from strengthening environmental regulations.[29]

The final hurdles are financial. The cost of water rights is increasing as water supplies shrink, demand grows, and markets expand. Because there is a direct correlation between water shortages and depleted streams, water prices are rising fastest in those regions with the greatest demand for environmental water. Funding to acquire water rights, however, remains limited. Water trusts must compete with other worthy organizations for philanthropic dollars from a limited set of individuals, foundations, and corporations interested in the geographic areas in which the trusts work. To stretch their funds, some water trusts now lease their water rights to farmers or other consumptive users during periods when instream flows are less ecologically important, providing funds that can then be used when the ecological needs are greater.[30]

IMPACT INVESTMENT FUNDS

The challenge of funding environmental water transactions through purely philanthropic donations has raised interest in impact investment funds. Impact funds seek to achieve measurable environmental or social benefits while also providing a financial return to their investors. The increasing interest of many investors in "doing good" has generated a wave of new impact funds over the last decade. In "impact first" funds, investors intentionally sacrifice a full market rate of return in order to provide environmental or social benefits, while in "investment first" funds, investors seek a full financial return. As of 2020, privately managed, measured-impact funds held almost $300 billion in investments.[31]

Conservation organizations have increasingly looked to impact investing as a potential mechanism for bringing new money to all forms of ecological protection, both aquatic and terrestrial. One recent study estimated that almost a trillion dollars might be needed by 2030 to avoid further biodiversity declines, while governmental spending and philanthropic funding are unlikely to exceed about $150 billion—leaving a deficit of up to $850 billion.

Conservation organizations hope that impact investing might partially fill this gap and have begun to work with investment groups to create environmental funds. TNC even created its own in-house impact investment wing known as NatureVest.[32]

The Walton Family Foundation took the first look at whether impact investing could enhance freshwater ecosystems in a 2005 report. The report sought to identify investments in the Colorado River basin, one of the foundation's priority geographies, that could "finance water resource solutions, generate related environmental benefits, and create a financial return." Setting out a thesis that has continued to animate impact investing in freshwater, the report saw an opportunity to achieve "sustainability goals for both human society and the natural world." The report examined nine different investment "blueprints" to determine their financial returns and their ability to improve watershed health, increase instream flow, raise groundwater levels, enhance water quality, and reduce water risk. Among the most promising blueprints were agricultural enhancements that could benefit ranchers and farmers, improve the freshwater environment, and yield market returns. Investments in sustainable ranching, for example, might provide significant returns while also making material differences in watershed health, water quality, and water risk. Crop conversion and agricultural infrastructure upgrades might earn even higher returns while appreciably increasing instream flows and reducing risks.[33]

As the 2005 report explicitly recognized, however, impact investments have often "failed in the face of unrealistic expectations." During the three years after publication of the report, the two institutional authors of the report (an investment company and a law firm), along with Trout Unlimited and a consortium of foundations, sought to implement the report's recommendations—with little success. In their final report in 2019, the group concluded that investment opportunities in sustainable water management were too new, too small, too disparate, too geography-specific, or too risky or required too much upfront development capital to attract mainstream investors. Government regulations, slow decision-making processes, and resistance to change also posed obstacles. In the group's view, demonstration projects are needed to overcome such barriers and build long-term investor interest. Philanthropy, government grants, and "risk tolerant capital derived from a limited pool of high-net-worth individuals and family offices" are needed to support these demonstration projects and to make needed freshwater investments until the field is finally ready for mainstream investors.[34]

TNC's NatureVest program has sought to make impact investment funds for freshwater ecosystems a reality today. In 2016, TNC announced its intent to launch a series of "Water Sharing Investment Partnerships." These partnerships would pay farmers to reduce their consumptive water use through deficit irrigation, improved soil management, crop switching, or other techniques. The partnerships would then dedicate part of this water to the environment while leasing or selling the remaining water to water consumers, benefiting both the environment and the water consumers. Through its leases and sales, the partnerships would also provide a market return to investors. The Murray Darling Basin Balanced Water Fund was TNC's pilot water sharing partnership. Although TNC originally estimated that water sharing partnerships could attract over $30 billion in capital, the Balanced Water Fund remains TNC's only water sharing partnership to date.[35]

In 2019, TNC and the Renewable Resources Group (a California-based investment firm with experience in water, energy, and agriculture) launched the Sustainable Water Impact Fund (SWIF). With $927 million under management, SWIF invests in farmland and water assets in California, Australia, and South America with the dual goal of making market returns and delivering "meaningful conservation outcomes," including the protection and restoration of freshwater ecosystems and instream flows needed by fish and wildlife. One of its first investments was former dairy land in an overdrafted groundwater basin of California's Central Valley, where SWIF planned to develop recharge facilities that would both improve groundwater sustainability and serve as wetland habitat for migratory birds on the Pacific Flyway. SWIF will continue to acquire and manage properties to advance water, land, and agricultural outcomes through 2030.[36]

The extent to which the private sector, both profit-making and nonprofit, will ultimately be able to restore and protect freshwater ecosystems through market mechanisms remains an unanswered question. Even local water trusts that use private donations to acquire small amounts of water for instream enhancement are making a significant difference and demonstrating how private organizations and markets can advance not only economic but also environmental goals. The question is whether the private sector can use markets to make significant improvements in aquatic environments.

Part of the answer will depend on the ability of organizations like TNC, Kilter Rural, and the Renewable Resources Group to identify investments that can provide significant financial returns while also making a material improvement in freshwater ecosystems. Investors are highly interested and motivated. The open question is how large a pipeline of potential investments exists. Current impact investment funds have identified significant low-hanging fruit: the ability in the Murray-Darling Basin to take the same water needed by wetlands in wet years and lease it to farmers in dry years, the ability to design groundwater recharge basins that provide critical habitat for bird species, the opportunity to reduce consumptive water needs through more profitable crops that use less water, and the opportunity to sell water at a profit to downstream water users and simultaneously increase instream flow above the new point of diversion. How many other opportunities exist, however, is uncertain. Scientific studies have not yet borne out many proposed ideas for increasing profits while reducing water use, such as rotational grazing. What is certain is that environmental nonprofits and investment firms will keep looking for ways to use market mechanisms to improve the freshwater environment.[37]

SIX

Thinking of Water as an Asset

Perspective matters. For years, businesses typically looked at water as an input, a waste product, or a flood risk. Water, in other words, was something that they had to pay for, get rid of, or avoid. Water markets and various governmental incentive programs are now leading businesses to think of water increasingly as an asset—something valuable that they should prize and try to optimize. This, in turn, has generated creative ideas for how to conserve, recycle, and store water that previously often went to waste. Water, of course, is not just an asset. As prior chapters have emphasized, it also is a human right and an environmental amenity. Governments must protect these public interests, and everyone has a responsibility to advance them. The next story, however, illustrates the value of thinking of water specifically as an asset.

The San Joaquin Valley in central California is one of the most productive agricultural regions in the world. It is also sinking. Literally. San Joaquin Valley farming outgrew local surface water in the early 1900s. When it did, it turned to groundwater and began to overdraft the local groundwater basins. The overdraft declined in the mid-twentieth century when federal and state water projects brought imported surface water into the Valley to help meet local demand. But it soon started to grow again as agriculture continued to

Figure 6.1 Photo of Dr. Joseph F. Poland in San Joaquin Valley southwest of Mendota, California. Source: US Geological Survey.

expand and new environmental regulations limited the imports. And the overdraft kept rising. Periodic droughts have further magnified the problem, as farmers have boosted their pumping in response to the shrinking surface supplies. In recent years, water users have annually exceeded the Valley's sustainable groundwater yield by nearly two million acre-feet—over three times the annual water supply of Los Angeles. Over the last century, groundwater tables have dropped by as much as one hundred feet in areas of the Valley, sometimes drying up shallow wells upon which local disadvantaged communities rely for drinking water. And in parts of the Valley, the surface has subsided by more than twenty-eight feet. In Figure 6.1, a US Geological Survey employee in 1977 stands next to a telephone pole marking the height of the land in 1925 and 1955.[1]

Terranova Ranch farms almost six thousand acres of land in the Kings River Basin, which lies near Fresno, California, in the heart of the San Joaquin Valley. Terranova is a diversified grower of fruit, vegetables, nuts, and seed crops. It plants significant amounts of land in permanent crops such as vineyards and nut trees (almonds, pistachios, and walnuts). Terranova prides itself on its environmental record. It supplies about a third of its power needs from solar arrays, partners with the Audubon Society to provide species habitat, and won the Governor's 2018 Environmental and Economy Leadership Award.[2]

After observing local water conditions, Don Cameron, vice president and general manager of Terranova Ranch, had an interesting idea for how to help solve the groundwater problem and improve Terranova's bottom line. Like the rest of the San Joaquin Valley, the Kings River Basin overdrafts its groundwater—by about 250,000 acre-feet per year. The Basin also sometimes floods. California suffers from climate whiplash. One year can be the driest on record, only to be followed by the rainiest. In wet periods, the Kings River can carry far more water than local farmers need or can use. The US Geological Survey calculates that over the forty-four years of available data, excess flood flows totaled 8.5 million acre-feet. And when the King River floods, the damage to communities in the basin and further downstream along the San Joaquin River can range as high as $1.5 million.[3]

Cameron's idea was to direct some of the flood flow onto Terranova's farmlands. The flood flows are unappropriated and thus available for diversion under California's system of water rights. Diverting the flows onto the Terranova farmland accomplishes multiple goals. First, it increases available groundwater. Once diverted to the farmland, the floodwater percolates down into the groundwater aquifer. Floodwater that otherwise would be lost becomes part of the groundwater supply, offsetting the overdraft, raising the local water table, and reducing or eliminating subsidence. Data for the Kings Basin indicates that flood flows exceed groundwater overdraft by about 40 percent and thus potentially could completely offset the current overdraft. Second, the reduction of flood flows diminishes downstream flood risk and damage as well as the risk that the levees built to contain the flood waters will fail. The controlled release of flood waters also can reduce flooding on the farm, help flush salt from the root zones, and provide wetlands habitat for migratory birds.[4]

To the degree that Terranova needs any water for irrigation during the period that flood flows are available, Terranova also can substitute flood waters for the groundwater that it otherwise would need to pump. This reduces Terranova's costs because using flood water for irrigation is only a third of the cost of groundwater pumping. And because the groundwater that Terranova would otherwise use remains in the aquifer, the substitution again reduces groundwater overdraft.[5]

The western United States has long engaged in "managed aquifer recharge" (MAR), in which water managers take excess water available in wet years and store that water in underground aquifers for later use in drier years. Many areas of the West enjoy significant groundwater storage capacity, and underground storage is cheaper, safer, and less environmentally damaging than surface storage. While new surface storage can cost $1,700 to $2,700 per acre-foot, recharge basins require far less land and infrastructure and therefore cost between $90 and $1,100 per acre-foot. All observers agree that MAR is a crucial method of ensuring sustainable water management in the West and will become even more important as the West continues to dry.[6]

Cameron's idea takes MAR one step further with AgMAR or "agricultural managed aquifer recharge." MAR has historically stored water by constructing large, centralized recharge ponds. AgMAR replaces these large ponds with decentralized farm fields, reducing the storage costs to as little as $36 per acre-foot and significantly increasing the total available recharge area. While MAR typically requires new conveyance infrastructure to bring available waters to the centralized recharge pond, AgMAR can often use existing farm infrastructure for needed conveyance. AgMAR is also flexible: it can be expanded or contracted based on the available water, with the total recharge capacity capped only by the total amount of land that farmers are willing to commit. About 3.6 million acres of farmland in the San Joaquin Valley have the potential for AgMAR.[7]

The first question that Cameron faced was how the flood waters would affect Terranova's crops because Cameron was not planning to take fields out of production before flooding them but instead intended to saturate fields planted in vines or nut trees. While some neighboring farmers thought that the idea of using active agricultural lands as recharge ponds was nuts (no pun intended), Cameron had grown up along the Sacramento River in northern California and recalled wild grapes flourishing along the river even when their thin roots were submerged in several inches of water. Studies at Terranova and elsewhere have now shown that flooding vineyards and nut trees does not appear to negatively impact quality or yield. Indeed, Cameron believes that flooding Terranova vineyards between January and May (the period of peak flood waters) may help grape yield by making the ground colder and thus providing the vines with enhanced dormancy conditions.[8]

Cameron's idea has attracted significant interest over the last decade. In 2011, Terranova flooded about 1,000 acres of its farmland, temporarily increasing the underlying water table by almost forty feet. Both the California Department of Water Resources and the US Department of Agriculture provided grants to study and expand the idea. The local groundwater sustainability agency, charged under state law with managing local groundwater, promotes AgMAR prominently as an important strategy for eliminating local overdraft. The Kings River area has contemplated enrolling as many as 16,000 acres of land in AgMAR, which could produce up to 30,000 acre-feet of recharge in a single month. Inspired by Terranova's work, the Almond Board of California published a report in 2021 touting AgMAR to its members. A scientific study commissioned by the Almond Board showed that almond trees can withstand two feet of flood water during their winter dormancy without any adverse effects on canopy development, root production, or tree yield. The California Department of Water Resources is now examining AgMAR as part of a larger effort to store flood waters in San Joaquin Valley groundwater basins.[9]

For years, farmers viewed flood waters as a nuisance that they should steer away from their property (what property law has long called a "common enemy"). Because California is facing a growing water shortage, however, Don Cameron asked whether flood waters could be an "asset"—a useful and valuable resource that, if managed properly, could help increase available groundwater supplies in dry years while reducing flood risks in wet years and improving the environment. Other farmers in California's Central Valley are now adopting Cameron's idea. Ninety percent of local farmers report that they are willing to flood their lands, so long as they retain discretion to decide when and how much flood water to take. Large food and beverage companies also like the idea. Companies like General Mills, Coca-Cola, and Molson Coors have invested in demonstration projects and studies. We still have a lot to learn about AgMAR, and there are many logistical and legal issues to resolve. But the idea and the favorable results to date demonstrate the importance of thinking about all water, including flood water, as a potential asset.[10]

STRETCHING AVAILABLE WATER

As earlier chapters have discussed, the two traditional sources of freshwater—surface waterways, such as rivers, streams, and lakes, and freshwater aquifers—are overburdened. The human quest for freshwater has left our surface waterways with inadequate environmental flows for the thousands of species reliant on them, while freshwater aquifers in a growing swath of the planet are in serious overdraft. The world's ability to sustainably meet growing water demands requires that we both reduce our withdrawals from the traditional sources of freshwater and find new sources of usable water. An important key to these goals is thinking of all water as an asset.

Most farmers, ranchers, and other industrial water users have long thought of water as a factor of production—an input needed to generate a product that they can sell for a profit. If water is merely a factor of production, water users may have an incentive to conserve, but only to save money or to meet impending water shortages. Water remains peripheral to the water users' core business, which is to produce wheat, cattle, or computer chips. The water users may worry about the risks of physical water shortages and, as discussed in Chapter 10, the risks to their business reputation and social license if others view them as using water unsustainably. But these water users are unlikely to think strategically or broadly about water conservation, AgMAR, or other means to increase water availability.[11]

Water markets, however, are leading a growing number of water users to think about their water as an asset. When water users do that, conservation becomes an opportunity to free up water that the water users can lease or sell. Farmers and ranchers ask whether there are ways that they can re-manage their land to make more money not only from their agricultural products but also from their water assets. In the process, water becomes an integrated element of their business, and water conservation becomes a strategic business focus.

Landowners have taken varying approaches to the opportunities that water conservation provides. Some have employed new technologies to reduce their water use—drip irrigation, micro-sprinklers, laser leveling of their fields, and smart irrigation controllers that incorporate weather and soil information with artificial intelligence to determine irrigation needs more precisely. Others have switched to crops that provide greater value per unit of water, maximizing their crop income while reducing water use. Still others have diversified their income streams through rotational fallowing in which they free up water for lease (and simultaneously give their soils a needed rest) by fallowing a different percentage of their fields each year while continuing to farm the rest. In all these cases, the saved water can meet new needs and reduce pressure on traditional freshwater sources.

Large water users sometimes hire in-house experts or consultants to help in the development and implementation of strategies to conserve and market water. These water users often experiment with new conservation tools and approaches. In other cases, organizations seeking to buy or market conserved water work with farmers or other water users to identify, test, and employ new ways to free up water. In Georgia, for example, The Nature Conservancy has worked with local farmers to redesign center-pivot irrigation with low-pressure nozzles, to increase soil moisture (and thus reduce irrigation needs) by reducing tillage, and to employ smart irrigation systems. Water Asset Management works with farmers in parts of the West to develop rotational fallowing programs that conserve water, enhance agriculture, and improve soil health.[12]

As Terranova illustrates, farmers are also increasingly interested in the opportunity to capture and store flood water in underground aquifers by MAR or AgMAR. One way to stretch available water resources is to capture excess water during wet periods and store it for later use. New surface storage, however, is expensive and challenging to get through environmental reviews and lawsuits; ideal locations for new surface storage are also limited. A far more effective approach is often to store the water in underground aquifers that are much less expensive and already exist. The current storage capacity of aquifers in states like California is at least eight times the capacity of existing surface reservoirs. All the better if the stored water is flood water that could otherwise pose a hazard.[13]

Governments have historically dominated aquifer recharge—constructing and operating enormous recharge basins in the western United States (e.g., in the lower San Joaquin Valley, Coachella Valley, and central Arizona), Australia, and Europe. Landowners and businesses, however, are increasingly adding private recharge capacity. A few large landowners have invested in the construction on their properties of large recharge basins that they can use for their own storage or for collaborative storage with other water users. Far more landowners are interested in the simpler, decentralized opportunity provided by AgMAR.[14]

Landowners' interest in using their property for aquifer recharge and their willingness to actively experiment with new recharge ideas depend on the incentive. In some cases, landowners have the right to withdraw some or all of the water that they store. In the Heyborne Ponds recharge project in Colorado, for example, the landowner receives "augmentation credits" under state law for a percentage of the groundwater stored; the landowner can then market those credits to other water users who need them to pump groundwater.

Storage credits, however, are meaningless in basins that do not limit groundwater withdrawals. Landowners in the Pajaro Valley near Monterey, California, can pump as much groundwater as they want but must pay a fee that the local water management agency uses to replenish the aquifer with recycled and imported water. To encourage local landowners to capture and recharge water draining off local hills, the local agency employs a novel program, known as Recharge Net Metering (ReNeM), that rebates pumping fees to the landowner in exchange for the recharge. Modeled after net metering for solar power, ReNeM has successfully engaged landowners in turning the local drainage water into an asset.[15]

Other businesses are recognizing that the wastewater they produce can be an asset. The factors that trigger this recognition vary, as does the amount of water made available for new uses. The Westin Cape Town Hotel, mentioned in Chapter 1, provides a small-scale example. Because the Westin is on reclaimed land at the edge of the Atlantic Ocean, a combination of groundwater and ocean water constantly threatens its basement levels. To avoid flooding, the hotel historically collected over 300,000 gallons of water from around its footings every day and pumped that water back into the ocean. Looking for a way to ensure that it and two neighboring hotels would not run out of water in the lead up to Day Zero, the Westin realized that it could cost-effectively desalinate this wastewater and turn it into an asset for the hotels. The Westin now produces about 25 million gallons of water every year for use by the Westin, the Tsogo Sun Waterfront, and the Tsogo Sun Cullinan. In a similar vein, many office buildings are now recognizing that they can save money by recycling their wastewater for reuse. San Francisco has created a grant program to assist buildings to connect their water systems with each other and develop area-wide water reuse projects.[16]

A growing number of petroleum producers are studying whether "produced water," the wastewater generated as a byproduct of oil and gas production, could be an asset. Treated produced water could potentially provide a sizable amount of water for other uses. For every gallon of oil they produce, petroleum companies generate ten times as much water—a total of almost three million acre-feet each year from current onshore wells in the United States. Producers reinject over 90 percent of the water deep underground, sometimes to enhance oil recovery but often just to get rid of it. Such injection not only is expensive but also poses earthquake and contamination risks. Producers can potentially earn revenue and reduce those risks by treating the water and selling it to local farmers, ranchers, industries, or even municipalities. Oil producers in California's San Joaquin Valley have sold treated produced water for agricultural use for over three decades, but interest is now growing elsewhere. In Montana and Wyoming, some petroleum companies now provide produced water from coalbed methane production to farmers, ranchers, and the environment, either by direct delivery or by releasing the treated byproduct into rivers or streams for downstream diversion and stream flows. New Mexico is currently working with the EPA to examine whether produced water could help relieve the growing demand for freshwater from rivers and aquifers.[17]

As freshwater grows scarcer, a growing number of farmers are also looking to brackish groundwater. Brackish water is high in salt (500 to 17,000 mg/liter) but not as salty as ocean water (over 30,000 mg/liter). Some brackish groundwater is usable for agriculture without treatment. Desalination is also significantly cheaper for brackish groundwater than for ocean water. Farmers, technology companies, and others are now studying the opportunity to employ mini-desalination plants at the individual farm level to produce freshwater usable for irrigation. The possibility that such plants might ultimately be able to remove lithium from the brackish groundwater for sale to manufacturers of batteries and electric cars has further increased interest.[18]

In all these cases, landowners and companies are helping to reduce water scarcity by capturing or reusing water that they previously ignored (brackish groundwater), written off as waste (produced water from petroleum fields), or even considered an affirmative nuisance (flood waters). In the case of AgMAR, landowners also are thinking creatively about how they can store and manage water for a drier climate, to their benefit and the benefit of their neighbors. Private water users, in short, are responding to growing water scarcity, water markets, and other financial incentives by identifying and pursuing new opportunities to increase water supplies while often improving their bottom lines. They are looking at water as an asset.

RISKS OF TREATING WATER AS AN ASSET

Looking at water as an asset is not a faultless virtue. While it can generate new ideas and opportunities, it can also raise new risks and challenges. In a quest to maximize profit, private actors might pursue ideas that risk injury to human and ecological health, water sustainability, or other public interests. Government's role is to ensure that does not happen.

Produced water from petroleum fields, as discussed, could provide a significant new source of water for agriculture. Farms are often located proximately to oil fields. If petroleum companies decide to recycle their produced water for sale to others, farmers are likely to be prime sales targets. Irrigating crops with produced water, however, also raises potential health and soil risks that neither the federal government nor most states have carefully and fully studied. Most states do not specifically regulate the use of produced water on farms.

The tremendous number and variety of contaminants found in produced water complicate the task of evaluating the safety of recycling it for irrigation. So does petroleum companies' reluctance to provide information about the makeup of the produced water from their fields. Produced water as a class contains approximately 1,200 different chemicals, including organic contaminants, suspended solids, heavy metals, inorganic compounds, and radioisotopes. Toxicology information is available for less than half of these contaminants, and approved monitoring and assessment techniques are available for fewer than a quarter. The content of produced water varies tremendously from field to field and well to well, depending on the local geology and the additives used to produce the petroleum, which are often subject to trade-secret laws and not disclosed. Without adequate monitoring, study, and analysis, applying produced water to agricultural fields thus poses a risk of harm to both humans and the local environment.[19]

As already noted, farmers in the San Joaquin Valley of California have used recycled produced water for decades. In 2016, the regional water-quality agency commissioned the first formal governmental study of the safety of irrigating crops with the treated water. After a five-year study, a panel of public and private experts in toxicology, food safety, agriculture, and public health released its report. The panel, assisted by an expert in water quality from Berkeley National Laboratory, concluded that the thirty-year use of produced water in local agriculture showed no evidence of increased risk to human health. The panel, however, identified gaps in existing data and issued recommendations for addressing them. The panel also recommended new measures for ensuring the continued safety of produced-water irrigation, including the development of a database of the additives used by the oil industry, their amounts, and their frequency of use. While some oil industry critics have challenged the panel's conclusions, a separate academic study of the use of produced water in the San Joaquin Valley also concluded that produced water is a safe source of irrigation water if properly treated and monitored.[20]

The California studies were unique to the historical use of produced water in the San Joaquin Valley. Other, more general evaluations of the safety of using produced water to irrigate crops have suggested caution until more information is available. One scientific study, for example, concluded that "[m]uch more research is required to safely reuse" produced water for other than energy-related uses. A workshop of scientists at ExxonMobil, the Environmental Defense Fund, and several academic institutions concluded that "decision makers are often ill-equipped to make informed decisions" on the use of produced water outside of oil fields and recommended careful identification and analysis of potential risks before any such use.[21]

AgMAR also can present health risks if not carefully regulated and implemented. Many farms in the past have used large quantities of fertilizer, leaving significant levels of nitrates in the soil. AgMAR could mobilize these legacy nitrates, as well as salts and other naturally occurring soil contaminants, and transport them into the groundwater. AgMAR could also lead to groundwater contamination where there is overfertilization of current crops. Elevated levels of nitrates in drinking water present a variety of health risks, including birth defects, blue-baby syndrome, and thyroid disease. AgMAR can avoid these safety concerns through careful planning. Indeed, if AgMAR recharges clean water into aquifers near local communities reliant on wells for drinking water, it can potentially reduce health risks by raising quality levels.[22]

Even conservation can pose problems when not properly regulated. "Wasted water" typically goes somewhere. If a farmer uses more water than needed, some of the water that is not consumed by the crops may flow into a local waterway or percolate down into a local groundwater aquifer. Other businesses or cities may subsequently use that water, the water might provide crucial instream flow, or it might support wetlands, lakes, or other freshwater ecosystems. If the farmer installs sprinklers or drip irrigation and then either makes a new consumptive use of the "conserved" water or sells it to other water users, the conservation can reduce the water previously available for other consumptive or environmental uses. "Gross conservation" (the amount by which farmers reduce their water use) is often much larger than "net conservation" (the amount of water actually "saved" after subtracting the amount of "wasted" water that previously went to other uses). For this reason, most states regulate the sale of conserved water to avoid harm to other water users or the environment.[23]

The development of previously ignored water can also impact sustainability. Brackish groundwater, for example, is often in the same aquifer as freshwater. In most cases, the brackish water sits underneath the freshwater. Many states, however, do not regulate brackish groundwater. If the government limits how much fresh groundwater can be used in order to avoid overdraft, groundwater users may be tempted to turn to brackish groundwater instead. Pumping the brackish groundwater, however, will still put stress on the aquifer. In a similar fashion, some California surface water users in the 1990s tried to sell their surface water for a profit and simply switch to groundwater, which was effectively unregulated at the time. Many counties responded by banning the practice. In short, unless the government effectively regulates all water sources, some water users may find it profitable to develop the unregulated sources even though the new use will add to an already unsustainable water system.[24]

These risks do not mean that it is unwise for farmers and other water users to think of water as an asset. Looking at water as an asset provides the perspective, incentive, and creativity to develop innovative solutions to water scarcity. Many private organizations are working to ensure that the ideas discussed in this chapter help solve water challenges without side effects. For example, Sustainable Conservation, a nonprofit that works with businesses to advance environmental sustainability, has developed water-quality guidance for AgMAR and works with farmers to implement the guidance.[25]

Government also has an important role in steering private ingenuity toward sustainable actions. Given the potential risks of unchecked private water initiatives, the creativity unleashed by thinking of water as an asset must be paired with governmental regulations that protect human health, the environment, and other public interests. As the Pajaro Valley "recharge net metering" program illustrates, governments also can provide incentives designed to encourage valuable water practices on private land that are consonant with public goals and interests. The disruptive and innovative ideas of the private sector are most beneficial when guided by governmental regulations, incentives, and education designed to protect and promote important public objectives.

PART III
TRANSFORMING
FRESHWATER MANAGEMENT

Private water suppliers and markets receive lots of attention, but they constitute only part of the private sector's growing involvement in water management. Technology companies, financial institutions, infrastructure firms, consultants, foundations, and nonprofits are transforming water management in other important ways. Here again, there are challenges. The public water sector, for example, is fragmented and conservative, limiting the ability of some companies, like technology firms, to make as large a contribution to water management as they might. The involvement of some companies, like private financial firms, raises concerns similar to those posed by private water suppliers, although opposition to their involvement has been more muted. All of these organizations, however, are helping to modernize and improve water management. This part investigates these organizations to see how they are helping to solve today's water challenges, what risks, if any, they pose, and how water policy can maximize the benefits that the organizations provide while minimizing the risks.

Chapter 7 examines the valuable and potentially disruptive contribution of private technology companies. Chapter 8 looks at how the private sector could help increase the financing available for critically needed water infrastructure. Chapter 9 turns to a trio of organizations that advise and influence the water sector—consultants, private foundations, and nonprofits—to see how they are changing freshwater management.

SEVEN

Innovative Technologies and Tools

Private technology firms will play a pivotal role in solving many of the water challenges currently facing the world. New water technologies can increase the affordability of reclaimed water, desalination, and other alternative sources of freshwater. They can reduce the amount of energy used by the water sector and the associated emissions of greenhouse gases. They can increase conservation and reduce water leaks. They can help detect and reduce harmful contaminants. They can improve water management by providing data and models that today are often lacking.

Technology firms do not generate the same type of commodification concerns that private water suppliers or markets do. Technology firms, however, often find it difficult to succeed in the water sector. The public water agencies that are the major customers for new technologies are often small, fragmented, conservative, and wedded to legacy technologies; because of low water prices, they also frequently cannot afford new technologies. But before looking at the obstacles that technology firms face in the United States (and much of the world), it is worth taking a look at how Singapore has actively embraced the private technology sector, helping the nation-state meet its water needs while creating a "hydrohub" of new technology firms.

When Sir Stamford Raffles established Singapore as a remote trading post for the British Empire in 1819, he never could have imagined that the island would someday become a nation of its own, the world's thirty-eighth largest economy, and home to over five million people. If he had thought about that possibility at all, he probably would have wondered how Singapore would get the water needed for such a feat. Singapore gets a lot of rain—over twice the global average. But it is an island (actually one large island and sixty-two smaller satellite islands), with no rivers and only miniscule amounts of groundwater. Its entire catchment area encompasses only 270 square miles. As a result, Singapore's native freshwater can meet only a small fraction of its current water requirements, and the United Nations classifies Singapore as one of the water-scarcest nations in the world, alongside nations such as Kuwait and the United Arab Emirates. Yet the island nation is known globally for providing universally accessible, reliable, plentiful, and affordable water.[1]

Singapore has successfully met its large and growing water needs through trade and innovation, two skills in which the country has long excelled. Singapore turned initially to trade, buying water from the Malay Peninsula across the Straits of Johor as an early pioneer of the type of market transactions discussed in Chapter 4. In 1927, while still part of the British Empire, Singapore convinced the Sultan Ibrahim of Johor to lease it 2,100 acres of land on the Malay Peninsula from which it could export freshwater

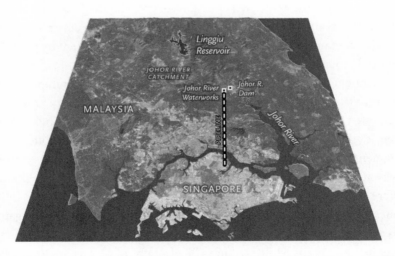

Figure 7.1 Singapore's Imports from the Johor River in Malaysia. Sources: Rafael Estrada; "Singapore and Malaysia: The Water Issue," Channel News Asia, info-graphics.channelnewsasia.com/interactive/waterissue/index.html.

by pipeline. About thirty-five years later, Singapore entered into a series of agreements with Malaysia for enough water to meet over half of Singapore's current water needs.[2]

Singapore's days of water trading, however, may be numbered. While its agreements with Malaysia do not expire until 2061, Singapore is hoping to be self-sufficient in water by then. Malaysia and Singapore have since the early 2000s been locked in a dispute over the price of the imported water. Singapore has also long feared that Malaysia might cut off water entirely if the two countries were in a heated political dispute. Both factors make it risky to remain reliant on Malaysia for water. And to Singapore, water is uniquely a matter of national security.[3]

In 2004, Singapore's environmental minister announced that the nation would rely on "Four National Taps" to meet its water needs moving forward. The first tap is the limited rainwater that Singapore captures in its local catchment and stores in its seventeen reservoirs. The second tap, for the moment, is the water that it imports from Malaysia. The final two taps are technological: reclaimed wastewater and desalination.[4]

Technological innovation has been central to the last two taps. Singapore first tried to reclaim wastewater in 1974, when it built an experimental recycling plant. Singapore, however, closed the plant within a year because it was too expensive and unreliable. As its water managers conceded, the "right technology" did not exist yet. Singapore therefore decided to wait for the technology to develop. Twenty-five years later, Singapore surveyed the reclamation field and decided that the needed technology was finally ready. Membrane technologies, along with auxiliary processes such as ultraviolet disinfection, had vastly improved over the quarter century. In 2002, Singapore successfully opened its first two full-scale water recycling facilities. Singapore followed a similar course of waiting for the right technology in its pursuit of desalination, opening its first ocean desalination plant in 2005.[5]

Singapore's reclaimed and desalinated water operations are today globally celebrated, and it has won multiple awards for its accomplishments. Singapore's national water supplier, the Public Utilities Board (PUB), operates five recycling facilities and five desalination plants, which are jointly capable of meeting up to 70 percent of the nation's current water demands. To gain public acceptance of its recycled wastewater, the PUB branded it "NEWater" (and even worked with a local craft brewery to launch NEWBrew). Even though national water demand in Singapore continues to expand, the PUB expects by 2060 to be able to meet up to 85 percent of that demand from its recycling and desalination facilities (about 50 percent from reclamation and 35 percent from desalination).[6]

Singapore's future success will depend on continued technological innovation by the private sector. Water reclamation and desalination currently require between five and seventeen times the energy required to treat rainwater, making both reclamation and desalination extremely expensive. In generating NEWater, the PUB's wastewater treatment facility also produces large volumes of sludge, disposing of which it is very costly. The PUB looks to the private sector and universities to help overcome these disadvantages and further lower the cost of recycling and desalination through new technologies and other innovations.[7]

The PUB has used several approaches to help strengthen its ties to the private sector and promote needed innovation. First, the PUB has developed close links with the private sector to stay abreast of new technological developments and often collaborates with the private sector on research and development. The PUB has been on constant lookout for new sources of innovation, even working with small local companies that have not yet developed a track record. Second, the PUB has turned to private companies to design and construct many of its reclamation and desalination plants in public-private partnerships. The PUB has pursued such partnerships to increase quality, lower costs, and take advantage of private innovation. Finally, recognizing the low level of R&D funding historically available to the water sector, the PUB has actively supported fundamental and applied research by private water companies and research institutions. Since 2002, the PUB and Singapore's National Research Council Foundation have invested over $670 million dollars in over six hundred water R&D projects in some thirty countries. The PUB also allows private companies to use its infrastructure to test and improve their innovations.[8]

In Singapore, private water companies have been not only a source of innovation in reclamation and desalination but also a growth industry that the government has actively nurtured. In 2006, Singapore's Research, Innovation, and Enterprise Council identified three economic growth areas that it believed were important for the nation to pursue: biomedical sciences, interactive and digital media, and water and the environment. Singapore believed that increased water shortages around the world would provide significant new business opportunities in the water field, particularly in the

Middle East and China. Singapore therefore launched the Environment and Water Industry Program Office in the late 2000s to turn the nation into a "global hydrohub." After this initial effort led to a successful expansion in Singapore's ecosystem of private water companies, the PUB more recently created the Singapore Water Exchange to allow those companies to collaborate and "push the frontiers of water innovation and business growth." Over 180 private water companies and twenty-six research centers now work in Singapore on new water technologies and services. Singapore's water technology sector provides over $2 billion in value added to the local economy and employs about fourteen thousand people.[9]

Companies in Singapore are already developing the next generation of technologies to reduce the cost and increase the efficiency of wastewater reclamation and ocean desalination. For example, Evoqua Water Technologies, a leading American supplier of water treatment technologies, is working with the PUB to demonstrate the commercial viability of electrodeionization, which uses electric currents to separate dissolved salts with potentially far less energy than used today by traditional reverse-osmosis plants (which separate salts by pushing saltwater through semipermeable membranes). Aquaporin, a Danish water company, is investigating the feasibility of using naturally occurring proteins and biomimetic membranes to lower the cost of reverse osmosis. EcoWorth Technology, a homegrown Singaporean company, has developed "carbon fiber aerogel"—a small, black, low-cost sponge that can absorb 190 times its weight in microplastics and other wastes and contaminants, is recyclable, and offers promise as a new means of filtering wastewater.[10]

Other companies operating in Singapore focus on water innovations that could save significant quantities of water, reducing the need for new water production. Several companies, for example, have developed free-swimming acoustic devices that, inserted into water mains, detect and analyze sounds that can determine the location and estimated size of leaks in the mains. By using such devices, Singapore has already reduced its water losses from leaks to just 5 percent of total water deliveries, one of the lowest leak rates in the world. Xylem, a global leader in water data, is developing advanced metering infrastructure that can improve operational efficiency, identify apparent leaks, and determine targeted interventions for nonpaying customers that can decrease both cutoffs and delinquent accounts.[11]

The story of how Singapore is addressing its dearth of natural freshwater illustrates how the public and private sector can work together to produce the type of water innovations needed to meet water challenges around the world. The PUB and other public agencies in Singapore have helped to fund and support research and development for new technological innovations by the private sector and have then collaborated with that sector, typically through public-private partnerships, to commercialize and use the new technology. This active governmental assistance has encouraged private entrepreneurs to start scores of new water companies and enabled both new and established companies to use their expertise and creativity to develop promising new inventions. The private sector, in turn, has raised significant capital through equity and debt to further support its work and has developed collaborative relationships with universities and other research institutions around the world.

THE IMPORTANCE OF TECHNOLOGICAL INNOVATION

The world needs more success stories like Singapore. Much of the water world suffers from what most observers believe to be an innovation deficit. New technologies and other innovations will be critical if the world is to successfully address the multiple water challenges that it faces. Yet water innovations and private companies' efforts to pursue promising new technologies face multiple hurdles and speed bumps in the United States and elsewhere. The structure and policies of public water supply systems often pose one of the challenges.[12]

Technological innovations have long been central to water suppliers' ability to provide reliable, safe, sustainable, and affordable drinking water and to reduce the harm from wastewater discharges. In the early nineteenth century, new purification techniques enabled urban water suppliers in the United States and Europe to protect their populations from contagious waterborne diseases like cholera and typhoid that had long led to deadly epidemics. The development of sewage treatment plants in the early twentieth century further improved water quality in the waterways from which water suppliers often pulled drinking water. And both the Clean Water Act of 1972 and the Safe Drinking Water Act of 1974 in the United States drove further technological improvements that enhanced the quality of the nation's waterways and drinking water.[13]

New technologies will continue to be important in improving water quality, cost, reliability, and efficiency. A host of factors, however, will make technological and other innovations even more important going forward than they have been in the past. Five factors will be particularly influential: (1) the aging of water infrastructure (and the opportunity to replace that infrastructure with a new generation of technologies), (2) increasing water scarcity, (3) climate change, (4) the need to reduce energy consumption, and (5) increasingly stringent water quality standards.

As Chapter 1 highlighted, the United States and many other developed nations are currently using aging, twentieth-century technologies to treat and convey water. Almost half of the water mains in the United States, for example, are at least fifty years old; in most urban centers around the world, they are even older. As existing infrastructure ages, water suppliers will need new technologies to maximize the continued performance of this infrastructure. Pipe leaks, for example, result in the loss of 20 to 35 percent of water in many cities (and loss rates as high as 70 percent in countries with low GDPs). Cities can help avoid such losses by deploying the type of free-floating acoustical devices used in Singapore that detect and predict pipe leaks, as well as a range of other new technologies that identify and analyze infrastructure failures at increasingly fine scales using low voltage conductivity, high-resolution cameras, and artificial intelligence. Water suppliers also can automate their systems to shut off pipes when leaks are detected. Leak avoidance technologies will continue to improve over time.[14]

When existing infrastructure needs to be replaced, the United States and much of the world will have the opportunity to replace that infrastructure with far more effective twenty-first-century technologies. If regions miss that opportunity, the twentieth-century technologies that linger will undermine those regions' ability to manage water more efficiently and effectively in the future. Maximizing the opportunity to upgrade aging water infrastructure will require that new technologies be available and that water suppliers trust the technologies' performance sufficiently to adopt them.[15]

Wastewater treatment plants illustrate the opportunity to upgrade existing technologies and improve future water management. The twentieth-century wastewater plants that are still in use treat water for safe discharge into waterways or the ocean. Newer plants, like those in Singapore, further treat the water for reuse. An emerging set of plants act as comprehensive resource recovery centers that not only convert wastewater into potable drinking water but also produce energy (from emissions of methane and other gases), biofuels, and other valuable constituents of wastewater such as nitrogen, phosphorus, and calcium. Wastewater can theoretically produce three times the amount of energy needed to run the typical wastewater treatment process. In the future, public health officials also will use the wastewater to detect pandemics at an early stage. (In recent years, public health officials have already used wastewater to gain new information about both Covid-19 and polio outbreaks.) Future resource recovery centers will operate at both large and small scales and provide off-grid wastewater solutions for rural areas. Although most of the technologies already exist for robust resource recovery centers, technology companies will need to perfect the technologies for broad commercial use, reduce the costs, and test and prove the technologies under field conditions.[16]

Growing water scarcity is a second factor that will contribute to the need for rapid technological innovation. Scarcity will call for technologies that can add to our existing water supplies, reduce waste, and increase conservation. Although most water users have improved their water efficiency over the last several decades, water demand continues to grow in many regions because of economic and population growth. At the same time that demand continues to grow, many regions have less water available from traditional sources to meet that demand. Some governments are restricting surface diversions to restore freshwater ecosystems and protect the fish and other species that inhabit them. Other governments are limiting how much users can pump from overstretched aquifers.[17]

While new desalination and recycling technologies will be the principal means of diversifying supplies, there are others. Atmospheric water harvesting (AWH) may supply water to some areas without access to either freshwater or saltwater. Water actually is all around us. The atmosphere holds approximately thirteen trillion liters of water—about 10 percent of the freshwater found in rivers, lakes, and other surface bodies. People have long used low-technology devices such as fog nets to collect atmospheric water in humid regions and have employed condensers to collect atmospheric water elsewhere. Seventy countries already sell commercial AWH devices of this nature. Devices like fog nets, however, have geographically limited use, while condensers consume high amounts of energy.[18]

New technologies may enable broader and less expensive AWH. Metal-organic frameworks and other desiccants—spongelike substances that absorb water from the air—have shown significant promise in the labora- tory and in prototype devices. Novel meshes and bioengineered coatings also have potential. While AWH is unlikely to ever furnish large amounts of water, it can increase water availability in shortage-prone areas without other options. Because devices such as metal-organic frameworks can be deployed in small-scale, distributed systems, AWH may also be able to pro- vide safe and affordable drinking water to rural areas around the world that lack improved water systems. One study estimates that solar-driven AWH could supply five liters of water per day to a billion people—about half of which currently lack reliable and affordable access to safe drinking water.[19]

The need to do more with less water will also require new information tools and technologies. Many regions manage water with surprisingly poor information about water availability and use. Historically, for example, many western states have not required groundwater users to report how much water they are extracting. The quantity of other types of information is declining. As a result of tightened budgets, we have fewer physical river gauges in operation today in many parts of the United States than we did at the start of the century. When water is plentiful, water managers can often muddle through without detailed and timely information. But when water grows scarce, timely access to information such as instream flows, environ- mental needs, groundwater availability, projected precipitation, amounts and timing of uses, conservation potential, trading opportunities, and water leaks becomes critical to officials wishing to manage that scarcity. Water consumers also can use better information to reduce their water use and eliminate unnecessary waste.[20]

Advances in remote sensing and monitoring and in artificial intelligence (AI) promise to increase the information that both water managers and con- sumers need to reduce water use. Systems that use "smart" water meters to track water use by time of day and look for anomalous use patterns can help both farmers and homeowners identify water leaks. Farmers can reduce their irrigation by using satellites and drones to evaluate crop conditions; employing wireless sensors to measure soil moisture, temperature, and hu- midity; and utilizing AI to determine precise irrigation needs.[21]

Climate change is yet a third factor increasing the need for innovative technologies. As discussed in Chapter 1, climate change will increase the odds and intensity of both droughts and floods in many regions. Harsher and more frequent droughts will again increase the need for technologies that can supply additional water or increase conservation. Climate change will also bring greater climate variability, which will require the development of better weather predictions and more flexible technologies that can adjust as conditions change. Satellite information and AI already have enabled us to predict precipitation more accurately and farther into the future. Further advances will be needed to manage multipurpose reservoirs that are used for both water storage and flood control and to anticipate and plan for flood events. Periods of increased precipitation will also call for new technologies that better enable regions to capture and store stormwater and reduce flood risks.[22]

The need to reduce societal energy use is yet another factor calling for new water technologies. The water sector is highly energy-dependent. In US cities, for example, wastewater facilities often consume more energy than any other single use. In California, water transportation, treatment, and use consume about 20 percent of the state's electricity and 30 percent of its natural gas. The water sector's energy use also continues to climb in some regions. In the United Kingdom, for example, water companies' energy use doubled between 1990 and 2015 and may double again by 2030, because of both higher water-quality standards and higher water demand. The water sector's high energy use not only contributes to climate change but also raises the cost of water. Reclaimed and desalinated water are expensive specifically because of their high energy use.[23]

New resource recovery centers, as discussed already, will not only reduce the energy used to treat wastewater but also become net energy contributors. New desalination technologies also promise significant energy savings. Reverse osmosis (RO) and, to a lesser degree, thermal desalination dominate the field of desalination today. While RO is less energy-consumptive than thermal desalination, it still uses tremendous energy and, as a result, is often not economically competitive with traditional methods of water production. Advances in the membranes used to separate water from salt (including new nanostructured membranes), new energy recovery devices, and energy-efficient pumps have already brought energy use and cost of RO down, and further developments could bring down energy cost by another 30 percent. Forward osmosis (which exploits the energy released when saltwater and freshwater mix), membrane distillation (in which water vapor passes through a microporous membrane), and electrochemical desalination (in which a small electrical field removes salts from seawater) all promise greater energy efficiency.[24]

Finally, water suppliers will need improved and innovative technologies to meet new drinking water standards. The ability to detect contaminants at lower concentrations as well as scientific studies suggesting that low levels frequently pose health risks are driving stricter standards. Newer contaminants, such as pharmaceuticals and personal care products, are also of growing concern and are triggering new standards. While water suppliers of all sizes will require new technologies to meet these standards, small water suppliers in particular will need help. As discussed in Chapter 3, small supply systems have limited funds and expertise and therefore account for a disproportionate share of federal violations.[25]

Nanotechnology offers an opportunity to create new water purification systems that are more efficient at removing a wide range of contaminants, more cost-effective, and more modular (and thus adaptable to different scales and communities). Nanotechnologies have higher surface-to-volume ratios that help increase the absorption of chemical and biological particles and separate contaminants at extremely low concentrations. While largely limited in the past to laboratory or pilot tests, nanomaterials are now being put to commercial use. Continued innovation in such purification technologies as well as innovative water monitoring systems will be needed to ensure safer water at a cost and level of complexity low enough to be acceptable to all water suppliers.[26]

Many of the new technologies needed to ensure that the United States and the world meet their growing water challenges can be classified into four groups, as shown in Table 7.1. Demand-side innovations are technologies that can help farmers, factories, and other water users to reduce their water demand and help water providers to reduce leaks and other system waste. Supply-side innovations are the technologies that will enable regions to develop new sources of water, like resource recovery centers, less expensive desalination, and atmospheric water harvesting, and to otherwise increase available supplies. Water purification innovations are technologies such as nanomembranes or nanoadsorbents that can further improve water quality in both our rivers and water supplies. Finally, new data and information systems cut across all three fields by offering better monitoring, assessment, and control.

Table 7.1 Categories of Technological Innovation.

Technology Type	Examples
Demand-Side Innovations	Precision irrigation systems; systems to monitor and detect consumer leaks; drought-resistant plants
Supply-Side Innovations	Wastewater resource recovery centers (water reuse); energy-efficient desalination; atmospheric water harvesting
Water Quality Innovations	Nanomembranes, nanoadsorbents, and nanostructured photocatalysts; photocatalytic water purification technology
New Data & Information Systems	Remote imaging from satellites, drones, and other aerial systems; wireless sensors; AI

Source: author.

AN INNOVATION DEFICIT

Despite the promise of and need for technological innovation, experts generally agree that the water industry in much of the world, including the United States, is suffering from an innovation deficit. Bursts of technological innovation, such as the new purification technologies that followed passage of the US Clean Water Act and Safe Drinking Water Act in the early 1970s, have been outliers. Except when new regulations or public funding have driven new innovations, water technologies have evolved slowly. Not only have there been fewer innovations than in many other fields, but innovations have generally been incremental, rather than radical and disruptive.[27]

There is no exact way to measure water innovation or, more importantly, to determine whether that level of innovation is too low or too high. Most efforts to measure innovation, however, suggest that the level of innovation in the water sector has been low and stagnant. One way to measure innovation is through the registration of new patents. While global water-related patents have grown significantly over the last twenty-five years, they have not increased as fast as inventions in other fields. Indeed, since 2008, the proportion of all inventions represented by water-related patents has declined slightly from a high of about 1.7 percent to something closer to 1.5 percent.

Over 70 percent of water inventions have been new water quality technologies—driven largely by increasingly strict water quality regulations.

The second-largest category of water patents, demand-side technologies, have focused on water distribution (e.g., pipes and leak detection devices) and technologies to reduce water use in power production. Supply-side innovations have long taken up the rear, contributing generally less than 5 percent of new water-related patents.[28]

Comparing new water and energy patents highlights the low rate of water innovation. Because both water and energy are critical societal resources, one might expect that the levels of innovation in the two sectors would be roughly similar. The number of new clean-energy patents in the United States, however, was roughly twice the number of new water-purification patents prior to around 2005. Energy patents, moreover, jumped from 2005 through 2009, probably because of new renewable energy incentives and regulations, such as renewable energy portfolio standards, and an infusion of private and public R&D funding into the renewable energy sector. With no similar increases in regulatory requirements or funding in the water arena, water patents flatlined during this same period. By 2011, the United States Patent and Trademark Office was granting approximately six times as many energy patents as water patents. This history both supports the conclusion that there is an innovation deficit in the water field and suggests two factors that likely influence innovation levels—regulation and funding.[29]

Given the close link between funding and innovation, another less direct means to compare innovation in the water and energy sectors is to compare R&D investment. In the last two decades, R&D investment in the clean energy sector has eclipsed investment in the water field by an order of magnitude, both in the United States and globally, no matter how R&D investment is measured. Energy R&D investments have far exceeded R&D investments in water, whether measured by venture capital, public R&D support, or corporate investments. From 2001 through 2014, for example, public agencies provided about $8 billion in funding for clean energy through grants, contracts, and loans, compared to only $28 million for the water sector.[30]

The innovation deficit in water has not precluded a wide variety of important water innovations. In recent years, for example, the value and importance of water data have driven a myriad of new innovations—from Open ET, which allows anyone in the United States to determine water use on specific parcels of land, to Xylem's SmartBall, which can swim through water pipes and detect structural conditions and potential leaks for up to eighteen hours at a time. The innovation deficit, however, means that the United States and the world are lagging in the invention, commercialization, and adoption of new technologies needed to solve the water problems that they face.

THE CHALLENGES FACED BY TECHNOLOGY FIRMS

Multiple factors have colluded against greater water innovation. Start with the two factors that helped to spur new innovations in renewable energy: regulation and funding. While the US Clean Water Act and Safe Drinking Water Act helped stimulate innovations in water purification in the twentieth century, changes in these laws' regulatory standards have occurred slowly, reducing the stimulus for further innovations. Governmental regulations, moreover, have largely focused on water quality, providing little, if any, impetus for innovations in water supply or conservation. Rather than promoting new technologies, regulations can sometimes even impede new technologies by adding to the cost of experimentation or by locking in current technological specifications. In a survey of innovation in the California wastewater sector, over a third of respondents called out regulatory compliance as one of the three greatest barriers to innovation.[31]

In the United States and many other countries, public R&D funding for new water technologies has also been low, particularly compared to similar funding for clean energy, biotechnology, information technology, and other important fields. As discussed above, public R&D funding for renewable energy is several orders of magnitude greater than that for water. Economists have long emphasized that public R&D funding is important in all fields, particularly for basic research, because innovation is a public good that private companies are unlikely to support at an efficient level. Public funding is even more important in the water field because many water technologies, by ensuring public health and safety, provide external benefits that water suppliers themselves may not fully internalize and because, as discussed below, water suppliers generally do not have their own R&D programs.[32]

Several factors depress public funding of water R&D in the United States. Because politicians see water as more a local than national issue, Congress and federal agencies do not devote as much attention to it as they do to energy and other technology-driven fields. There is no federal Department of Water, for instance. New water technologies, such as reclamation and de-salination, also have not captured the public imagination in the same way as solar panels, new vaccines, or advances in telecommunications. There is no water equivalent of Tesla to inspire the imagination.[33]

One must probe deeper than regulations and R&D funding, however, to fully explain and understand the low level of water innovation in the United States and much of the world. Even when new technologies exist and appear valuable, water suppliers often fail to adopt them, or they adopt them slowly. The immense importance of water to public health, the heavy use of in-frastructure in the delivery of water, and the structure of the water-supply sector all contribute to lower levels of water innovation. Water's importance to public health, for example, leads to an innate and understandable conser-vatism toward new technologies. Water managers openly admit that they and their agencies are risk-averse and look for close to 100 percent reliability. Water suppliers do not want to adopt new technologies that might harm their customers, nor do they want to rely on technologies that might fail to deliver water to customers when they need it. The reliable delivery of safe drinking water is imperative, and system failure is unacceptable. This natural risk aversion, not surprisingly, deters the deployment of untested technologies that could threaten deliveries or safety. Regions can recover from failures in solar farms; failures in a water treatment facility, by contrast, could lead to irremediable disease outbreaks. Inventors, however, often cannot locate test beds at which to test their technologies.[34]

Water supply systems also use massive infrastructure with lengthy lives—thirty, forty, fifty years or longer. Such long lives pose a variety of obstacles to the adoption of new and disruptive technologies. First, long life means infrequent windows for the adoption of new technologies. Water suppliers, with large investments in existing infrastructure, are reluctant to replace infrastructure until the end of its life. Indeed, with tight bud-gets, most water suppliers continue to use existing infrastructure long after its projected lifespan. Sunk costs become an impediment to frequent updating.[35]

Second, water suppliers seldom consider replacing an entire system at one time. New technologies therefore must mesh with the existing infra-structure and physical layout, creating a strong path dependency. Many water systems today, for example, are highly centralized, making it more difficult for suppliers to consider and adopt more decentralized approaches.

When parts of a system wear out, the tendency is often simply to replace those parts, leading to incremental innovation at best.[36]

Third, water suppliers often favor technologies that resemble the existing technologies with which they are familiar and have operational expertise. New technologies can require the development of new skills and operational capacity, which water suppliers may not have the resources to support. Identifying new technological approaches also often involves an expensive search, further contributing to an inertia that favors the existing technology. And managers know that the old technologies work, minimizing the regulatory and performance risk that water suppliers face.[37]

Water suppliers' technological choices also can affect the technological options of their customers. Sewage treatment agencies, for example, typically size their wastewater systems for expected sewage volumes. Building owners, large corporations, or colleges might want to develop decentralized recycling systems, but that could undermine the operational effectiveness of the centralized wastewater systems by materially reducing the volume of sewage. As a result, local governments are sometimes hesitant to encourage or even allow the adoption of decentralized recycling technologies.[38]

While water managers readily acknowledge the importance of technological innovation to the future sustainability and resilience of the water sector, they have been slow to pursue and adopt new technologies. In several surveys of US and global water and wastewater managers, almost all respondents agreed that innovation was likely to improve water quality, performance, and costs, particularly in the long run. Yet most of the surveyed water managers reported that they were not effective at leveraging innovation and spent less time on the uptake of innovation than they should. As one consultant to water suppliers in both the United States and the United Kingdom has observed, the "water industry is notoriously slow to implement change, often embracing tradition and tried-and-true methods for achieving their goals."[39]

The structure of the water sector is itself biased against innovation. Water supply systems are a natural monopoly, reducing the competitive incentives that help encourage innovations in other fields. As previous chapters have discussed, the water supply sector in the United States also has a relatively unique structure. Public agencies dominate in the supply of water and the disposal of wastewater, in contrast to the electricity sector, where investor-owned utilities dominate. Some of the water and wastewater agencies are city or county offices, while others are special governmental districts. The water supply industry, moreover, is highly fragmented. About 152,000 drinking-water systems and 15,000 wastewater systems currently provide water and wastewater services in the United States. While three large public utilities (Pacific Gas & Electric, San Diego Gas & Electric, and Southern California Edison) provide virtually all of California's electricity, over 275 cities, 125 county districts, 525 special districts, 125 investor-owned utilities, and 1,200 mutual water companies provide California's water. As discussed below, these three characteristics of the water supply sector—lack of competition, dominance of public agencies, and extreme fragmentation—all suppress the degree of technological innovation.[40]

Competition helps drive innovation in many business sectors, as companies look for new ways to produce better products at lower cost. But water entities are natural monopolies who are generally protected both legally and economically from competition. While electricity providers share similar characteristics, the right of power generators to sell into the same distribution system increases competition and thus enhances energy innovation. Many people have the option to buy renewable energy from their electricity provider; no water user has the option to buy recycled or desalinated water.[41]

The dominance of public agencies in the water sector has had several effects. First, it has held down water rates. Public managers are generally very responsive to local voters, almost all of whom want low water rates. As a result, the price of water in the United States is lower than in most other societies and, more importantly, less than the water's actual cost to society. Water consumers in the United States generally do not pay for water; they pay only for the cost of treating, conveying, and delivering water. US states generally give away the water itself, reflecting the historical view that water is a public good for which people should not have to pay. Holders of state water rights do not have to pay anything for their water, other than occasional administrative fees. But water has an opportunity cost; water that is diverted for offstream use can harm the environment and is water that cannot be used for a different, potentially more productive purpose. Because cities and counties sometimes subsidize water rates through property taxes or other funding sources, consumers may not even pay the full cost of treating, conveying, and delivering water.[42]

While low water rates advance affordability, they unfortunately can undercut innovation in several ways. First, the low rates reduce the availability of funding for innovation. Even if innovations prove less costly in the long run, water agencies must have the funds to identify, buy, and install the innovations. In many cases, however, water agencies simply do not have the financial resources needed to do so. With budgets already stressed, new technologies often are an unaffordable luxury. As a result of belt-tightening, water agencies continue to use their aging technologies. That, however, can reduce revenue and increase costs (for instance, because of water losses from leaking pipes), further reducing discretionary funds and depressing innovation. In the survey of California wastewater agencies, almost three-quarters of the respondents cited cost or financing as a barrier to innovation.[43]

Low water rates also reduce the attractiveness of water innovations to venture capital firms and other funding sources. Investments in both energy and water innovations are risky, but energy investments often promise a large payoff if successful. Not only are water innovations less likely to be adopted, but their profitability is smaller. Partly for this reason, less than 5 percent of all venture capital investments in the cleantech area have annually gone to water technology companies.[44]

Water consumers also have less incentive to invest in innovative new conservation technologies when faced with low water prices. High energy prices have stimulated energy consumers to invest in new technologies to reduce energy use. The failure of some water suppliers to even meter customer water use has further eroded the incentive to invest in conservation innovation, since reduced water use results in no change in water bills at all.[45]

Low prices have an impact not only on conservation by domestic consumers but, more importantly, on agricultural innovation. Agricultural water rates are often much lower than urban rates. Although this is partly because of lower infrastructure costs, the federal government also highly subsidizes water delivered through federal reclamation projects. As discussed in Chapter 4, water markets can encourage investments in conservation innovation by giving farmers an opportunity to sell conserved water, but in much of the United States the markets are rudimentary or nonexistent.[46]

Public water agencies also tend to invest less in innovation for reasons unrelated to cost. Public water managers, for example, tend to focus more on short-term than long-term goals. The public pays attention to short-term performance, not how well water managers are planning for the future. Short-term objectives such as keeping prices down, meeting regulatory requirements, and ensuring reliability can squeeze out innovation, which water managers perceive as paying off, if at all, only in the long run. In the survey of California wastewater managers, respondents were far more likely to believe that innovations would lead to long-term performance improvements than to short-term benefits. Short planning cycles and budgeting horizons further undermine investments in innovations.[47]

Because many public water agencies have not historically pursued new technologies, innovation also is often not part of their culture, and they are not typically structured to support innovation. Unlike many private companies, most public water agencies do not have R&D offices or programs. Only about 40 percent of California wastewater agencies, for example, have in-house R&D capabilities or track new technology trends; only 10 percent budget for new technologies. European and global percentages are even lower. Even when they exist, R&D budgets are often very small; globally, water utilities dedicate less than 1 percent of their budgets to innovation programs. To the degree that public water agencies are interested in identifying available technologies, they tend to rely on outside consultants. This can undercut the development of an internal innovation culture. Few public water agencies formally reward employees who engage in significant innovation. And because they have no tradition of innovative change, public agencies often do not have expertise on how to sell new innovations to their customers.[48]

Public water agencies can also face challenges in financing innovations. New technologies may not work as designed. Public water agencies, however, rely heavily on governmental bonds to finance new infrastructure, and those bonds require high levels of certainty to maintain their low interest rates. Because the water industry has high capital needs, many public water agencies also operate close to their capital limits, restricting how much debt they can incur for innovative new technology. And constrained revenues, resulting from low water rates and increasing costs, have sometimes jeopardized the public water sector's credit quality. Not surprisingly, public water agencies identify financing as yet another major barrier to innovation.[49]

Fragmentation of the water industry, both in the United States and elsewhere, reinforces many of these challenges to innovation. Small water agencies often have neither the revenue nor the expertise to identify, acquire, and operate innovative technologies. Entrepreneurs wishing to market new technologies also must contact and work with hundreds or thousands of separate agencies, rather than working with one large entity. And diffusion of new technologies takes longer because multiple agencies must learn of and acquire the technologies. Finally, because water agencies frequently service only a small geographic area, there is the chance that an agency's customers, while bearing all the costs of a new technology, will not receive all the benefits. Many beneficiaries of a new water quality technology, for example, might live downstream of the water supply, giving rise to externalities that can undermine the adoption of the technology.[50]

Trade associations can help reduce some of these challenges by providing a forum in which water agencies can trade information and perhaps even a mechanism by which water agencies can share in the cost of evaluating and testing new innovations. Only a small percentage of water agencies, however, belong to water research groups, partly because of the cost in time and money to do so. The Water Research Foundation, for example, provides industry-related research for US drinking water agencies, but has only about 800 members out of the more than 150,000 US public water systems. The Water Environment Research Foundation, which provides similar research for the wastewater industry, has fewer than 200 members.[51]

For all these reasons, most water agencies, not only in the United States but throughout much of the world, are slow to adopt new technologies, particularly those that are radical or disruptive. The reluctance of the agencies to adopt new technologies in turn suppresses research into and development of new innovations.

THE WATER TECHNOLOGY INDUSTRY

As a result of these and other influences, the industry resembles a barbell: giant technology corporations that can best overcome the challenges at one end, a small number of medium-sized companies in the middle, and a large and growing number of startups and small early-stage companies at the other end. The large corporations tend to buy up the small companies with greatest potential before they get to be medium-sized.[52]

A small number of large multinational corporations have long dominated the water technology industry. France (Suez Water Technologies & Solutions and Veolia Water Technologies), Japan (Kurita), the Netherlands (Royal HaskoningDHV and Skion Water), and the United States (Evoqua Water Technologies and Xylem) are currently home to the largest companies.

While a few companies such as Royal HaskoningDHV and Veolia also have significant non-water arms, most focus on water. Because they tend to grow through acquisition, many have multiple subsidiaries—Skion has over 310 subsidiaries, Evoqua over 175, and Veolia over 150.[53]

While water startups are growing in number, they face significant funding and commercialization challenges. A recent survey of 132 California water startups found that virtually all were still at either seed or early stages, far from the IPO stage. As already noted, venture funding is often hard to obtain. Water technology has a low success rate; globally, less than 10 percent of patents are ultimately licensed. If success comes, it occurs slowly; testing can take five to eight years, while successful adoption can take twelve to sixteen years. The VC community, however, looks for an exit after seven to ten years. And returns are lower than for most other VC investments; there are no "unicorn" startups in the water field. Water technology also is subject to regulatory risk, which is not as common in other VC fields. To succeed, moreover, technology startups must frequently prove their technologies in the field. Yet many startups, starved for cash already, cannot afford the high cost of demonstration projects.[54]

Startups frequently find needed support from the large corporations that dominate the field. Large corporations can provide startups with both longer-term capital and enhanced access to markets and distribution. Startups provide large corporations with targeted R&D and potential growth. The support that large corporations provide startups takes multiple forms, including acquisitions, equity investments, joint ventures, and channel and sales partnerships. Xylem, for example, follows a strategy that it labels "M&A as a proxy for R&D," searching for and acquiring companies with valuable intellectual property that helps Xylem expand its portfolio of water products.[55]

POLICIES TO PROMOTE TECHNOLOGICAL INNOVATION

Governments can promote greater innovation in the water field in at least four ways. First, governments can ensure that regulations promote rather than impede innovation. Second, governments can adopt water pricing policies that promote innovation by both water utilities and users. Third, governments can reduce fragmentation in the water sector and encourage the adoption of new innovations. Finally, governments can create offices and programs to promote water innovation.

Given the hesitation of many water utilities to pursue new technological innovations, states should consider requiring utilities to adopt, or at least consider, specific technologies. Renewable portfolio standards in the United States have successfully encouraged the adoption of renewable energy technologies—and thereby reduced greenhouse gas emissions. Similar regulations could encourage technological innovation in water. In the most direct parallel, governments could require utilities, by a fixed date, to use recycled water to meet a fixed percentage of their water demand or to supply specific uses such as golf courses or public irrigation. Less prescriptively, governments could require water suppliers to examine the potential value of new technologies to the resilience of their systems, perhaps as part of periodic urban water plans, or to evaluate technological alternatives when the suppliers replace or enlarge portions of their systems.[56]

Governments also should ensure that regulations do not unnecessarily hinder new technologies. Regulatory uncertainty poses one of the greatest obstacles to the adoption of new technologies. Water utilities hesitate to spend large sums on a new technology when future regulations might require them to adopt a different technological approach. The challenge of meeting multiple, often inconsistent regulatory standards, frequently imposed by different levels of government, can also dissuade water utilities from adopting new technologies. Jurisdictions, for example, impose differing standards for recycled water, impeding its use. In addition, utilities generally hesitate to test new technologies with little or no track record if there is a risk that the test will violate regulatory requirements. Regulatory agencies can eliminate these and other barriers: they can promise a reasonable period of regulatory certainty for the implementation of new technologies, coordinate among themselves on regulatory standards, and offer regulatory safe harbors for carefully managed tests of new technologies. In general, regulatory agencies should work actively with utilities and technology companies to understand regulatory trends and ensure that their regulations promote rather than hinder useful innovations.[57]

Price reform can both encourage water users to adopt innovative conservation technologies and ensure adequate funding for technology R&D, testing, and adoption by water utilities. As noted earlier, most water systems do not confront consumers with the actual cost of the water they are receiving, undercutting the incentive to conserve; some systems still charge flat fees no matter how much water a consumer uses. Price reform, of course, should protect those consumers who cannot afford higher rates. Water is a human right, and all consumers should be able to afford basic domestic water. Several types of price reform, however, can increase the incentive for innovation while protecting against water unaffordability. Inclining block rate structures that charge consumers more per unit of water as their consumption increases can send stronger conservation signals to those consumers who can most easily reduce their water use while protecting poorer consumers who use little water and have little ability to further reduce their use. Alternatively, water suppliers can raise rates but subsidize rates for households under specific income levels.[58]

The imposition of a state-wide "public benefits charge" on water use (or a requirement that local utilities include such a charge in their water rates) could also ensure rates closer to the actual cost of water and provide funds for technology R&D, testing, and adoption. As discussed earlier, most water prices do not account for the opportunity cost of water use—the environmental, recreational, and aesthetic cost of lower instream flows and the benefits foregone by not using the water for other purposes. A public benefits charge would help correct this underpricing. The state or local governments could then use the funds to support innovation, mediate environmental impacts, and address other public water interests. A similar charge on electricity sales has long allowed California to advance renewable energy research and implementation. Affordability programs could again protect those who cannot afford the higher water rates that a public benefits charge would generate.[59]

Fragmented water systems, as already discussed, not only undermine innovation but increase costs and undermine performance. If run privately, small water systems would more frequently merge to achieve an efficient scale. Public agencies can also merge through consolidation or annexation but are frequently hesitant to do so. Governments may therefore need to require smaller suppliers to consolidate into larger regional water authorities (as the United Kingdom government did in the 1970s). Less ambitiously, governments can require all the suppliers in a geographic area to create a regional water authority to pursue new technological opportunities, such as resource recovery centers, for the collective benefit of all local suppliers.[60]

Governments can also address the problem of fragmentation by helping to organize and support technology clusters that bring together technology firms, utilities, science research institutions, and regulators to promote the development and adoption of new technologies in a region. Clusters can ensure effective collaboration among key parties and provide for joint testing and demonstrations. In 2012, the US EPA launched a program to develop water technology clusters; after successfully launching several clusters, the EPA handed the program off to the Water Environment Federation, an association of water quality professionals. Additional clusters could further speed innovation.[61]

Governments also can try to increase the ability and willingness of water utilities to evaluate and adopt new technologies. Culture change is difficult and often requires leaders at the top dedicated to innovation. Governments, however, can use incentives and other mechanisms to nudge water managers toward greater innovation. Governments, for example, can link new infrastructure funding to the consideration or adoption of new technologies or cover any unexpected costs of adopting new technologies. They also can require larger water agencies to participate in technology R&D groups or dedicate a percentage of their revenues to technology R&D. Water utilities themselves, however, are in the best position to change their innovation culture. Utilities can consider innovation as a factor in hiring and promoting employees and setting their salaries and can also adopt formal innovation programs.[62]

Governments can pursue these and other reforms more systematically by creating offices with the specific task of promoting water innovation. Europe experimented successfully with an E.U.-wide innovation partnership for water from 2012 to 2020. In the United States, the federal government has offices and agencies tasked with promoting innovation in energy technology; many states do as well. A water innovation office, whether part of an existing or new agency, could fund innovation efforts, support the adoption of regional demonstration test beds, work with other agencies to lower regulatory barriers, assist in marketing and promoting new technologies, and promote other changes supportive of innovation. A water innovation office also could help companies to develop technologies that are consistent with key regulatory requirements and management frameworks, helping to ensure the technologies' usefulness and value.[63]

Singapore has done many of these things in creating its hub for water technology innovation. Singapore created the Environment and Water Industry Program Office to promote technological innovation through grants and demonstration sites at which companies can test their new technologies.

It also adopted a comprehensive framework of supportive policies, regulations, and codes of practice. To encourage new conservation technology and help fund supply-side innovations, Singapore also reformed its water pricing policies and imposed a conservation tax on water use. Most importantly, Singapore's public water supplier, the PUB, works actively with private technology companies through public-private partnerships to develop, test, and adopt innovative new technologies. Singapore provides a successful example of how the public and private sectors can work together to help solve water challenges through innovation.[64]

EIGHT

New Financing Options

The private sector can also play an important role in addressing the freshwater crisis by providing water suppliers with new financing sources and tools. As discussed in Chapter 1, there is an increasing gap between how much water suppliers are investing in infrastructure and the amount they need to invest. By 2039, the cumulative gap could be over $2 trillion. Private investment dollars could help reduce this gap, often through novel financial mechanisms. Traditional municipal bonds remain the primary mechanism by which cities and other water suppliers finance their infrastructure, and bond financing remains limited. This chapter explores both traditional and emerging financing options, beginning with the story of how Washington, D.C., financed a new "green" approach to stormwater.[1]

Stormwater is a challenge for most cities. When there's heavy precipitation, the runoff can flood neighborhoods and damage property. For centuries, cities have responded by installing stormwater drainage systems that collect and convey the stormwater for discharge to rivers, estuaries, or other water bodies. As the stormwater flows across streets, parking lots, lawns, and other surfaces, however, it can pick up harmful contaminants, including oil, grease, pesticides, bacteria, and heavy metals. The US Clean Water Act therefore generally requires cities to treat this stormwater before discharge into waterways.[2]

Many cities have two wastewater systems—a sewage system that collects and treats wastewater from homes and other buildings and a stormwater system that collects and treats stormwater. Some older cities, however, have combined systems that use the same infrastructure to collect and treat both sewage and stormwater. In the United States, over 750 cities, mostly in the Northeast and Great Lakes region, employ combined systems. Unfortunately, extremely heavy precipitation can overwhelm combined systems and cause both sewage and stormwater to spew untreated into local waterways and the environment. In 2014 alone, almost 1,500 overflows occurred in the Great Lakes region, spilling over twenty billion gallons of untreated wastewater. Over the last three decades, the EPA has required cities like Chicago, Cleveland, and Detroit that have combined systems to enlarge or replace them to avoid untreated discharges—at a cost to date of over $30 billion.[3]

The US capital was once a poster child for the problems of combined systems. Lawsuits brought by the EPA and the Anacostia Watershed Society, a D.C. environmental group, led to a 2005 consent decree in which the District of Columbia Water & Sewage Authority (known today by its catchier name of "DC Water") promised to fix its problems. Under the decree, DC Water agreed to install three massive new storage tunnels for the watersheds of the Anacostia River, the Potomac River, and Rock Creek. The DC Clean Rivers Project, of which these tunnels were a central part, would cost $2.7 billion. Reevaluating its strategy after several years, DC Water decided it might be able to eliminate the Rock Creek storage tunnel and reduce the size of the Potomac River tunnel by using "green infrastructure"—saving DC Water and its ratepayers money.[4]

Green infrastructure uses nature rather than tunnels and pipes ("grey infrastructure") to manage stormwater. Cities face greater stormwater problems than rural areas because of their high percentage of impervious surfaces such as roads and parking lots. These surfaces prevent water from soaking into the ground and instead direct the stormwater into storm drains. Indeed, the EPA estimates that the typical city generates five times the runoff of a similarly sized woodland. The goal of green infrastructure is to reduce stormwater runoff by increasing the percentage of permeable surfaces, adding new "bioretention" areas like rain gardens and planting strips and directing floodwater into parks where the floodwater can sink into the ground. Green infrastructure not only reduces and slows runoff, but it also helps to filter and clean the stormwater and beautify neighborhoods. Where green infrastructure

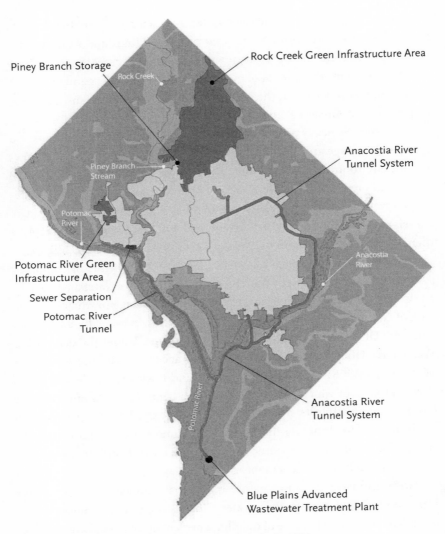

Figure 8.1 DC Water Infrastructure Plan. Source: DC Water.

increases groundwater recharge, it can lead to an increase in local groundwater availability. Studies of different approaches to stormwater also have shown that green infrastructure can be significantly cheaper than grey infrastructure. A growing set of cities, from Seattle to New York, have therefore turned to green infrastructure to help solve their stormwater challenges.[5]

To pivot toward green infrastructure, DC Water first had to get EPA approval to modify its consent decree. The only problem was that no one knew

1 Disconnected downspout
with rain barrel

2 Curb extension bioretention

3 Permeable parking lane

4 Planter bioretention

5 Permeable Alley

Figure 8.2 Types of Green Infrastructure Used to Capture Stormwater. Source: DC Water.

for sure whether green infrastructure would achieve the level of water quality demanded by the Clean Water Act. The EPA therefore agreed to a revised consent decree under which DC Water would construct a pilot project in the Rock Creek watershed. If the pilot proved effective, DC Water would complete four additional green projects. If the pilot was a failure, DC Water would need to return to its original plan or develop and implement other solutions.

DC Water next had to raise the financing needed to pay for its pilot project. DC Water wanted to minimize the project's costs, but it also worried that, if the pilot were unsuccessful, it would need financing for an alternative solution. DC Water, in short, needed to protect itself from the financial risk of failure. Working with two investment companies (Goldman Sachs Urban Investment Group and Calvert Foundation) and a capital market consultant (Quantified Ventures), DC Water created a novel environmental impact bond (EIB) that reduced the water authority's risk while providing low-interest municipal bond financing.[6]

At the core of the EIB was a thirty-year, $25 million municipal bond that DC Water could pay off, if it wished, through a "mandatory tender" after five years. Like other tax-exempt municipal bonds, the EIB had a low interest rate—only 3.43 percent. The genius of the EIB was the amount that

DC Water had to pay to tender its bonds at the end of the first five years. DC Water agreed to rigorously evaluate the success of its completed pilot project in reducing stormwater runoff per acre. If the project reduced runoff within the range that experts expected (18.6 to 41.3 percent), DC Water would make its final interest payment and pay off the full $25 million in principal—just as it would with any other municipal bond. If the project underperformed, however, the investors agreed to accept $3.3 million less, providing DC Water with funds that it could use to help pay for an alternative solution. If the project overperformed, by contrast, DC Water would pay the investors $3.3 million more, reflecting the higher benefits that the project achieved and compensating the investors for the risk they were taking that they would get less if the project underperformed.[7]

The private investors, in short, agreed to share the risk of the novel green infrastructure approach that DC Water was trying. The EIB was a variation on a "social impact bond." First launched in England in 2010, social impact bonds encourage governments to pursue innovative approaches to social challenges by requiring full payback only if the approach succeeds. Under the EIB's "pay for success" structure, DC Water would pay back less if the green infrastructure proved unsuccessful, but more if the green approach were super successful. By packaging the funding as a tax-exempt municipal bond, the EIB was also able to tap federal tax support and thus offer a low interest rate. The project evaluation that the EIB required to determine the final payback also would provide useful lessons for DC Water's future green infrastructure projects.[8]

In 2021, DC Water announced that its pilot green infrastructure project was successfully performing within the expected range, reducing stormwater runoff per acre by about 20 percent. In the same announcement, DC Water revealed that, having proven the success of its "natural" approach to stormwater, it would proceed with the next phase of its green infrastructure program. This new phase would incorporate a variety of lessons learned from the detailed evaluation of the pilot project that the EIB required DC Water to complete. DC Water praised the EIB financing structure that had allowed it to share the risk of failure with private investors. In DC Water's words, its EIB provides a "replicable and scalable approach to financing green infrastructure for other communities across the country." Indeed, Quantified Ventures, the consulting firm that helped DC Water design the EIB, has now developed the first publicly offered environmental impact bond. This bond will help Atlanta finance new stormwater infrastructure for low-income communities that have often found it difficult to access any financing at all.[9]

DC Water's EIB illustrates the innovation currently occurring in the financing of water infrastructure in the United States. New bond products, from EIBs to forest resilience bonds, are helping to finance green infrastructure. Creative public-private partnerships are also financing large, complex infrastructure projects like desalination plants and water imports.

Financing, however, still lags critical infrastructure needs in the United States by billions of dollars. Ninety-nine percent of financing, moreover, still comes from a combination of government coffers and traditional municipal bonds. This is for two main reasons. First, the same institutional fragmentation, low water rates, and conservatism that are hindering technological innovation also undermine both the ability of water suppliers to obtain financing and the water suppliers' interest in less traditional, often more expensive, forms of financing. Large cities and water suppliers are the primary source of financial innovation. Second, federal and state financing programs, including tax exemptions for municipal debt, make other sources of financing comparatively less appealing. The key questions are how to increase needed financing capacity, how to extend financing to water suppliers currently unable to access it, and how to design financial instruments that better meet water suppliers' requirements.

GOVERNMENTAL FINANCING IS LIMITED

Governments have long dominated the construction of major water infrastructure in the United States, just as they have the supplying of water. While private water utilities and "carrier ditch companies" built infrastructure for cities and farms in the late nineteenth century, their role in the twentieth century shrank as the nation's water ambitions grew. The US Bureau of Reclamation and the Army Corps of Engineers as well as states like California, Montana, and Texas constructed the aqueducts, dams, reservoirs, and pumps needed to store millions of acre-feet of water and move it hundreds of miles. Cities and other public water suppliers also built their own massive water import projects as well as the treatment facilities and pipelines needed to purify and distribute drinking water to their growing populations and to collect and dispose of wastewater.[10]

As discussed already, much of this infrastructure is aging and needs replacement. Water suppliers will also need to invest in new infrastructure to address the needs of growing populations, climate change, and tightening regulatory standards. The investment needed to bring US water infrastructure up to snuff will grow each year. The American Society of Civil Engineers (ASCE) has estimated that the annual capital investment needed for water and wastewater infrastructure in the United States will rise sharply in real terms from about $140 billion today to almost $200 billion by 2039.[11]

A critical question is how water agencies will obtain the necessary money. The agencies face two related fiscal challenges—finding the *funding* to pay for the infrastructure and arranging the upfront *financing* they need to build the infrastructure. To fund the costs of needed infrastructure, water agencies have historically relied on water rates and taxes. Unfortunately, as mentioned, politics and legal constraints have made it difficult for many water suppliers to raise adequate funds to meet their infrastructure needs, and that has played a big role in the nation's infrastructure crisis. Regardless of the methods by which suppliers ultimately fund their infrastructure, they also must finance the upfront cost of the infrastructure. While some water agencies "pay as they go" and try to support infrastructure costs out of current rates or taxes, most obtain separate financing for the upfront cost of their infrastructure and then pay the cost back over time. That financing is the focus of this chapter.[12]

Governmental coffers provide a major source of financing. The US government, for example, has long relied on its enormous borrowing power and its ability to deficit-spend to finance the construction of new water infrastructure like the Central Arizona Project (which brings Colorado River water to Phoenix and Tucson) or the Missouri River Mainstem Reservoir System (which stores water, reduces flood risk, and produces hydropower in the Missouri River basin).

The federal government also helps finance local infrastructure. To enable cities to comply with the 1972 Clean Water Act, for example, the United States originally provided construction grants for the facilities needed to treat wastewater. To reduce federal expenditures, however, Congress switched in the 1990s to a revolving fund from which cities can borrow money to finance their wastewater infrastructure. Congress created a similar revolving fund for the infrastructure needed to meet the requirements of the Safe Drinking Water Act. Such federal programs, however, have never been the primary source of financing for local water infrastructure. Federal financing peaked in the 1970s and early 1980s, when Congress provided Clean Water Act grants, and then failed to grow (even in nominal dollars) for many years.[13]

The federal government has recently taken a greater interest in helping to finance local water infrastructure. In 2014, Congress passed the Water Infrastructure Finance and Innovation Act (WIFIA) to provide partial loans at the federal borrowing rate for large water projects of over $20 million. The 2021 Bipartisan Infrastructure Law also provided a $55 billion increase over five years in federal financing. More than $43 billion goes to the revolving funds for the Clean Water and Drinking Water Acts, with a priority for the replacement of lead pipes and the control of emerging contaminants. New dollars are available for stormwater infrastructure (including that needed to address sewer overflow problems), infrastructure resiliency, and the drinking water needs of Native American reservations.[14]

In recent years states have played a far larger role than the federal government in financing local water infrastructure. All states financially supplement the federal revolving funds, which require at least a 20 percent state match, through either direct budget allocations or state bond revenues. Many states also provide their own grant and loan programs for local infrastructure. Texas offers subsidized loans, and in 2021, California appropriated over $1.5 billion for new water infrastructure, with a priority for drinking water projects in disadvantaged communities. California also uses voter-approved bond measures to finance needed water infrastructure—primarily storage facilities but also drinking water, recycling, and stormwater projects. Since 2000, California voters have approved eight water bonds totaling almost $30 billion in financing.[15]

MUNICIPAL BONDS REMAIN KEY

Even combined federal and state dollars, however, are insufficient to meet the growing infrastructure needs of local water suppliers. Since the 1990s, local suppliers have turned increasingly to financial markets, meeting over half their infrastructure needs with private funds. Municipal bonds, which provide over $100 billion annually for water infrastructure, are water suppliers' favored source.[16]

Municipal bonds have two major advantages for the two thousand water systems of sufficient size and financial stability to successfully issue them.

Municipal bonds are well suited for long-lived public infrastructure be-cause their maturity dates are staggered over many years, with the option of an early call. Because their interest is exempt from federal and some state income taxes, municipal bonds also offer rates that are almost two hundred basis points lower than corporate bonds of similar quality and with similar features. The lower rates, in turn, help increase the amount of financing that water suppliers can afford.[17]

The private sector is key to the municipal bond market. Municipal bonds raise money primarily from household investors attracted by the safe and predictable long-term yields and from insurance companies and other in-stitutional investors with risk portfolios that must be backed by safe long-term assets. Private businesses also facilitate water suppliers' ability to issue bonds at competitive rates. Investment banking firms and other financial intermediaries advise water suppliers on financing opportunities and help develop bonds that best meet the suppliers' requirements. Private bond in-surers play a hidden but critical role in evaluating and backing the credit-worthiness of water suppliers, lowering the interest rate that the suppliers pay. Indeed, a temporary decline in the number of insurers able to back new municipal bonds after the 2007–2008 financial crash led to an increase in borrowing costs of twenty-six to twenty-eight basis points for munici-palities seeking to finance drinking water infrastructure, which probably resulted in a billion-dollar reduction in water infrastructure investment.[18]

The municipal bond sector, while often viewed as overly cautious by investors, has engaged in significant innovation over the last two decades. Some innovations have reduced the costs of issuing traditional municipal debt. Private placement bonds, for example, which investment banks sell directly to accredited investors, reduce issuance cost, in part by avoiding the normal financial disclosure requirements of municipal bonds. Between 2010 and 2017, private placement of municipal bonds increased almost 400 percent.[19]

Private firms have also helped to design bonds that better meet the unique needs of innovative new infrastructure projects and that can attract new investors. Green infrastructure bonds are a prominent example. Green infrastructure projects are often riskier than traditional projects. Environ-mental impact bonds like that issued by DC Water for its Rock Creek project allow water suppliers to offload part of that risk to investors by varying the final payment based on the degree of success.

Firms also have designed new bonds to address the greater complexity of many green infrastructure projects. Green projects, for example, can involve multiple beneficiaries and implementation partners. Forest restoration, for example, can benefit multiple parties by providing cleaner, more reliable water for downstream water suppliers, while also reducing flood and fire risks. At the same time, federal, state, and private forest owners may all need to engage in the needed forest work. Blue Forest Conservation, a California-based nonprofit, has developed and successfully tested the first forest resilience bond to support a forest restoration project in California's North Yuba River watershed with exactly these complexities. Environmental impact bonds, forest resilience bonds, and other such bonds not only meet the specific needs of green infrastructure projects but also attract new investors interested in encouraging innovative green approaches and sometimes willing to accept lower returns to do so.[20]

FINANCING THROUGH PUBLIC-PRIVATE PARTNERSHIPS

Public-private partnerships (PPPs) provide water suppliers with yet another mechanism for financing infrastructure. As briefly discussed in Chapter 3, a private company agrees in a PPP to finance, build, and sometimes operate water infrastructure for a public water supplier. PPPs offer at least four possible benefits as a financing mechanism. First, because private infrastructure firms typically bring significant expertise and experience to the design and management of infrastructure projects, PPPs can potentially reduce the cost of developing, constructing, and, where relevant, operating the projects. Second, PPPs can shift financial risks from the public water supplier to the private company. These risks include cost risks (the danger that construction or operating costs may exceed budget), demand risks (the possibility that demand for the infrastructure may be lower than expected), and revenue risks (the chance that funding from fees or taxes will not fully materialize). Private companies may be willing to assume some or all of these risks for a higher financial return. Third, the higher rate of return can attract new financial investors and thus increase the pool of private capital available for water infrastructure. Finally, PPPs can provide financing for water suppliers that are unable to use municipal bonds because of debt limitations, credit difficulties, or other fiscal constraints. Because the water industry has high capital needs, many water agencies operate close to their capital limits, restricting how much debt they can incur. Constrained revenue also has sometimes jeopardized the credit quality of public water agencies.[21]

The Vista Ridge Regional Water Supply Project for San Antonio, Texas, is the largest PPP infrastructure deal involving water to date. One of the fastest-growing cities in the United States, San Antonio suffers from an extremely limited local water supply. The Vista Ridge project, completed on time in 2020, collects groundwater from the Carrizo-Wilcox Aquifer system 150 miles away and pipes the water to San Antonio, increasing the city's water supply by about 20 percent. The project involves 18 production wells, 7.5 miles of pipeline, a high-service pump station, 142 miles of transportation pipeline, and a 10-million-gallon storage tank at the pipeline terminus. To give a sense of financial size, the project cost was comparable to the cost of redeveloping LaGuardia Airport, another PPP, in the same time period.[22]

In 2014, a private consortium led by Garney Construction agreed to construct the project, obtain all necessary permits, and operate the project for at least thirty years. After that, the San Antonio Water System (SAWS) will assume full ownership. In return for the consortium's commitments, SAWS agreed to a take-and-pay contract under which it will pay $1,606 an acre-foot for up to 50,000 acre-feet per year of Vista Ridge water. The consortium assumed most major risks, including the risks that the project would be unable to obtain needed rights-of-way and permits; that the project would be unable to continuously pump and supply 50,000 acre-feet of water per year for the length of the agreement; and that construction, operation, and financing costs would be higher than planned. Initial five-year financing came from a consortium of nine banks led by Sumitomo Mitsui Banking Group, which provided favorable loan terms based on the strong credit rating enjoyed by SAWS, Garney's performance track record, and the project's business fundamentals. All the parties to the Vista Ridge PPP are pleased with the results (although environmental groups worry that the imported water might increase local growth). A 2021 refinancing of the original loan was oversubscribed by about four million dollars.[23]

PPPs are particularly suited for large, complex infrastructure projects. For this reason, the largest developer of desalination projects in the United States, Poseidon Resources Corporation, has used PPPs to finance its projects for over two decades. In 2012, a joint venture between Poseidon and Stonepeak Infrastructure Partners agreed to build and operate the biggest desalination plant in the United States in Carlsbad, California, in return for a take-and-pay agreement with the San Diego County Water Authority. Completed in 2015 with a capacity of fifty million gallons per day, the plant now supplies about 10 percent of the regional water demand. The joint venture effectively assumed all risks, except for the risk of demand shortfalls. The joint venture financed the plant with a combination of equity and about $750 million in tax-exempt private activity bonds.[24]

PPPs are as varied as the infrastructure projects and goals that they support. In an early PPP with the City of Seattle, for example, CH2M Hill designed, financed, built, and operated a new water filtration plant in return for a share of water utility rate payments. Rather than dictating a particular technology, the PPP agreement linked CH2M Hill's compensation to the water quality that CH2M Hill achieved—leaving it up to CH2M Hill to experiment with and decide on the best technology.[25]

Despite their potential advantages, PPPs have been slow to develop in the water field and currently finance less than 1 percent of new water infrastructure in the United States. The small role of PPPs stems in part from the availability of direct federal financing for water infrastructure and of tax-exempt municipal bonds, both of which are financially more attractive to water suppliers than PPPs. Studies estimate that PPPs are typically 130 to 220 basis points more expensive than bonds, depending on the mix of financing that a PPP uses. Even water suppliers in the United States that do not currently have inexpensive financing may choose to wait, rather than engaging in a PPP, in the hope that new governmental financing will open up. Water suppliers in Australia, Britain, Canada, and Europe, which do not have the same government-subsidized portfolio of financing alternatives, make significantly greater use of PPPs.

Some privatization opponents also worry that PPPs may be the first step in that direction. Although water managers maintain control over key decisions such as water rates and over the remainder of their water supply systems, PPPs still allow private companies to play a significant role in a historically public field. Water suppliers engaged in PPPs also must worry about the risk of private sector failure. Garney Construction had to take over the Vista Ridge PPP consortium after the Spanish company that originally put together the consortium went bankrupt. Finally, PPPs are inherently more complex than bonds and direct governmental financing—requiring the participants to work out the details of risk allocation and operational responsibilities.[26]

Some of the claimed benefits of PPPs are also uncertain. Empirical studies, for example, have not shown that PPPs result in materially lower construction or operating costs (although cost overruns and schedule delays are less common). It also is unclear whether PPPs attract a significant quantity of new investors to the financing of water infrastructure. PPPs often rely on private activity bonds to raise needed financing because, like municipal bonds, the interest is tax-exempt and generally low. While such bonds reduce the financing cost of PPPs, their low return is unlikely to attract many new investors.[27]

Private infrastructure companies also frequently worry about participating in water PPPs. Because the water sector is highly political and tightly regulated, PPPs present infrastructure companies accustomed to working in more stable fields with significant risks and higher costs. Poseidon, for example, has frequently encountered strong public opposition to its desalination plants. Poseidon tried for a quarter of a century to build a desalination plant in Huntington Beach, California, before the California Coastal Commission in May 2022 voted to reject it. Some private companies also have found public water agencies to be bureaucratic and challenging, again raising risks and costs.[28]

Despite these problems, PPP activity has begun to increase as both public water suppliers and private infrastructure companies have grown more comfortable with the mechanism. From 2012 to 2017, PPP activity in the water field grew at an annual rate of 26 percent. Interest has grown particularly in PPPs that offer environmental, social, or governance (ESG) benefits. Further growth will depend on the willingness of public water managers to engage in often novel partnerships with private businesses. The future of PPPs also will depend on the ability of private investment firms to address water suppliers' natural price sensitivity and to deliver cost savings.[29]

THREE KEY FINANCING ISSUES

While private firms have helped increase the amount and diversity of financing available to water suppliers, the gap in available financing for water infrastructure remains. Most water suppliers continue to face large and growing financing needs for new infrastructure, leading to three questions. First, how can the federal government best contribute to financing the increasing US infrastructure gap? The federal government's largest financial contribution remains the tax exemption on municipal bonds. This exemption, however, is not the most effective way for the United States to support water infrastructure for at least two reasons. Because the value of municipal bonds' tax exemption varies among investors based on their tax rates, municipalities do not receive the full benefit of the exemption; for the same cost to the federal treasury, a direct subsidy would provide greater monetary support for infrastructure. The federal government tested this proposition with "Build America Bonds," authorized in the 2009 federal stimulus bill, which provided a 35 percent subsidy to issuers rather than tax benefits to investors. Analyses showed that the bonds lowered issuers' borrowing costs by thirty to eighty basis points.

The value of the tax exemption for municipal bond interest, moreover, goes primarily to large and relatively wealthy water suppliers because only they are generally able to issue municipal bonds. Smaller and poorer water agencies often are unable to issue municipal bonds even though they have the greatest need of financing assistance. A more equitable and effective federal policy would replace the current tax exemption with direct subsidies to those water agencies that most need federal assistance, perhaps through "viability gap funding" that would determine and provide the money needed to make a PPP or other financing proposal work.[30]

Change in federal policy, however, is unlikely to come soon. Large municipalities and the municipal bond industry, having a strong stake in the current tax exemption, are likely to fight any change. Water suppliers also believe that the current tax exemption is better protected from congressional budgetary cuts than a direct subsidy would be, because the tax exemption does not require regular appropriations. For this reason, municipalities opposed reauthorization of Build America Bonds, which lapsed after a year of experimentation.[31]

Second, how can the nation broaden the availability of financing to those water suppliers that historically have had the most difficulty accessing traditional financing? High fragmentation among water suppliers can undermine financial viability and expertise. This, along with low water rates, undermines the ability of many water suppliers to take advantage of available financing. Less than 5 percent of community water suppliers in the United States, for example, are currently able to issue municipal bonds at a competitive interest rate. Others simply do not have the needed size or creditworthiness.

One obvious answer is to provide greater governmental support for those communities that currently are unable to access municipal bonds or other financing. In the 2021 Bipartisan Infrastructure Law, Congress specifically prioritized financing for those rural and disadvantaged communities that need federal assistance the most. Much of the new funding for the revolving loan funds under the Clean Water and Drinking Water Acts is forgivable. Other federal and state programs, like the federal Bureau of Reclamation's Rural Water Supply Program and HUD's Community Development Block Grants, also direct financing to more marginal suppliers that need greater support.[32]

Small water suppliers often lack the capacity and expertise to take advantage of even these governmental programs. New nonprofits, such as the Water Finance Exchange (WFX) and Moonshot Missions, have therefore stepped in to help smaller suppliers apply for and obtain governmental financing and to help find affordable private financing. The WFX, for example, helps suppliers to develop fundable infrastructure projects, mitigate the risks that often preclude financing, and build relationships with the financing community.[33]

The private sector can also help to expand financing options for small water suppliers by developing more effective approaches to the challenges that those suppliers face. Potential investors might collaborate with small suppliers to consolidate their infrastructure needs into larger portfolios that can be more readily financed. Bond insurers might similarly reduce unsystematic risks by bundling diversified infrastructure projects into more insurable portfolios. Community-based PPPs that seek not only to finance needed infrastructure but also to benefit the community where the infrastructure is built might better meet the needs of water suppliers in disadvantaged communities.[34]

Finally, how can the public and private sectors work together to make additional private financing available for water infrastructure? Governments have taken multiple steps over the last decade to do so. The EPA created the Water Infrastructure and Resiliency Finance Center. California, Oregon, Washington, and British Columbia put together the West Coast Infrastructure Exchange to help redesign the way they plan, build, and finance public infrastructure. The private sector must similarly engage in active experimentation. Only by working together can the private and public sectors succeed in addressing the nation's infrastructure challenges.

NINE

Change Agents and Experts

Solving the world's freshwater crisis will require expert analysis and design. The challenges are complex and will not be solved without the input of hydrologists, economists, and other experts. Effective solutions also will require change agents who can overcome political inertia and foster support for needed new approaches. Three groups within the private sector—consultants, private foundations, and nonprofits—are meeting these needs. Hundreds of consulting firms are helping water managers to understand the challenges they face and how to solve them; many consultants are also encouraging water managers to take the innovative actions necessary for improvement. Philanthropic foundations are funding the analyses and tools that are needed to ensure a more sustainable and equitable water future, and a growing number are orchestrating affirmative campaigns for change. Nonprofits are bringing water to poor communities around the world, pushing to protect the environment, advising policymakers on how to better promote the public interest, and lobbying all levels of government for needed change. The history of California's Sustainable Groundwater Management Act illustrates the critical role that all three groups can play—and have played—in helping California address its unsustainable use of groundwater.

California was the last state in the American West to adopt statewide groundwater regulation. Initially, none of the western states regulated groundwater effectively. States wanted to encourage water use, not regulate it. Groundwater was also a hidden resource that seldom caught legislators' attention, and groundwater use was modest until the invention of the high-speed centrifugal pump in 1937. In the three decades after World War II, however, groundwater extractions in the West more than doubled, and the region began to experience the ills of overdraft. Groundwater tables dropped, overlying lands subsided, coastal aquifers suffered salt-water intrusion, and groundwater-dependent ecosystems dried up. Most western states responded with new laws and regulations, some more effective than others, to protect their groundwater resources.[1]

Not California. While California's common law had long limited aggregate pumping from an aquifer to its safe yield, the state provided no effective enforcement mechanism. When California created a state water regulator in 1914, the legislature gave it authority over surface water but not groundwater. Groundwater users could seek judicial intervention through a formal legal proceeding known as a groundwater adjudication, but the adjudications were complex, costly, and unending. The proceedings, which frequently involved the rights of hundreds or even thousands of potential groundwater users, could take more than a decade to resolve and consume millions of dollars in legal and expert fees.[2]

While a handful of adjudications occurred despite these obstacles, groundwater pumping remained unregulated in much of California through the first decade of this century. The resulting free-for-all led to massive overdraft, as illustrated by the story about Terranova Farms in Chapter 6. Farmers and other groundwater users, enjoying the ability to pump as much groundwater as they needed whenever they wanted, opposed legislative change on the topic, particularly any bill that would provide for state rather than local regulation. Groundwater users did not trust the state to understand their needs. As a result, legislative reforms consistently failed to pass. Even proposals to require groundwater users to report their groundwater extractions failed.[3]

In 2011, two private California foundations, the S. D. Bechtel, Jr. Foundation and the Pisces Foundation, created a new entity, the California Water Foundation, to spearhead California water reform through strategic initiatives. Headed by Lester Snow, a well-regarded former head of the state's Department of Water Resources, the California Water Foundation chose to pursue more effective groundwater management as its first major initiative.

The timing seemed perfect for groundwater reform. California governor Jerry Brown had long supported groundwater reform. And the state was in the initial stages of a new and serious drought that, like all droughts, had the effect of galvanizing public attention to water. Serious challenges, however, remained. Groundwater users remained opposed to any meaningful legislative reforms. The state lacked good data on the extent and consequences of the groundwater problem. And the public and most legislators did not even know there was a groundwater problem.[4]

The California Water Foundation set out to compile information showing the importance of statewide regulation, create public awareness of the issue, and generate needed political support for legislative reform. To show the importance of new legislation, the foundation commissioned studies on the impacts of groundwater overdraft in California, including the extent of the subsidence that had occurred, the resulting damage to surface infrastructure, and the added energy costs of pumping groundwater from lowered groundwater tables. To promote public support for new legislation, the foundation published reports and op-eds on groundwater overdraft in California, its dire consequences, and its relevance to the ongoing California drought. To develop political support, the foundation first met with agricultural groups, because they were the likely core of any opposition. The foundation argued to the farm community that state legislation of some kind was inevitable and that, if the farmers did not engage, others would end up controlling the legislation's shape and details. The strategy worked. With a core group of farmers willing to discuss legislation, the foundation brought together all the key interest groups—agriculture, cities, environmental organizations, environmental justice advocates, and water managers—in a series of meetings to develop the contours of the legislation. Throughout this process, the foundation remained in close contact with legislators of both major parties.[5]

The Water Foundation's campaign succeeded. In September 2014, the California legislature passed, and Governor Brown signed, the Sustainable Groundwater Management Act (SGMA). Under the legislation, local groundwater sustainability agencies (GSAs) manage the groundwater in the state's various groundwater basins. GSAs develop groundwater sustainability plans (GSPs) that will ensure sustainable management of the local basin within twenty years. The state Department of Water Resources (DWR) reviews the GSPs for adequacy. If a GSA fails to prepare an acceptable GSP, the state can prepare and enforce its own plan for the basin. SGMA's underlying precept is thus "trust but verify": the state gives local regulation a chance but stands ready in the wings to manage groundwater basins if needed to ensure adequate protection.[6]

SGMA's passage was just the start of a lengthy process to protect California's groundwater. The state next needed to implement SGMA. The first step was to agree on the boundaries of each groundwater basin. Stakeholders in each basin then had to designate one or more GSAs to manage the basin. Once formed, GSAs had to prepare their GSPs, and the DWR had to review the GSPs. The GSAs would then need to execute their GSPs by taking the actions needed to ensure sustainable groundwater. Making implementation harder, SGMA set out an aggressive schedule for completing most of these tasks: initial basin boundaries had to be determined by January 31, 2015, GSAs formed by June 30, 2017, and GSPs submitted to the DWR by January 31, 2020 (in the case of critically overdrafted basins) or January 31, 2022 (in the case of all other high-priority or medium-priority basins).[7]

The DWR was responsible for SGMA's overall implementation, but it had never managed a major groundwater regulation program—let alone a complex multiyear program involving virtually every major groundwater basin in the state. The DWR quickly pulled together a top internal team. But to help the team complete its responsibilities within the aggressive deadlines set by SGMA, the DWR turned when needed to outside consultants. For example, the DWR hired a national environmental engineering firm, GEI Consultants, to help streamline its regulatory processes and publish best practices for sustainable groundwater management.[8]

The GSAs faced an even tougher task than the DWR. The GSAs needed to develop governance rules, construct hydrogeologic models, determine local groundwater conditions, create water budgets, establish the criteria they would use for sustainable groundwater management, identify the actions and programs they would pursue to achieve sustainability, and create groundwater monitoring systems to evaluate results and adapt if needed—all in just a few years. Most of the GSAs were local water agencies with almost no relevant experience or expertise in these tasks. Many of the terms and concepts, ranging from "measurable objectives" to "groundwater-dependent ecosystems," were foreign to the managers, boards, and stakeholders. To further complicate the lives of the newly created GSAs, needed data was not always readily available or easy to access.[9]

The GSAs therefore brought in consultants to advise them on what the Act required, pull together and analyze available data, build new models, identify actions that the GSAs might take to reduce groundwater use or increase groundwater supplies, and help the GSAs develop GSPs that met SGMA's requirements. Over twenty different environmental and hydrologic consulting firms, ranging from local firms with one or two employees to national firms with a thousand or more, signed up as consultants. As one consultant observed, SGMA created a "gold rush" for consulting firms. Consulting firms outside California "swarmed to open local offices while established consulting firms worked to secure 'their territory.'" Some GSAs signed up multiple engineering firms, as well as economic consultants, to help them complete their work. A few GSAs also hired private facilitators to assist them in running meetings, gathering public comments, and resolving disagreements among stakeholders regarding the terms of the GSPs.[10]

Convinced that market incentives could be a useful tool under SGMA, the Bechtel Foundation provided $2 million in funding to explore and promote market mechanisms. One grant recipient, the Environmental Defense Fund (EDF), worked to create local groundwater markets that, as discussed in Chapter 4, can both encourage conservation and reduce the economic impact of groundwater restrictions by allowing those who need more water to buy water from those who can get by with less. Working with groundwater managers and stakeholders in the Rosedale–Rio Bravo Water Storage District, EDF created an innovative open-source water trading and accounting platform for the seriously overdrafted Kern County basin. Using this system, water managers and basin landowners can track water supplies and groundwater use, create water budgets, and engage in groundwater trading. EDF has since teamed with the DWR and other state agencies to enhance and scale the platform for broader use. The Nature Conservancy worked with another GSA, the Fox Canyon Groundwater Management Agency, to develop a pilot groundwater market in the Ventura area of Southern California.[11]

Because SGMA will require reducing water use in California's San Joaquin Valley, SGMA's next major challenge will be deciding how to retire significant amounts of local farmland. The sustainable groundwater yield in the Valley unfortunately cannot support all the currently irrigated farmland. Importing more water for recharge will be able to address only part of the shortage. As a result, at least 10 percent of the farmland, about 500,000 acres, will probably need to convert to other uses. EDF and TNC have again spearheaded efforts to develop thoughtful, coordinated ways to transition local farms out of agriculture. Both organizations have advanced the idea of restoring at least some farmlands to natural habitat in return for land-owner compensation. TNC calls it "rewilding" the San Joaquin Valley. Some farmlands would become intermittent wetlands for migrating birds, other farmlands would revert to riparian habitat (reducing flood risks), and still other lands would become upland habitat for imperiled species like the San Joaquin kit fox and the giant kangaroo rat. To kickstart this idea, EDF successfully proposed and lobbied for new state legislation to fund a land re-purposing program.[12]

By anyone's definition of "public," SGMA is a public effort. The California legislature enacted the law, the governor supported and signed it, state governmental agencies are overseeing it, and public GSAs are implementing it. Yet the fingerprints of private entities are all over SGMA. Most California groundwater basins would still be under critical threat today if it had not been for the private foundations that helped overcome years of political opposition to statewide groundwater regulation, the private consulting firms that have supplied the scientific and managerial expertise needed to implement SGMA, and the environmental nonprofits that have brainstormed creative new ways to enable groundwater users to live with a more limited water supply. (Private involvement, moreover, has not stopped there. Private lawyers have also helped GSAs to interpret SGMA and determine what is needed to comply with its requirements.) Philanthropic foundations, consultants, and nonprofits influence water management in multiple ways without ultimately controlling it. They are a critical but often invisible segment of the private water sector.

CONSULTING FIRMS

Since the late twentieth century, consulting firms have been ubiquitous in virtually every private and public walk of life. Indeed, social scientists have suggested that we are in an age of "consultocracy." Engineering consultancies arose initially in the mid-1800s to assist in the design and construction of railroads. By the end of the nineteenth century, industrial firms in Europe and the United States were also turning to engineering firms like Arthur D. Little and Stone & Webster to provide needed technical expertise. Efforts to achieve managerial efficiency in the early twentieth century produced management consulting groups like Booz Allen Hamilton and McKinsey & Company. Governments began hiring consulting firms in the mid- twentieth century to improve their efficiency in everything from agency structure to military procurement. The consulting sector grew rapidly in the late twentieth century as a result of modern information technology, increased specialization, globalization, and a host of other factors. The market for consulting firms continues to grow today. Indeed, total consulting revenue has increased in recent years by about 20 percent a year.[13]

While consulting firms are important in every sector, consultants play an outsized role in water. There are at least two reasons. The first is the water industry's fragmentation, already discussed in prior chapters. Many water suppliers are too small to have the experts on their staff needed to plan for climate change and other future contingencies, design and manage new infrastructure projects, and take the multiple other actions that modern water systems require. Small water suppliers turn to consultants to provide the needed expertise and analysis.

The second reason for the importance of consultants in water is the large set of planning and regulatory requirements that water suppliers must meet. Water managers face a larger and more complicated set of requirements than most administrators. Depending on the state, US drinking water suppliers may need to develop local water management plans, integrated regional plans, drought contingency plans, conservation plans, hazard mitigation plans, and water quality assurance plans. Water suppliers also must navigate the complex and expanding set of standards under the federal Safe Drinking Water Act and its state equivalents, and they must simultaneously comply with the Clean Water Act, state water quality regulations, endangered species protections, and requirements for environmental assessments.[14]

Water consulting is a large and diverse industry. The global revenue from water consulting is uncertain but probably about $10 billion or more each year. No one tracks revenue specifically from water consulting. The global environmental consulting sector as a whole exceeded $30 billion in revenue in 2020 (and, according to some sources, was at least twice that size). While environmental consulting includes work for multiple industries, including transportation, energy, mining, manufacturing, and the built environment, surveys suggest that water is the largest consulting area and probably accounts for about 30 percent of the sector's revenue. While large firms such as AECOM, Jacobs, Tetra Tech, and Veolia overshadow the industry, smaller regional firms—many with only a handful of employees—do most of the work. As described earlier, the consulting firms that helped California's groundwater sustainability agencies to develop their SGMA plans were a broad mix of large national or global consulting firms and smaller local companies.[15]

Water consultants provide an extremely broad range of services to the water sector. Management consultants, for example, help identify and develop improved water strategies for governments, water suppliers, and private companies. Management consultants often draw on their experience in other industries such as energy (which offers important lessons for water) and on their ability to amass and analyze enormous amounts of quantitative and qualitative data.

Engineering consultants help water suppliers, governments, and others to design and manage innovative new infrastructure projects. Cities, for example, have enlisted consultants for help in capturing and storing stormwater for future use—an important way that cities can expand and diversify their water supplies. Geosyntec, a global engineering firm, led a team of consultants to help the Los Angeles Department of Water and Power (LADWP) develop a stormwater capture master plan. Geosyntec pulled together and synthesized local stormwater plans throughout Los Angeles County, calculated available stormwater in the county's sub-watersheds, and identified the constraints that a large stormwater capture program would face. Geosyntec then analyzed and prioritized alternative policies and projects for the LADWP and assembled an implementation roadmap.

Other cities have sought the help of consultants in designing and constructing formative new water facilities such as water purification plants, recycling plants, and desalination facilities. Recall, from Chapter 8, San Antonio's effort to import groundwater almost 150 miles from the Carrizo-Wilcox Aquifer system. That groundwater unfortunately is too saline for direct use. To treat the brackish groundwater, Tetra Tech, another global engineering company, designed an innovative reverse osmosis plant. Utilizing its expertise in membrane technology, 3D modeling, and interdisciplinary-design platforms, Tetra Tech successfully halved the amount of concentrated brine waste that the plant produces. Engineering firms sometimes go on to either construct the facility they have designed or administer the bid and construction process. Rather than designing and constructing new projects, still other consultants help water suppliers to identify, evaluate, and select new technologies that are most appropriate for their needs.[16]

Consulting firms also help improve regulatory compliance. Firms are not only helping groundwater sustainability agencies in California to comply with SGMA but advising water suppliers how to comply with the Safe Drinking Water Act and how to protect the habitat of endangered species. The LADWP's struggles with Owens Lake in the Eastern Sierra of California illustrate both the breadth of environmental issues that water suppliers face and the methods consultants use to address them. The LAD-WP's exports of water from the region have emptied Owens Lake. Winds can pick up dust from the dry lake bed, making the lake the largest source of dust in North America and putting the region on the USEPA's list of "serious non-attainment areas" under the Clean Air Act. The Cordoba Corporation, a California-based engineering consulting firm, and Colorado-based Air Sciences, Inc., have been helping the LADWP comply with air quality standards. The consulting team has monitored air quality, planned and engineered dust-suppression methods, and implemented demonstration projects. Shallow flooding of the lake bed has proven most effective. In response to drought conditions, the consulting team has also shown the effectiveness of tilling the lake bed, saving the LADWP 26,000 acre-feet of water per year.[17]

Studies also suggest that environmental consultants are an important intermediary between their clients and regulatory agencies. Consultants help explain regulatory requirements to their clients and translate those requirements into implementable actions. They also alert their clients to expected regulatory changes, allowing the clients to anticipate and get ahead of the changes. Environmental consultants, moreover, often help improve relationships between their clients and regulators, ensuring a greater understanding of their respective goals and concerns. When regulatory requirements are not working well, consultants also provide feedback to regulatory agencies that can lead to regulatory improvements. Many consultants consciously promote the public interest. Although consultants work for their clients, they often view themselves as public stewards too. A study by Dave Owen of UC College of the Law, San Francisco, found that environmental consultants "often embrace the public spirited values underlying the regulatory programs they implement and view advancing those values as part of their professional role."[18]

While water consulting is generally uncontentious, it is not totally free of controversy. Consultants have significant sway over the decisions of their clients, raising concerns about potential biases. Some consultants, for example, may fall back on prior experience and advice rather than spending the extra time to investigate new options, undermining innovation and experimentation. Large engineering firms may recommend proprietary technologies, creating a barrier to alternative options. The lure of additional revenue may tempt consultants to recommend actions that call for future consulting assistance. More importantly, consultants may highlight the technical issues on which they are experts, such as financial or engineering viability, to the detriment of political or equitable considerations. Consultants may thus unintentionally or intentionally "depoliticize" water decisions that inherently present political or equitable issues. Finally, some political scientists have worried that the ready availability of external consultants may lead to the hollowing out of internal expertise, making water agencies even more dependent on consultants and undermining the agencies' ability to evaluate the consulting advice they receive.[19]

Political scientists also have lamented that consulting typically occurs outside the public limelight and can be completely invisible to the public. Even worse, in their view, consultants have often become a shadow government—a consultocracy, as noted earlier—that provides advice without public involvement and without an appreciation for public opinion. In this fashion, consultants may be undermining the democratic legitimacy of public decisions. These concerns are particularly troubling in the water realm where the human right to water and other important public interests are critical. Finally, where water suppliers and other governmental agencies depend on consulting firms for important managerial decisions, that reliance can also undermine public accountability.[20]

These are all legitimate concerns. Actual practice, however, suggests that they are overstated, at least in the US water industry. While consultants have provided advice to California's groundwater sustainability agencies on almost every key issue, the GSAs made the ultimate decisions based on substantial public input, not just on the consultants' advice. The SGMA process provided multiple opportunities for public meetings and comments. Indeed, consultants frequently helped in structuring effective public processes and amassing public input for the GSAs. Consulting work also does not appear to have undermined the political legitimacy of other key managerial decisions made by public water agencies in the United States or reduced the agencies' accountability for those decisions. While consultants' work is often invisible to the public, so is the work of most internal experts. Any written work by the consultants is typically open to public request under freedom of information laws. More importantly, managers, boards, and public officials typically make their decisions based on all the information in front of them, including public input, and they remain responsible for the consequences.

PRIVATE FOUNDATIONS

Foundations were slow to engage with water issues. A handful of private foundations in the late twentieth century considered whether to set up water programs, but few decided to do so. Politics dominates water management to a far greater extent than many other fields, leaving some foundations uncomfortable about becoming involved and others wondering whether their dollars could make a difference. Because of entrenched political interests, water policies often seemed unlikely to change—certainly within the time horizon in which most foundations work. Finally, because water policies are typically local, foundations seldom had the ability to scale their efforts. Change, if it was to come, was always likely to be one city, one state, and one nation at a time.[21]

In the early 2000s, however, several private foundations, including the Bechtel Foundation, became interested in water issues. The Bechtel Foundation's interest, like that of many foundations working in the water field today, was personal. Stephen Bechtel was an avid duck hunter and had helped to conserve over 4,000 acres of waterfowl habitat in California. The experience of trying to preserve wetlands opened Bechtel's eyes to the problems of California water management and the need for reform.

The Bechtel Foundation quickly realized that other foundations would also need to step forward if philanthropy was to effectively improve water management. The foundation therefore helped to organize the Water Funders Initiative (WFI), now known as the Water Table, to bring together the few foundations then working on water issues and to encourage other foundations to become involved. Partly because of the WFI, at least a dozen foundations now support significant US water work, including the Gates Family, Hewlett, Lyda Hill, Laural, Mitchell, Moore, Pisces, and Walton foundations. Ironically, Bechtel had long planned to spend down its endowment and closed shop in 2020.[22]

Because the Bechtel Foundation knew that it would be going out of business, it created new institutions to continue to advance improved water management after Bechtel was gone. One of those institutions is WFI, which tries to leverage the limited philanthropic dollars going into water by developing shared priorities and collaborations among foundations. As noted earlier, Bechtel and Pisces also created the California Water Foundation to undertake strategic change in the western United States. Now known simply as, the Water Foundation, it has helped pass multiple reform laws in California, including SGMA, the Safe and Affordable Drinking Water Fund, and the Open and Transparent Water Data Act. Bechtel also started or funded a variety of other nonprofits that are changing the California water landscape. One is the Water Solutions Network, which is training a new generation of water leaders how to collaboratively solve problems and is building a cross-sector network of water leaders. Another is the Water Hub, which promotes water justice and resilience through story-based communications.[23]

Like Bechtel, most foundations working on water issues are pursuing a strategic approach. In the twentieth century, most private foundations engaged in "responsive grantmaking." Each foundation established programmatic criteria and then chose among grantees and projects based on the strength of the grantees' proposals and the alignment of the proposals with the foundation's criteria. Grantees, not foundations, typically developed the strategies and tactics. Current water programs, by contrast, reflect a movement toward "strategic grantmaking," in which foundations set detailed and often measurable goals and then develop their own programs to accomplish those goals. Foundations choose grantees based on their ability to implement the foundations' strategies. Under strategic grantmaking, philanthropy has become more top-down. Foundations still seek strategic input from their grantees and are receptive to the grantees' ideas. The foundations, however, generally play the key role in developing the water strategies of civil society.[24]

Foundations have adopted a variety of strategies to improve water management in the United States. One strategy, illustrated by the successful passage of SGMA, is legislative reform. A second strategy is to develop the data and scientific knowledge needed to inform more effective water management. Water managers have long made decisions based on surprisingly paltry information. State agencies, for example, often have minimal real-time data on how much water is available, who is using it, how much they are using, or what the quality of the water is like. Data, like the water sector itself, is often fragmented, with different organizations collecting different information. This fragmentation makes it difficult to find and use needed information. Several foundations have therefore set out to improve information availability and drive better decisions by water managers and consumers alike.[25]

An innovative example of the effort to improve information is OpenET. The amount of water used on agricultural fields and other lands is often not known, making it difficult to manage limited water supplies, enforce water rights, or improve irrigation practices. Satellites, however, can measure evapotranspiration (ET) levels on individual parcels of land, and computer models can then translate ET measurements into reasonably accurate estimates of water use. The Moore, Walton, and Bechtel foundations funded a project involving Google and NASA to collect the relevant satellite data, translate it into usable water information, and make that information available to everyone. (If you are interested in examining water use in a particular region, just go to www.openetdata.org and zoom in to that region. OpenET is interesting and free.) Groundwater sustainability agencies are using OpenET to manage their limited groundwater supplies; the Navajo Nation is using it to evaluate drought conditions across its reservation; Arizona's Salt River Project is using it to identify concentrated stands of vegetation that need thinning to reduce wildfire risk. The same foundations, along with others, are now supporting the Internet of Water (IoW) Coalition that is working to advance a publicly accessible platform for US water data.[26]

Recognizing that water policy is always local, a handful of foundations are trying to improve specific waterways and watersheds. The Campbell Foundation is helping to improve conditions in Chesapeake Bay, the William Penn Foundation funds the Delaware River Watershed Initiative, and the Charles Stewart Mott Foundation works in the Great Lakes. Since 2013, Walton and five other foundations have channeled almost $30 million per year of philanthropic support into the Colorado River, the lifeblood of the American Southwest. They have promoted collaboration throughout the basin by strengthening planning processes, sharing information, and improving the capacity of local organizations. They also have encouraged water conservation by promoting markets and other incentive programs, insuring farmers against the financial risks of experimental crop-shifting efforts that can reduce water use, and trying to reverse the "use it or lose it" doctrine under which water consumers can lose water rights they don't use. Demonstrating the Walton Foundation's impact in the Colorado River, policymakers often treat the foundation as an important stakeholder in its own right.[27]

As these examples show, foundations have focused over the last twenty years on many of the traditional pillars of good water management: (1) strong data and science, (2) effective communications, (3) collaboration, (4) adaptive management, and (5) innovation. Three important new themes are also now emerging. First, foundations are working to increase the involvement of disadvantaged communities and Native American nations in water management. The Walton Foundation, for example, supports the Water and Tribes Initiative that seeks to enhance tribal input on Colorado River policy. Second, foundations are seeking to ensure that water managers address climate change. The San Diego Foundation, for example, has publicized the need for greater water resilience in the face of climate change and has funded local projects to pursue resilience. Finally, philanthropies are increasing their support of nature-based solutions to water problems. The Water Foundation, for example, is working to replenish aquifers, filter pollutants, and ease floods through the restoration and protection of watersheds; other foundations are seeking to improve forest management in important watersheds.[28]

Like consulting firms, foundations have had a large impact on water management. They have helped to achieve important legislative reforms, increased public understanding of water policy, expanded available information, strengthened the capacity of civic organizations to participate in management decisions, launched programs to enhance collaboration, and promoted integrated, basin-wide management of major rivers. Without foundation support, many nonprofits, particularly those focused on environmental justice, would be unable to participate as actively in water decision-making. Foundations also have brought their own expertise and experience to water policy. While philanthropic support of improved water management has been small compared to governmental funding, foundations have achieved sizable impacts by focusing their attention on a limited set of critical issues and regions.[29]

Foundations have not been immune from criticism. One dominant concern has been that foundations, historically governed by wealthy white boards, tend to support mainstream interest groups and solutions to the detriment of more radical or diverse groups and ideas. Foundations have taken a largely business and neoliberal approach to water management. The makeup of foundation boards is changing, however, although the exact degree of change remains to be seen. And as noted, foundations have increased their support of disadvantaged communities and water democracy as part of a more general trend toward diversity, equity, and inclusion. Foundations still tend to support mainstream rather than radical approaches to water issues, but largely because they reasonably believe that mainstream strategies are more effective.[30]

Social scientists also worry that foundations, because of the sizable funding that they bring to public issues, have an undue sway on policy agendas and can influence the work of interest groups, journalists, and research organizations. This worry has grown as foundations have increasingly turned to strategic grantmaking in which they are the primary architects and to coordinating mechanisms such as the WFI discussed above. This concern blends into the broader debate over the legitimacy and accountability of private foundations. Private foundations are creatures of the extremely rich, allowing them to use their wealth to achieve an outsized influence on policy. Private foundations are also free to pursue any public objectives they wish using whatever strategy they feel is best. They are financially independent and are not responsible to voters, public shareholders, or members. Governments impose virtually no obligations on foundations other than negligible reporting. Foundations' management and boards therefore have significant discretion, yet potentially enormous influence. This discretion has given foundations the freedom to pursue new, innovative, and often effective strategies, but it raises accountability concerns. A frequent lack of transparency into internal decisions further heightens concerns about accountability.[31]

NONPROFIT ADVOCATES

Nonprofit organizations have long sought to advance and protect public interests in water and are another example of the growing role of the private sector in water policy and management. The first nonprofits to address water in the United States were environmental nonprofits, and their focus was less on water than on the species that rely on water and the impact that large water projects can have on landscapes. The Sierra Club undertook perhaps the nonprofit sector's first environmental water fight in the early 1900s when, under John Muir's leadership, it unsuccessfully fought San Francisco's efforts to dam the Tuolumne River in Yosemite National Park and turn the Hetch Hetchy Valley into a large reservoir. Muir's concern, however, was the Hetch Hetchy Valley, which he considered a "second Yosemite" owing to its natural beauty, not the Tuolumne River itself. The first environmental nonprofits with strong interests in water were Ducks Unlimited, created in 1937 to protect ducks and their wetland habitat, and Trout Unlimited, formed by sixteen fishermen in 1959 to promote wild trout populations. Here again, the nonprofits cared first and foremost about the species; water issues were secondary. Environmental organizations that focused primarily on waterways did not arise until the enactment of federal environmental laws like the Wild and Scenic Rivers Act of 1968 and the Clean Water Act of 1972, which provided an opportunity to advance water-specific goals.[32]

Over six thousand environmental nonprofits exist in the United States today. Only a small percentage of them focus on water. A handful of the water-focused nonprofits, like American Rivers, Clean Water Action, and the Waterkeeper Alliance, are national. Most, like the Bay Institute of San Francisco, the Chesapeake Bay Foundation, Friends of the Columbia River Gorge, and Missouri River Relief, seek to protect specific waterways or regions. Almost all large environmental nonprofits, however, have sizable freshwater programs. Fish and waterfowl groups like Trout Unlimited and Ducks Unlimited—the "cast and blast" crowd—spend much of their time working to improve water management because water is crucial to the species they seek to promote. But the Audubon Society, Defenders of Wildlife, the Environmental Defense Fund, Environmental Justice, the Natural Resources Defense Council, the National Wildlife Federation, the Sierra Club, and The Nature Conservancy also all have large programs that seek to protect waterways, water-dependent ecosystems, and water quality.

Environmental groups use multiple tools to influence water policy and practice. Advocacy before legislatures, agencies, and courts has long been a favored device. By focusing their lobbying efforts on a limited number of important legislative bills and enlisting the support of their sizable membership, environmental groups over the last half century have helped to pass major national and state laws protecting environmental interests in water. As noted earlier, EDF was responsible for the enactment of California's

Multibenefit Land Repurposing Program, which will help convert irrigated agricultural lands to less water-intensive uses. EDF began with a multi-stakeholder workshop to establish the need for a financial incentive program, helped draft the legislation, and then mobilized support for the law. The California legislature passed it unanimously.[33]

Environmental groups are also active participants in administrative processes, where their expertise can provide strong leverage. Having helped pass California's Land Repurposing Program, for example, EDF is now working to make it a success by advertising the availability of grants and establishing best practices for local implementation. A coalition of five environmental organizations led by TNC has been analyzing all draft groundwater sustainability plans submitted for review to the California Department of Water Resources. Using their scientific expertise, the nonprofits have provided detailed comments on the plans, making it difficult for the state to ignore potential deficiencies in the plans. When the Trump administration considered whether to cut back on wetlands protections under the federal Clean Water Act, the Natural Resources Defense Council (NRDC) filed lengthy comments "on behalf of [its] more than three million members and online activists" that detailed the scientific and legal objections to the proposed rule.[34]

Environmental groups also have used courts to establish long-lasting victories. When the Tennessee Valley Authority chose to move forward with a dam in the 1970s that would harm the downstream habitat of a small fish known as the snail darter (*Percina tanasi*), Hiram Hill and the Audubon Council of Tennessee sued to block the dam. In a 1978 opinion that would enshrine the Endangered Species Act as one of the most protective environmental laws in the nation, the US Supreme Court held that the costs of protecting endangered species play no role under the Act because "Congress viewed the value of endangered species as 'incalculable.'" When the water usage of Los Angeles threatened to drain Mono Lake in the Eastern Sierra in the same time period, the Mono Lake Committee and National Audubon Society in 1979 sued Los Angeles under the public trust doctrine, which no court had ever applied to water diversions. In 1983, the California Supreme Court, holding that the doctrine did apply, required state agencies to protect the environment "whenever feasible" in managing water, providing environmental groups with another weapon to protect instream flows.[35]

Environmental groups now use a broad set of strategies in addition to formal advocacy. Many environmental nonprofits have turned to market mechanisms to help protect the environment. As already discussed, EDF, TNC, and a growing set of land trusts are using markets and financial incentives to encourage conservation, take pressure off surface waterways and groundwater aquifers, and return water to the environment. As Chapter 5 highlighted, TNC has turned to impact investing. And TNC, WWF, and other international environmental nonprofits have helped create "water funds" in Central and South America where water users pay the residents of watersheds to protect the natural ecosystem because of the benefits that well-maintained watersheds can provide to downstream water consumers. These water funds are an example of environmental nonprofits' growing interest in "natural capital."[36]

Environmental nonprofits are also reaching across traditional political battlelines and international borders to improve water management. Sustainable Conservation, a California-based nonprofit, collaborates with private businesses. The organization, for example, works with farmers to promote AgMAR and other projects to replenish depleted groundwater aquifers. Environmental nonprofits are engaging internationally on the Colorado River. The Colorado River Delta, as discussed in Chapter 5, has been largely dry since the early 1980s because of upstream diversions in both the United States and Mexico. To address this problem, nonprofits from both countries helped to negotiate two "minutes" to the 1944 Mexico–United States Water Treaty, authorizing "pulse flows" from the river's reservoirs to help restore parts of the Delta ecosystem.[37]

Environmental groups are no longer the only public interest groups working to change water policy. The last twenty years have seen the growth of the environmental justice movement and the creation of several nonprofits focused exclusively on access to drinking water, including the Community Water Center and the Environmental Justice Coalition for Water. As Chapter 1 highlighted, over 2.1 million people in the United States lack access to affordable and safe drinking water. Environmental justice groups are fighting to ensure such access and to provide disadvantaged communities with a meaningful voice in water management. In California, these efforts resulted in the 2012 passage of legislation recognizing the human right to water and, more recently, state funding to help actualize that right. The Community Water Center is now working to put members of disadvantaged communities on the boards of the water districts that service them. White men have historically dominated water boards, in part because no one ever contested their seats. The Community Water Center is helping interested community members to build their technical and governance skills and encouraging them to run for board seats; voters have already elected several center-sponsored candidates.[38]

A larger, longer-established set of nonprofits has been working for decades to provide affordable and safe drinking water, as well as sanitation services, to the developing world. As Chapter 1 described, the challenge is enormous, with over 700 million people living in water poverty and over two billion without sanitation. Global nonprofits are taking varied and complementary approaches, most rooted in business concepts, to water, sanitation, and hygiene (WASH). Most of the nonprofits seek to help build drinking water and sanitation infrastructure. Charity:Water, for example, partners with local organizations around the world to develop community-owned water projects. Water for People develops water projects through a market-based approach that it calls "Everyone Forever." To ensure that projects are sustainable in the long run, it carefully plans each project based on local needs and capabilities, strengthens the community's capacity to manage and run its system, advocates for any needed policy changes, and insists on local co-financing for buy-in. Drop in the Bucket provides wells and latrines for schools.

Water.org, by contrast, seeks to help fill the $114 billion funding gap that the World Bank estimates is needed to meet the United Nations sustainable development goals for water and sanitation. Working with local organizations, Water.org provides microfinancing that local households can use to obtain safe drinking water, a latrine, or a toilet. Water.org also works with commercial banks to lend money for WASH activities at multiple scales, from individual households to local water utilities. While intergovernmental organizations like the World Bank bring far greater funding and capacity to WASH goals, nonprofits estimate that they have helped over fifty million people obtain acceptable access to water or sanitation.[39]

While not as publicly visible as private water suppliers or technology companies, consultants, foundations, and nonprofits strongly influence virtually all aspects of water management. Because of their past involvement, current water management is stronger than it otherwise would be, with smarter decisions, better data, more robust analysis, and enhanced inventiveness. Going forward, they will play a major role in how legislators, regulators, and water managers address freshwater challenges. Because their activities can raise legitimacy and transparency concerns, all three groups must ensure that their decisions and activities are fully visible to the public and open to evaluation and criticism. With appropriate protections, however, they will continue to play an indispensable role in solving today's freshwater crisis.

PART IV
TOWARD A SUSTAINABLE WATER FUTURE

The final two chapters look at how business and government can together promote more sustainable water management. Chapter 10 looks at how businesses are addressing their own water use. As Chapter 2 explained, businesses are the largest users of water, and their engagement in water management is therefore essential to a sustainable freshwater future. Because of the various risks that water scarcity and pollution pose to businesses, large corporations are adopting water stewardship programs to reduce and offset their water use and improve the quality of their wastewater. Many corporations also are working with nonprofits and governments to improve water management outside their corporate walls, recognizing that even the best internal programs will fail to reduce corporate risks if external governance is inadequate. These stewardship programs, if meaningful, promise benefits not only to the corporations themselves but to society.

Chapter 11 reflects on four important ways that businesses and governments can improve the contributions that the private sector is making to water management and simultaneously protect the critical public interests in water. Governments, for example, can make needed reforms to the public sector and appropriately regulate private involvement. Businesses can recognize and pursue their unique ethical responsibilities in the water field. Most importantly, governments and businesses can work in closer partnership to jointly achieve a sustainable water future.

TEN

Corporate Water Stewardship

The success of many businesses depends on effective water management, both within the company and in the regions in which they operate. As Chapter 2 discussed, water presents a variety of business risks. Water shortages and pollution can pose a physical risk to companies' operations and supply chains. The perception that a corporation is harming a region's supply can lead to new regulations, public protests, poor public reputation, and loss of a company's social license to operate. For these reasons, investors are increasingly evaluating a company's water risks when deciding whether to invest in the company. In response to all these factors, a growing number of corporations have adopted water stewardship programs, almost always as part of broader sustainability initiatives, that are likely to play a major role in addressing water challenges around the world. Many observers trace water stewardship programs to the Coca-Cola Company and the water protests it encountered in India in the early 2000s.

Kaladera is a small town of about fifteen thousand residents in a semiarid region of Rajasthan, India. Agriculture is the mainstay of the local economy. Farmers grow a variety of crops, some of which, like wheat and groundnuts, are water-intensive. Because surface water is scarce, farmers primarily rely on groundwater for irrigation. Because the government subsidizes energy, groundwater pumping is relatively inexpensive, encouraging overwatering and the growing of water-intensive crops. Because electricity is unreliable, many farmers let their pumps run continually, getting water when they can. Unconstrained pumping, along with growth and urbanization, has led to sizable overdraft of the local aquifer, with withdrawals exceeding sustainable yield by anywhere from 33 to 150 percent. From 1990 to 2000, groundwater levels dropped about ten feet.[1]

In 2000, the Coca-Cola Company opened a new bottling plant in Kaladera, even though the facility promised to further strain the already overexploited aquifer. Hoping to turn Kaladera into an industrial hub, Rajasthan had offered tax incentives to Coca-Cola to locate there. If Coca-Cola had any concerns about water sufficiency, Rajasthan's financial inducements overrode them. Within two years, Coca-Cola found itself mired in a major water dispute with colonial and human rights overtones. Local farmers complained that groundwater levels fell dramatically after Coca-Cola arrived, drying up their wells and threatening their livelihood. While Coca-Cola's pumping probably averaged only 1 percent of local withdrawals, it was the largest pumper, and its pumping peaked in late spring when the water stress was most acute. Coke did not reach out effectively to address the community's water concerns, and farmers did not trust the company's assurances that it was operating only two borewells. As rumors flew, residents formed a "Struggle Committee" and demanded that Coca-Cola shutter its plant.[2]

The Kaladera plant was not Coke's only facility under challenge in India. Farmers in an arid region of the southern Indian state of Kerala objected that the local Coca-Cola plant had not only dried up their wells but also polluted the groundwater basin. Residents surrounded the plant in protest for hundreds of days. In response, the village council canceled the plant's permit in 2004. Coca-Cola sued. A judge approved the cancelation, ruling that the government had a public trust obligation to protect against groundwater overdraft, only to be overturned by a panel of judges who concluded that the plant was not actually at fault for the local groundwater ills. With protests continuing, Coca-Cola voluntarily closed the plant. Coca-Cola plants in the states of Uttar Pradesh and Maharashtra soon faced similar accusations of water depletion and degradation (mixed with additional complaints about labor practices and land ownership).[3]

Coke's problems in India soon drew international attention. Amit Srivastava, a California-based activist, began publicizing the story, attracting twenty thousand visitors a month to his website. The tale of a giant international corporation "stealing" groundwater from impoverished farmers in India struck a chord with college students, who began demanding the removal of Coca-Cola products from their campuses. The University of Michigan, Bard, Carleton, and Oberlin all temporarily banned Coca-Cola. The *Wall Street Journal* published a front-page story on the bottling plants, with Srivastava playing David to Coca-Cola's Goliath. The problem threatened to sully Coke's highly regarded brand name both domestically and globally and risked turning the company into a symbol of corporate irresponsibility.[4]

Coca-Cola realized that it was facing a water crisis. And an internal analysis suggested that Coke's water-related risks were not limited to India. Water is a central ingredient of Coca-Cola. Eighty percent of a half-liter bottle of Coca-Cola is water. To save distribution costs, Coca-Cola produces and bottles its beverages at over nine hundred bottling plants around the world. About a third of those plants are in water-stressed regions like Kaladera and thus run similar risks of provoking a water conflict. The 0.4 liters of water in each half-liter bottle of Coke is also only 1 percent of the total water footprint of that bottle. Sugar beets, which Coke uses as a sweetener, require far more water (about twenty-three liters per bottle). Because Coca-Cola buys from farmers all over the world, its supply chain presents another global water risk. Producing the packaging for Coke also requires water. One writer has estimated that the water used across all Coke's operations would meet the annual domestic needs of over two billion people, fully a quarter of the world's population.[5]

Coke realized that it needed to address and manage its water risks, both in India and elsewhere around the world. In 2002, Coke published its first environmental report. Two years later, the company launched a Global Water Initiative and created a department to manage its water operations. Coca-Cola also conducted a detailed analysis of the potential water risks facing each of its bottling plants. One of its first goals was to improve the water efficiency of its plants. To allow the company and the public to track Coke's progress in reducing water use, it started to report water efficiency for its global bottling system. In 2010, the company announced a goal to improve water efficiency over the following decade in its manufacturing facilities by 25 percent. By 2019, it had succeeded in reducing water use through technological and operational improvements by 19 percent—not quite its goal but a significant accomplishment nonetheless.[6]

Although water efficiency reduced Coca-Cola's footprint, it did not eliminate it. For communities like Kaladera, *any* water withdrawals threatened local groundwater users. In 2007, Coke therefore announced that it would pursue "water neutrality" in an initiative it dubbed "Replenish." As explained by E. Neville Isdell, the company's CEO at the time, Coke would "replace every drop of water we use in our beverages and their production to achieve balance in communities and in nature with the water we use." Coca-Cola would not only reduce its water use but offset that use—much as corporations buy carbon credits to offset carbon emissions.[7]

Coke had already taken steps in India to offset its local water consumption. Using a traditional system of groundwater recharge, the company had dug ground shafts to capture rainwater and allow it to percolate into groundwater basins. Coke also supported the construction and rehabilitation of stepwells known as *bawari* and similar projects designed to capture more water. And the company helped defray the cost to local farmers of drip irrigation, reducing local agricultural use. Although critics complained that Coca-Cola overstated the benefits of these actions, the company had become the first major corporation to try to offset its water impact.[8]

At a global level, Coke set a goal of offsetting 100 percent of its production water by 2020. The company met its goal in 2015, five years early, becoming the first Fortune 500 company to replenish all direct water use. To meet that goal, Coke undertook more than 200 community projects in over seventy countries. Coca-Cola installed check dams to induce infiltration into aquifers, restored the storage capacity of floodplains, harvested rainwater, removed thirsty invasive plants from watersheds, recycled process water for community reuse, and conserved water through upgrades in irrigation equipment and other infrastructure. The Nature Conservancy and Limno-Tech, an engineering firm, verified each project and calculated the water credit Coke could claim. By 2020, Coca-Cola was replenishing almost twice the amount of water it used in its operations.[9]

Critics complained that Coke's water stewardship practices were not quite as exceptional as the company implied and, more importantly, did not always protect the local communities that it impacted. Under its Replenish program, Coke offset only the water that it used directly in its product and its bottling plants. The company chose at an early stage not even to try to offset the vast volume of water used to grow sugar beets and other syrup ingredients. Being "water neutral" at a company-wide level, moreover, did not mean that Coca-Cola was offsetting its water use in every location where it operated a bottling plant. Coke replenished water in regions with the greatest opportunity and impact. As a result, Coke still used more water in some regions than it replenished. At the same time that Coke announced success in replenishing 100 percent of its operating water globally, it had to abandon or cancel plans for several new plants in India because of continued local opposition to its bottling plants activities.[10]

Coca-Cola has continued to enhance its water stewardship program. Finally addressing its supply chain, the company in 2013 released "Sustainable Agriculture Guiding Principles" for its farm suppliers. Coke has encouraged its midwestern farmers to adopt advanced irrigation techniques, trained Indian farmers to practice more sustainable farming of sugarcane, and provided recycled wastewater to its farmers in China. In its new 2030 Water Strategy, Coke identifies "priority sourcing watersheds"—regions with both water scarcity and water-intensive agricultural production—where it will actively engage with its suppliers to "ensure water-sustainable ingredients and landscapes." In its 2030 strategy, Coke also pledges to achieve "water neutrality" not only company-wide but also in "leadership locations" where water risks are particularly high. Not all bottling plants will be "water neutral," and Coke will not actively reduce water use in all portions of its supply chain. But Coke promises to do better "in the areas where it matters most."[11]

Coke is also addressing water quality. As part of its expansive water stewardship program, the company treats 100 percent of the wastewater from its facilities. Coke seeks to ensure that the water that its plants discharge into the environment is clean enough to support aquatic life, even if local governments set a lower standard. To meet its corporate standard, Coke has worked with multiple technology companies to develop innovative new treatment systems.[12]

At a relatively early stage, Coca-Cola also moved beyond the impact of its own facilities and suppliers to tackle broader water challenges in partnership with governments, nonprofits, and other businesses. In Coke's Replenish Africa Initiative (RAIN), which the Coca-Cola Foundation began in 2009 with a $65 million commitment, the company works to provide clean drinking water and sanitation services to African communities, and it restores and protects African watersheds through water funds that enhance downstream water supplies while providing economic benefits to watershed communities. According to Coke, RAIN has helped over 6 million people in forty-one African nations. In another initiative, Coca-Cola has worked with WWF and local land trusts to reduce agricultural pollution in the East Anglia region of England and to restore the River Nar.[13]

Building on initiatives like RAIN, Coca-Cola is increasingly focused on improving water governance in the regions in which it or businesses in its supply chain operate. While continuing to embrace internal water efficiency and replenishment, Coke's 2030 Water Strategy prioritizes far broader external issues: "reducing shared water challenges around the world," "enhancing community water resilience with a focus on women and children," and improving priority watersheds. Anticipating future water threats, the company also promises to help communities "adapt to the water-related impacts of climate change." Coca-Cola's "priority levers" include "advocacy" for "good water governance," "collaboration," and "collective action."[14]

After years of protests, Coca-Cola finally closed its Kaladera plant in 2016. Most of the bottling plants that Coca-Cola closed in the face of water protests remain shut down (although the Kerala facility found a useful second life in 2021 as a temporary Covid hospital). The decaying foundations of those buildings, however, have given birth to a major global movement focused on corporate water stewardship. According to Coca-Cola, its "water leadership was born in India." As a result of the company's experiences in India, Coke "learned what is now well-accepted: that the availability of freshwater is a defining issue of our times—one that poses risk to a company's license to operate" but also provides "opportunities to make a positive impact on lives and livelihoods around the globe."[15]

Coke's program is serving as the model for water stewardship programs at a growing number of other major corporations. By virtually everyone's account, Coca-Cola's water stewardship program is one of the most aggressive and successful in the world. In 2021, Ceres, a nonprofit focused on encouraging corporate sustainability, ranked Coke as the leader in water sustainability.

Through its efforts, Coca-Cola provides another illustration of how private businesses can help address the multiple water challenges that the world faces today.[16] Yet Coke's critics have not disappeared. There are still areas of the world where Coke's net impact is negative. To Coke's critics, the company's engagement in programs like RAIN and global water replenishment is simply bluewashing for the local harm it is still causing. As Coca-Cola has become more engaged in water partnerships and policy, a handful of critics have also begun to worry about the potential ability of large corporations like Coca-Cola to use water stewardship programs to influence the global water agenda. What began as an effort by a major corporation to address its own water impacts has evolved into an effort to help improve global water governance. And Coke's engagement with broader governance issues is once again raising questions about the appropriate role of private companies in the management of a public resource.[17]

THE GROWTH OF CORPORATE STEWARDSHIP PROGRAMS

As the Coca-Cola story illustrates, corporate water stewardship programs increasingly involve both internal and external elements. Internally, many corporations are reducing their water use and wastewater discharges. Externally, a smaller yet growing number of corporations seek to improve water conditions in the communities in which they operate, whether the corporation is responsible for the water problems or not, and to improve general water governance. To these companies, corporate water stewardship extends beyond the company's walls and includes partnerships with governments, nonprofits, and local stakeholders designed to ensure sustainable water management at a watershed scale or even broader scope.

Corporate water stewardship (CWS) is a relatively nascent movement that is still growing and evolving. Far more corporations engage in programs that address climate change or general corporate sustainability than water stewardship. The number of corporations that have joined the United Nations' CEO Water Mandate provides one measure of the growth in CWS. Companies that sign the CEO Water Mandate commit to actively pursue water stewardship in six contexts: direct operations, supply chain, collective action with stakeholders, support of effective public policies, community engagement, and transparency. Twenty-four companies, including Coca-Cola, committed to the CEO Water Mandate when it launched in 2008. As shown in Figure 10.1, commitments have grown slowly. Today there are still only about two hundred corporate members. By comparison, over fifteen thousand companies participate in the United Nations Global Compact on Sustainability, of which the CEO Water Mandate is a part.

CDP (formerly the Carbon Disclosure Project) also provides insight into the growth of water stewardship. Since 2010, CDP has tracked global companies that disclose key water data about their operations. In 2010, 176 companies provided information (see Figure 10.2). By 2021, that number had

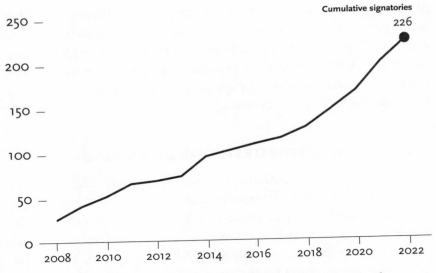

Figure 10.1 CEO Water Mandate Signatories. Source: CEO Water Mandate, UN Global Compact, ceowatermandate.org.

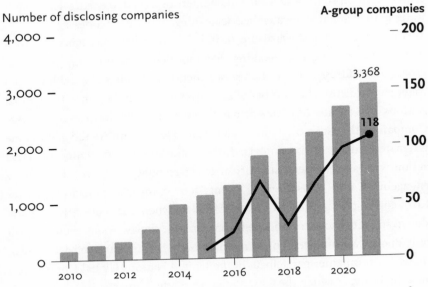

Figure 10.2 CDP Water Participation. Source: CDP Global Water Reports and related news releases, cdp.net.

grown to 3,368 companies—an impressive number of companies, although only a quarter of the number of companies that made climate disclosures, and most of the water disclosures were partial. CDP also grades companies each year based on the extent of their disclosures, their management programs, and their progress toward meaningful change. From 2016 to 2021, CDP's water "A List"—those companies that went beyond basic awareness and management to become action leaders in water security—had grown from 8 to 118 (about half the number of companies on CDP's climate change A List).

CWS has grown faster in some business sectors than in others. A company's total water use, its brand value, and its need to operate in water-scarce regions all influence the company's interest in CWS. Not surprisingly, companies in the global beverage, consumer food, and textile industries are CWS leaders. All three sectors depend heavily on water and are brand-sensitive. By contrast, local farming companies, even when they are of significant size, have less brand sensitivity and are therefore less likely to practice water stewardship, even though agriculture accounts for over 70 percent of freshwater withdrawals. The mining industry, which has little choice about where they locate mines, is a more recent convert to CWS. Large corporations in virtually every sector, however, have significant CWS programs today, including information technology (Google), medical equipment (Abbott Laboratories), motor vehicles (Nissan), paper products (Kimberly-Clark), petroleum (BP), and pharmaceuticals (Bayer).[18]

CWS programs vary tremendously across corporations. As the Coca-Cola story illustrates, a company's CWS program evolves over time as the company gains experience, learns from initial successes and failures, and responds to new issues. Most companies begin by gathering and evaluating information about their water use and risks. Coca-Cola, for example, began by requiring its bottling plants to conduct source vulnerability assessments. Companies then typically focus on three internal activities designed to diminish their water risks. First, they reduce their internal water use. All the major beverage companies—Coke, Pepsi, AB InBev, Nestlé—have significantly lowered the volume of water they use in their facilities to produce each bottle or can of product (known as their water use ratio). Such conservation efforts have led to sizable improvements in corporate water efficiency. Second, companies reduce and treat their wastewater discharges to minimize harm to the environment and human health. Finally, companies look for ways, like insurance and alternative water supplies, to decrease the potential economic impact of water shortages and other water disruptions to their operations.[19]

Once companies have begun to successfully address internal operations, they often move beyond the walls of their facilities. Some companies, for example, work to improve water efficiency and sustainability in their supply chains, which as mentioned often account for a majority of the companies' water use and pollution. Supply chains are of particular importance to consumer sectors such as beverages, food products, and textiles that rely heavily on agriculture. PepsiCo, for example, has established conservation standards for its agricultural suppliers and teaches them more efficient irrigation practices; AB InBev provides irrigation advice to its suppliers based on analyses of field data. While critically important to water stewardship, supply chains pose a major challenge for many companies because of the sheer size of the water footprint and the challenges of managing hundreds or thousands of individuals suppliers.[20]

A growing number of companies also seek to offset their remaining water use—a policy known today as "Water Positive." Coca-Cola's Replenish program was the first such program and the most successful to date. In 2021, a host of other companies, including BP, Facebook, Gap, Microsoft, and PepsiCo, pledged to become Water Positive. In Water Positive programs, corporations offset their own water use by recycling their wastewater, removing invasive phreatophytes that consume water from rivers, capturing stormwater and using that water to recharge groundwater aquifers, reforesting areas ravaged by wildfires, paying to retire other water uses, and otherwise increasing water supply or reducing demand. Through such programs, corporations often take a first step toward engaging in broader water management with nonprofits and governmental agencies.[21]

In the most interesting evolution of CWS, many companies have begun long-term and active collaborations with governments and external stakeholders to address water issues beyond their own water footprint. In some cases, companies work with nonprofits and governmental agencies to achieve specific philanthropic goals, such as improved access to safe water and sanitation or restored freshwater ecosystems. In 2017, for example, Gap joined the US Agency for International Development in a $32 million partnership, named Women + Water, to improve water and sanitation access for thousands of women in cotton-growing communities in India. A growing number of companies are working to ensure domestic water access and sanitation services for their own employees. Where this work is not related to a company's own water use, companies frequently use their philanthropic wings to support it.[22]

Companies are also increasingly working with local governments and stakeholders to improve local, national, and even international water governance. In the Jaguari River basin of Brazil, for example, AB InBev is collaborating with numerous nonprofits and governmental entities, including the City of Jaguariuna, Agência das Bacias PCJ, and the Agência Nacional de Águas, to increase water availability and better manage seasonal flows. As we shall see, involvement in governance can be controversial because it raises questions about the potential influence of private businesses over fundamentally public issues of water management. But companies often believe that it is imperative to engage on governance if they want to ensure sustainable water systems.[23]

Many proponents of CWS see these various elements of CWS as a natural progression in corporations' engagement with water security. As Figure 10.3 illustrates, WWF views corporate programs as progressing along

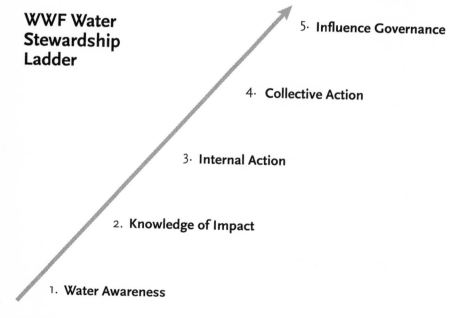

WWF Water Stewardship Ladder

5. **Influence Governance**

4. **Collective Action**

3. **Internal Action**

2. **Knowledge of Impact**

1. **Water Awareness**

Figure 10.3 WWF Water Stewardship Ladder. Source: Alexis Morgan, "Water Stewardship Revisited: Shifting the Narrative from Risk to Value Creation," WWF Germany, 2018.

five steps. In the first two steps, the corporation gains an understanding of its water needs and the impacts of its water use. In the third step, the company addresses internal water management, including both water use and wastewater discharge. In the fourth, the company engages with external stakeholders to pursue collective projects to improve water management in the regions in which it operates. And in the final step, the corporation works to improve water governance, recognizing that governance is central to achieving sustainable water management. While the first three steps are common to virtually all CWS programs, many corporations have not undertaken the final two steps—and may never pursue them—given the greater costs, complexities, and risks involved.[24]

Another element of advanced CWS programs is transparency. Corporations provide varying levels and types of information and data about their water use, water risks, and stewardship projects. Virtually every corporation engaged in CWS touts its water programs and accomplishments in its annual sustainability report (an increasingly common corporate publication) and on a web page devoted specifically to water stewardship, but the goal is often marketing rather than transparency. A growing number of companies also publish their responses to CDP's annual water questionnaire, which provides more detailed and objective information about the companies' water activities. Companies increasingly provide data on their water use and the impacts of their CWS programs. The Global Reporting Initiative, which promotes best practices for impact reporting, has issued standards for water reporting that call for data on water withdrawals, water recycling and reuse, water discharges, and key characteristics of impacted waterbodies such as biodiversity. Some industries have adopted their own standards. Members of the international mining industry, for example, comply with the industry's "Practical Guide to Consistent Water Reporting," which requires data on everything from water efficiency to a company's "water risk profile."[25]

WHY CORPORATIONS ENGAGE IN WATER STEWARDSHIP

Private companies engage in CWS for at least four reasons. The first, and for many companies the most important, is to avoid the business risks that unsustainable water use and local water shortages pose. As Chapter 2 explored, an increasing number of companies throughout the world view water as a serious business risk. In 2014, the World Economic Forum ranked water scarcity among the top three global systemic risks based on its annual survey of business, government, academia, and nonprofit leaders. The World Economic Forum has ranked water crises as one of the top ten business risks in at least half of the last ten years. In a 2019 CDP survey of almost 2,500 global companies, over 45 percent reported that "inherent water-related risks" could have "substantive financial or strategic impact" on their businesses. Over 70 percent of the companies in fossil fuels, power generation, and mineral extraction reported serious water risks; 55 percent of the companies in the food, beverage, and agricultural sectors did the same. Only a fraction of these companies tried to estimate the business value at risk, but even those estimates totaled over $400 billion. A 2021 CDP survey of just 357 companies found that the cost of water insecurity to those companies was over $300 billion, about six times what it would cost to eliminate the water risks.[26]

Studies often separate out three distinct types of water risks: physical risks, regulatory risks, and reputational risks. Water shortages or pollution problems that prevent a business from operating or limit its production are a *physical* risk. Companies that do not have an adequate and sustainable water supply may, in the short run, be forced to shut down temporarily or reduce production and, in the long run, to close and relocate. Even when a company enjoys sufficient water for its own operations, physical or quality limits elsewhere in the world can impact the company's supply chain by reducing supplies or increasing prices. The global character of today's supply chains puts businesses at often far-flung geographic risks from droughts or other water challenges. McKinsey & Company estimates that two-thirds of businesses face substantial physical risk in either their direct operations or supply chains.[27]

Poor access to safe drinking water and sanitation services for a company's employees also can pose a physical business risk. Poor water access and sanitation can increase sick days, reduce employee productivity, undermine work quality, and increase turnover. While rigorous quantitative studies of these costs are lacking, a growing number of case studies suggest that the costs can be significant. According to these studies, every dollar invested in water access can potentially return two dollars in economic benefits, and every dollar invested in sanitation can return $5.50.[28]

Companies that operate in water-scarce regions or produce significant effluent also can face *regulatory* risks. The failure of mining companies to carefully address the water impacts of new mines has frequently led to costly project delays and even to the denial and cancelation of mining permits. While regulatory risks are particularly severe for mining companies because mines cannot move to less restrictive jurisdictions, other industries also face regulatory risks. Nestlé's bottled water operations in the United States triggered multiple lawsuits and regulatory investigations before Nestlé sold its US operations. Businesses that appear to threaten water sustainability also can lose their social license to operate. Coca-Cola's Indian experience again provides an illustration. As described in Chapter 2, Constellation Brands found itself unable to build a new brewery in Mexicali, Mexico, when water concerns led local voters to ban the brewery by plebiscite.[29]

As Coca-Cola discovered in India, businesses also can face *reputational* risks if they utilize substantial amounts of water in water-scarce regions or discharge harmful effluent. Over half of the complaints that local communities lodge against mining companies with the International Finance Corporation focus on water. Complaints that begin locally often spread rapidly through the internet, global media, and nonprofit networks. For companies that depend on their global brand image for consumer sales or to win government concessions, major water disputes can cause significant economic harm.[30]

Pressure from stakeholders—buyers, investors, employees, and civil society—is a second, less prevalent reason that corporations engage in CWS. Among stakeholders, large corporate customers have had the greatest influence so far on water stewardship. Global corporations are increasingly demanding that their suppliers improve water efficiency and address other water risks, often as part of the corporations' CWS programs. The average retail customer, by contrast, does not appear to have taken a strong interest in water sustainability. In contrast to other environmental impacts, water concerns have not yet given rise to consumer certification programs. Nor are corporate water practices readily apparent to most retail customers.[31]

Financial investors could ultimately prove a major force for CWS, but their current influence is uncertain. Investors are increasingly expressing interest in whether and how corporations are addressing water risks. In 2021, a CDP survey revealed that almost six hundred investors with over $100 trillion in assets had asked companies in the prior year to disclose their impacts on water security and take steps to reduce those effects—up from approximately five hundred investors the year before. A recent study of Dutch investors, however, revealed that, while most of the surveyed investors considered water stewardship in making investment decisions, the investors did not employ a consistent or rigorous approach. The US Securities and Exchange Commission addresses disclosure of water data only as part of its climate guidance. The degree to which investors are driving CWS is therefore unclear, although companies that have higher debt leverage and therefore may undergo greater financial scrutiny appear to engage in greater water stewardship.[32]

Third, some corporations may see CWS as an important business opportunity. A growing number of companies, including food and drink companies such as Diageo, Nestlé, and Pepsi, view emerging economies as an important new market. In water-stressed regions of Africa or Asia, companies that improve the local population's access to water and sanitation will often enjoy a brand advantage. While the average retail consumer in the United States or Europe might not worry about water impacts elsewhere in the world, consumers in emerging regions will often be aware of, and care about, local stewardship. Corporations with a strong history of water stewardship are also more likely to obtain needed concessions and permits to operate in water-stressed regions. A few corporations also see CWS programs as an opportunity to identify new technological opportunities. AB InBev, Coca-Cola, Colgate-Palmolive, and Unilever, for example, are jointly pursuing new sustainable water technologies arising out of their CWS programs.[33]

Finally, a corporate leader's belief in the societal importance of sustainability can inspire both the adoption and the enhancement of a strong CWS program. Corporations, of course, are ultimately responsible to their shareholders. For this reason, studies of CWS and broader corporate sustainability programs often assume that the personal convictions and altruistic instincts of corporate leaders play little, if any, role in a corporation's water or sustainability policies. In confidential interviews, however, corporate leaders often speak at greater length (and more passionately) about the societal importance of their CWS programs than about the advantage in reducing business risks, responding to stakeholder demands, or opening new markets. Case studies of corporate sustainability programs also frequently highlight the views of corporate leaders, and some emerging studies have also suggested their importance.[34]

THE CORPORATE STEWARDSHIP SUPPORT NETWORK

An expanding network of private organizations both supports and influences CWS. Some of these organizations provide corporations with the tools needed to evaluate and manage their water impacts. A second group nudges corporations to move beyond their internal walls and engage in external partnerships designed to improve water governance more broadly. Both sets of organizations are largely private. And both sets shape how corporations around the world think about their proper role in water governance and the water activities in which they engage.

The Water Footprint Network illustrates the first category of organizations, those that provide the tools that corporations need to design and implement CWS programs. Corporations that wish to reduce their water impact need tools to identify, measure, and track that impact. In the late twentieth century, British geographer Tony Allan provided the theoretical underpinning for such a tool when he observed that all products, whether an orange or a car, contain "virtual water"—the water used to produce the product. In 2002, Arjen Hoekstra converted the idea of virtual water into a product's "water footprint." That footprint consists of blue water (the water withdrawn from a waterway or groundwater basin to make the product), green water (the rainfall consumed in making it), and grey water (the water polluted in the production process). A product's water footprint consists of both the water used directly in a product's creation and the water used in the product's supply chain. In 2008, Hoekstra, along with various businesses, nonprofits, and academics, launched the Water Footprint Network to promote, refine, and support water footprint assessments. Extensively used today, these assessments can help corporations quantify their total water impact and identify the water risks that they face.[35]

Water footprints are one of dozens of water stewardship tools that nonprofits and businesses have developed to help corporations identify, characterize, measure, and manage their water consumption, impacts, and risks. WWF maintains a water risk filter that corporations can use to map, analyze, and prioritize the water risks that they face both internally and in their supply chains. The World Resources Institute maintains a similar set of maps and tools that allow businesses to identify and evaluate water risks. McKinsey uses cost curves to analyze and compare methods to reduce water use. CDP and the Global Reporting Initiative have created standards for corporate water reporting. Other nonprofits and consulting firms offer their own proprietary tools.[36]

This CWS "support industry," through its choice and design of tools, influences the ways in which corporations perceive and engage in water stewardship—and thus significantly shapes CWS, for good or bad. Some analysts, for example, have criticized water footprints for emphasizing only volumetric water use and discharges—not local water availability and competing needs for the water that the corporation uses. As these analysts argue, the goal of stewardship is not simply to reduce a corporation's water footprint but to achieve a footprint that respects human rights, protects the environment, and is sustainable over time. The standard footprint assessment addresses none of these goals. Other water experts worry that by focusing on the identification and diagnosis of water risks, most existing CWS tools fail to highlight the affirmative opportunities that CWS can provide a company and thus truncate the scope of CWS programs.[37]

An influential group of other civic organizations have pushed corporations to address water issues beyond their internal walls, shaped corporations' external activities, and defined their underlying normative precepts. A variety of large international nonprofits, including TNC, WWF, and WaterAid, have used corporate interest in water stewardship to bolster the water missions of the nonprofits. TNC and WWF have encouraged corporations to invest in and support nature-based solutions to water shortages, such as reforestation, wetlands restoration, and watershed protection. WaterAid, which promotes water access, has enlisted companies in projects designed to provide clean water, decent toilets, and good hygiene to communities around the world.[38]

Partnerships between nonprofits and corporations provide synergetic benefits to both groups. The corporations bring funding and other resources to the nonprofits' missions. (It may not be coincidental that many of the partnerships arose in the wake of the 2008 recession, when nonprofits were seeking new sources of revenue.) Companies also can bring valuable business and financial expertise to the nonprofits. Finally, the corporations can reach powerful governmental officials to which the nonprofits might not otherwise have access. While nonprofits might have good connections with environmental or water ministers, those are relatively junior positions in most governments; corporations, by contrast, can often reach the more powerful ministers of finance, development, or agriculture and, in some cases, even the head of state. By working with nonprofits, corporations gain critical new expertise on water issues and solutions. More importantly, corporations can help legitimize their water stewardship efforts and gain valuable credibility.[39]

A handful of global organizations, led by the Alliance for Water Stewardship (AWS), the CEO Water Mandate, and the 2030 Water Resources Group, work to advance and shape CWS programs. While these organizations all arose at approximately the same time, each has slightly different goals and structure. A group of nonprofits and the United Nations Environment Programme launched the AWS in 2009 to provide an independent membership organization, open to all interested companies and stakeholders, for the support and advancement of CWS. The AWS has created a five-step standard for CWS programs (now in version 2.0 and compliant with international guidelines for standards systems), a certification program to provide corporations with a credible means to validate their programs, and a network of professionally credentialed experts to support corporations in their stewardship work. Companies in over forty nations now use the AWS Standard.[40]

The UN Global Compact, which UN Secretary-General Kofi Annan launched in 2000, promotes general corporate sustainability and unveiled the CEO Water Mandate in 2007. With over two hundred members, the Mandate provides a knowledge platform for CWS and encourages corporations to engage with local communities, nonprofits, and governments to improve water resilience around the world. The Mandate, for example, urges corporations to improve water policy by contributing recommendations on new government regulations, advocating for "water sustainability in global and local policy discussions," and joining policy groups. It also encourages corporations to advance local water and sanitation agendas, to partner with local communities in support of adequate water infrastructure, to offer water-resource education, and to advance public awareness of water issues. On World Water Day in 2020, the Mandate unveiled the new Water Resilience Coalition to further promote resilience in the world's water-stressed geographies.[41]

The World Economic Forum launched the 2030 Water Resources Group at its Davos forum in January 2010. The ambitious goal of the 2030 Group, a multi-stakeholder partnership now hosted by the World Bank, is to "catalyze transformative change and impact at scale" by facilitating collective action among governments, private businesses, and nonprofits. Underlying its work is a belief that collective action can help overcome the capacity constraints and political limits of purely governmental action. To date, over 1,000 organizations (including over 350 businesses) have worked together as part of the 2030 Water Resources Group on innovative water projects and policy reforms in over a dozen countries. Projects have increased water security in rain-fed cotton farming communities of India, reduced municipal water leakage in South Africa, and developed a water valuation methodology for Mongolia.[42]

CORPORATE ENGAGEMENT IN WATER GOVERNANCE

The newest and most interesting development in CWS has been its turn toward external water governance. A growing number of businesses are partnering with nonprofits, governments, and local stakeholders to pursue public water projects such as water and sanitation access, infrastructure improvements, groundwater recharge, stormwater capture, watershed reforestation, and wetlands protection. Businesses also are sharing expertise and insights with local communities on subjects ranging from improved irrigation to sanitation practices. Finally, corporations are convening water discussions and seeking to influence water policies at multiple scales, often through collective partnerships like the 2030 Water Resources Group.[43]

This evolution in corporate stewardship is unsurprising. Corporations have often found that they cannot fully meet their CWS goals without external involvement and engagement. Some goals, like employee access at home to clean water and sanitation, typically require external action. Other goals, like Positive Water, are often easier to achieve in partnership with nonprofits and governments. The most effective replenishment projects frequently involve natural solutions, such as watershed protection, that require or benefit from the involvement of governments or environmental groups like TNC and WWF. Indeed, virtually all CWS goals require some level of external engagement. No matter how well a corporation manages internal water use, it will continue to face physical, regulatory, and reputational risks if local water resources are mismanaged. Beverage companies like Coca-Cola, for example, will continue to face business risks in water-stressed regions, even if they fully replenish their own water use, if groundwater overdraft continues or if climate change or environmental degradation threatens local surface supplies.[44]

The evolving language of water stewardship reflects the difficulties of separating the business risks that water poses from broader societal water challenges. Corporations first described corporate water risks as "business risks." They later began to call them "shared risks," a term that emphasizes both the common harms from poor water management and the difficulty of addressing water challenges through an entirely internal strategy. In recent years, the terminology has further evolved to "shared water security," emphasizing that private businesses, local populations, governments, and non-profits share common goals, not just common problems.[45]

CWS, in short, inevitably pushes corporations toward external engagement in water governance. The only question for corporations is whether they are willing to undertake the inherent costs and risks of external engagement. Many CWS advocates, like AWS, the Global Water Compact, and the 2030 Water Resources Group, believe that water stewardship programs are inherently incomplete if they do not seek to solve water challenges beyond the corporation's walls. Will Sarni, one of the world's leading experts in CWS, has publicly worried that many corporations' CWS programs have "stalled" and has argued that corporations must move toward a more "transformative" model that seeks to improve water policies and that partners for "scalable actions." WWF also has expressed concern that too many corporations have failed to go beyond internal measures.[46]

External engagement, however, is not costless. Corporations must develop new relationships and undertake activities that are often outside their traditional expertise. They must commit to long-term involvement. They must share internal data with new partners that they may not fully trust. And they must engage in consensus processes far different from their traditional internal decision-making. Active involvement in external water projects or policy discussions also poses reputational risks if the projects fail or the corporation's goals are questioned. For all these reasons, corporations that do not see much upside to external engagement are likely to stop at their own walls.[47]

Industries for which water stewardship is critical, however, have increasingly engaged in external water governance. The beverage industry was the first to step beyond the corporate walls. All the major beverage companies, including Coca-Cola, AB InBev, Nestlé, and PepsiCo partner with nonprofits on water security projects. Coke has launched water projects with WWF to restore watersheds and increase water access; AB InBev has worked with TNC and WWF to launch new water funds; Nestle has undertaken multiple water access projects through the 2030 Water Resources Group. In 2017, a third of the international mining industry committed to support sustainable water management through collaborative action with governments, local communities, and other businesses.[48]

THREE MAJOR QUESTIONS GOING FORWARD

Corporate water stewardship raises three broad policy questions. First, will CWS programs measurably improve global water sustainability and security? While the number of CWS programs is increasing, reported corporate water withdrawals have continued to climb. In every year from 2015 to 2019, an increasing number of companies participating in CDP's annual water survey reported higher water withdrawals. Although the number fell in 2020 (the first year of the Covid pandemic), one-fifth of the companies with high water dependency still reported increased water withdrawals that year. It also is not clear whether aggregate water quality is substantially improving. According to CDP, less than 5 percent of survey respondents in 2021 set and reported progress against pollution reduction targets. CWS has tremendous potential, and many corporations' CWS programs have led to meaningful, and in some cases dramatic, improvements in water performance. Greater progress is needed, however, if CWS is to make a major difference in overall water sustainability.[49]

Greater impact is likely to come with time. Many major corporations either have not yet adopted CWS programs or are in the early days of implementation. Existing CWS programs are often still ad hoc rather than strategic. In the view of many experts, transformative change will also occur only as CWS programs evolve to include more external engagement than they do today. As more corporations adopt CWS programs and as those programs grow and evolve, results should increase.

CWS, however, may also be inherently limited outside those industries— like food, beverages, and mining—that face large water risks. For many corporations, improving water efficiency, being Water Positive, reducing water discharges, and enhancing water governance may not be important enough to justify the significant cost involved in voluntarily addressing these issues through a robust CWS program.

Time will tell how large an impact the CWS movement will have on global water sustainability. The infrastructure for effective CWS programs—standards, certification programs, expertise—is in place. The most important determinant of CWS's future impact is likely to be whether investors or other significant stakeholders demand that corporations adopt and implement comprehensive and meaningful CWS programs. In the meantime, governments should not see CWS as a replacement for strong laws and regulations requiring conservation, ensuring equitable water sharing, and protecting water quality.[50]

This raises a second issue: do CWS programs risk undermining effective laws and regulations? Some observers worry that CWS might either undermine the perceived need for better water governance or change the shape of policy discussions. If corporations voluntarily pursue water conservation or water quality, local governments might decide that new governmental limits on water use or wastewater discharges are unnecessary, even if governmental regulations would be more effective. By focusing on scarcity, efficiency, and business risks, CWS programs might also divert attention away from political questions such as how water is allocated among members of society; CWS might "depoliticize" water management and make it into a purely technocratic issue. Finally, CWS might privilege large corporations and others who can afford to offset their water use. None of these risks justifies abandoning or downplaying CWS. Groups like the AWS and the CEO Water Mandate, moreover, recognize and work to guard against these risks. The risks, however, require constant vigilance by governments and civil society.[51]

Finally, as corporations increasingly engage in water governance as part of their CWS programs, can CWS effectively navigate the critical line between private and public interests? As emphasized in earlier chapters, businesses are private entities—non-elected, nondemocratic, and ultimately responsive to their shareholders—while water is an innately public resource. CWS assumes that corporations will recognize that they have a shared interest in equitable and environmentally sustainable water governance, eliminating or reducing the conflict between private and public, but that is still an untested hypothesis. The most common definition of water stewardship, adopted by the AWS and others, is the "use of water that is socially equitable, environmentally sustainable, *and economically beneficial*," yet some might object that the final criterion can conflict with the first two. Even if corporations pursue appropriate objectives, they are likely to favor solutions that are consistent with their business approach to other problems, like markets, pricing, and technological solutions, to the potential exclusion of regulatory approaches. The influence that businesses often have over governmental decisions increases the importance of these concerns.[52]

Recognizing these concerns, the CWS movement has emphasized that the appropriate corporate role is to augment governmental authority rather than to displace it, to help build governmental capacity rather than substitute for it. Corporations must accept that governments are the appropriate decision-makers and confine the corporate role to enhancement and support. Governments and businesses can help avoid potential conflicts between private and public interests through transparency, inclusivity, and collaboration. Transparency can provide a window into the content of corporate advocacy, while inclusivity and collaboration can provide corporations with a broader perspective on water issues and enhance other voices. Governments also have a responsibility to maintain control of water policy, rather than relying on private businesses to define or implement that policy.[53]

CWS, in summary, is one of the most exciting and promising ways in which the private sector is addressing today's water challenges. Businesses have a far larger impact on water resources than domestic users, so meaningful efforts by businesses to reduce and mitigate their impact can produce potentially outsized results. In its broadest versions, CWS could also generate innovative solutions to water challenges as businesses focus on how best to solve those challenges and strengthen water governance. Whether CWS delivers its promised benefits will depend on the actions of other parties. Investors and other stakeholders with significant influence over corporate behavior must insist that corporations pursue effective CWS. Governments must also ensure that greater corporate involvement in water governance does not drown out other voices or undermine the public interest.

ELEVEN

Conclusion: Four Policy Recommendations

Like the rest of the world, the United States is facing an expanding freshwater crisis. That crisis is the result of multiple factors, including climate change, continued growth, unsustainable water use, environmental degradation, aging infrastructure, and society's historical failure to ensure that everyone has affordable and reliable access to freshwater. The public sector, which has long dominated water management, is playing a central role in addressing these challenges. Public agencies are working to replace and improve infrastructure, to increase access to clean drinking water, to protect river health, to develop new water sources, to constrain groundwater pumping, and to achieve other public goals. They are also making progress toward these goals.

The private sector, as this book has shown, is also providing critical help in solving these water challenges. Technology companies are developing innovations that will make recycled and desalinated water more affordable. Information firms are offering increasingly sophisticated tools to monitor and analyze water data and to improve water decisions. Infrastructure firms are financing, and sharing the risks of, both grey infrastructure (like desalination plants) and green infrastructure (like DC Water's stormwater control program). Water markets are reducing the economic impact of groundwater restrictions and of ever more frequent and severe droughts. Consulting firms are helping local governments sustainably manage groundwater. Impact investment firms are identifying ways to simultaneously enhance wetlands, and provide water to farmers. Farmers are using their fields as groundwater recharge ponds. Foundations and nonprofits are helping to pass stronger legislative protections. The list of important contributions by the private sector is long and getting longer.

Private organizations bring valuable attributes to this work. One of the most important is innovation, which will be critical in meeting the growing list of water challenges. The public sector can often be resistant to change, risk-averse, and hierarchical, all traits unconducive to innovation. While many public water agencies are highly creative and have made crucial advances in water management, innovation is a comparative strength of private companies. The need to succeed in a competitive environment generally drives private firms to be innovative (as well as efficient). Indeed, innovation is often central to private businesses' growth. The private sector attracts business by bringing new products, services, and ideas to water management. When new companies enter the water sector, they are not invested in traditional solutions and therefore frequently bring original and sometimes disruptive ideas and perspectives to existing water challenges. Innovation and creativity are among the most exciting aspects of the private sector's involvement—and among its greatest values.[1]

Private organizations also often bring useful knowledge from other sectors and fields to their water work. Infrastructure firms, for example, may draw on their experience with infrastructure projects in transportation and power. Technology firms may draw on their experience in renewable energy, information technology, and remote monitoring. Investor-owned utilities increasingly span multiple utility services because of the crossover value. Environmental impact bonds in water have built on financial firms' experience with social impact bonds. Ideas from other sectors increase the degree of innovation in the water field by reframing problems and offering fresh solutions. Where private companies work for multiple public agencies, they also can share innovations across those agencies, increasing the spread of best practices.

For these and other reasons, the private sector's growing involvement in water offers significant opportunities to improve water management. Prior chapters have looked at many of the specific roles that the private sector is playing and offered particularized lessons on how the private sector can help solve water challenges without risk to the public interests inherent in water. This chapter sets out four more general lessons. These include the need to restructure the public water sector, the importance of regulatory policy, the unique ethical responsibilities of private companies working in the water field, and the importance of partnerships between the private and public sectors.

NEEDED REFORMS IN THE PUBLIC SECTOR

As discussed throughout this book, the structure and practices of the public water sector both drive and impede private involvement in water management. Two specific characteristics have had a particular impact. As prior chapters have emphasized, US public water suppliers are highly fragmented and frequently fail to charge a water rate that fully accounts for their operational and infrastructure needs and for water's opportunity cost. Insufficient scale and inadequate revenues have sometimes led cities to privatize, with private utilities promising to eliminate inefficiencies, balance budgets, and invest in needed infrastructure. Unless water rates are sufficient to pay for all costs and infrastructure needs, however, privatization is unlikely to achieve these promises. Yet higher rates can lead to dissatisfaction and calls for municipalization and, if not carefully designed, can undermine the goal of equitable water access for low-income consumers.

Beyond their influence on privatization, fragmentation and inadequate water rates can impede the efforts of many other private water companies to improve water management. As discussed in Chapter 7, they can undercut the technological innovation needed to improve water management, reduce water use, and ensure future supplies. Low rates weaken the market incentive to develop new technologies, while fragmentation undermines the adoption and diffusion of new technologies. Both fragmentation and inadequate rates also have made it difficult for water suppliers to take advantage of private financing, whether traditional municipal bonds or more innovative public-private partnerships.

Fragmentation and low rates also weaken overall water management because many public water agencies are neither sufficiently large nor financially viable enough to be effective. Small, underfunded water suppliers, for example, are often unable to replace their aging infrastructure and meet environmental regulatory requirements. Poor water management in turn risks the wellbeing of domestic users and the local economy.

For all these reasons, water supply consolidation and rate reform are high policy priorities. Neither goal will be easy to achieve. While consolidation is possible, state efforts to promote consolidation have achieved mixed success. Most states have made little progress, although Kentucky reportedly reduced the number of its water supply agencies by 81 percent in the late twentieth century, and California has recently embarked on a new program to encourage small struggling systems to consolidate with larger neighbors. Consolidation faces not only political distrust among neighboring jurisdictions but also a substantial risk of both physical and financial failure. Despite states' best efforts, fragmentation is likely to remain a problem in modernizing the US water industry and maximizing the benefits that technology firms and other private organizations can contribute to water management.[2]

So long as fragmentation persists, policy workarounds will be necessary. As discussed in Chapter 7, states can support technological R&D efforts through grants, state-led demonstration projects, and accelerators. States can also help smaller suppliers identify and adopt useful innovations. Bond issuers, as Chapter 8 suggests, can develop financeable portfolios of infrastructure projects involving multiple local agencies. Organizations like the Water Finance Exchange and Moonshot Missions can help small suppliers apply for and receive needed financial support. Consultants can provide small agencies with crucial expertise, including lessons learned from larger agencies.

Rate reform will be even more challenging. Local political pressure often makes it difficult to charge adequate water rates, even when higher rates are needed to fund accumulating infrastructure needs and operational deficits. No one happily admits that their water rate is too low. Any rate revision must also deal with affordability. Increasing block rate structures, which charge consumers more for each unit of water as their total consumption grows, are one way to increase rates while protecting affordability. Alternatively, local governments can adopt affordability programs that directly subsidize water consumers with low incomes. While these and other approaches can solve affordability, the underlying political hurdle to rate increases remains.

Given the challenges of local rate increases, states should consider the adoption of a "public benefits charge" on water, as described in Chapter 7.

States could use the resulting funds to promote innovative technologies, provide infrastructure financing to communities that otherwise cannot afford to replace and update their water systems, and ensure sufficient instream flows for the environment—all costs that local water rates should support but currently do not. Political opposition will again be a challenge, although the greater separation between the charge and water rates might help defuse general voter opposition.[3]

RETHINKING REGULATIONS

Regulatory policies are also essential to the effective involvement of the private sector in solving today's water challenges. Regulations are critical to ensuring that private businesses do not negatively impact the human right to water, the environment, and other public interests. Water, as emphasized throughout this book, is a uniquely public resource. While most business leaders want to improve water management and serve public interests, profit motives can lead businesses astray. Effective regulations are the best way to protect public interests while allowing private companies to help improve water management. Regulation can ensure that water transfers do not harm other water users or the environment, that recycled water is safe for use, that investor-owned utilities do not abuse their natural monopolies by charging excessive prices, and that desalination facilities do not injure marine systems.

Not only can regulations prevent harm, but they can also increase the benefits of private involvement. Regulations can boost participation in water markets by providing security and access to market data. Public utility commissions can improve the performance of private water supply systems (and, in some contexts, even make them superior to public systems) by requiring adequate investments in infrastructure, conservation-promoting price reforms, and affordability programs. Regulations, in short, both protect the public interest and shape the quality of private services.

Regulations also can promote the demand for the products and services of private businesses. The federal laws requiring safe drinking water and clean water in the nation's rivers and lakes encouraged the development of a new generation of water purification technology. New regulations requiring golf courses and other large water consumers to use recycled water can similarly drive more efficient recycling technology. California's

Sustainable Groundwater Management Act has generated demand both for new groundwater markets and for the services of expert consultants in sustainably managing groundwater. The Endangered Species Act and governmental instream-flow regulations generate demand for environmental water transactions.[4]

In other situations, however, regulations can unnecessarily impede valuable private activity. Governmental regulation of US water markets, while furnishing important protections, has historically been far costlier than needed, discouraging valuable trades. In addition, government regulation of water rights and markets makes it difficult in many states for water trusts to purchase rights for instream flows. Existing environmental regulations can pose a hurdle for innovative technologies by creating regulatory uncertainty or inconsistency and by giving an advantage to legacy technologies and incumbent firms.

For all these reasons, legislators and administrative agencies must pay greater attention to the design of regulations that promote the effective involvement of the private sector in water management. Current regulations are insufficiently protective in some areas but overly constrictive in others. Government officials must think comprehensively about how existing laws and regulations are influencing the value that private businesses can bring to water management, just as they have in the energy sector.

THE ETHICAL OBLIGATIONS OF BUSINESS

Articles in popular and business journals often cast water as the hot business market of the future (or today)—a get-rich-quick opportunity. In the view of such articles, water is the "new gold, a big commodity bet." Water is also the "new oil." Water is a "hot market" and a "21st century winner." Growing global water shortages will "guarantee price appreciation for this ever-scarcer commodity." Water in the future will "become more valuable than oil." The private water sector has a bit of the western frontier to it, and it tends to attract its share of business cowboys (or cowhands). This is unfortunate.[5]

Successful water businesses will not be cowboys out for a fast buck. Instead, they will be businesses that seek to improve water management and that recognize and reflect the ethical dimensions of the water field. As emphasized in prior chapters, water is different from other resources. Neither gold nor energy invokes strong moral obligations. One can pursue a killing in gold and energy without worrying (too much) about potential injury to the public. Water, however, is a human right and a public trust. Public interests permeate water management. Any business wishing to survive and prosper must understand this core difference and operate with that difference in mind.

Private corporations have a fiduciary duty to their shareholders to return a profit. For some corporations, this may mean staying within regulatory strictures but otherwise maximizing corporate profits. Corporations that fail to go beyond regulatory requirements in the water field, however, risk frequent public controversies and are unlikely to attract public-agency customers. They are thus unlikely to be sustainable in the long run. Water corporations' fiduciary obligations to their shareholders closely parallel the interests of the public and other stakeholders.

Corporations that consume significant amounts of water are increasingly adopting corporate stewardship plans and joining global pacts for water sustainability, as discussed in Chapter 10. These pacts explicitly recognize the public interest in water and commit companies to support that interest. The Alliance for Water Stewardship, for example, encourages the "use of water that is socially and culturally equitable, environmentally sustainable and economically beneficial." Companies that join the CEO Water Mandate commit to contribute toward the UN Sustainable Development Goals (SDGs) in water. Members of the 2030 Water Resources Group support both the SDGs and sustainable water management. These are the emerging ethical commitments of corporate water consumers. Companies that *work* in the water field, from water suppliers to technology companies, have an even greater impact on water management and must commit to at least the same level of equitable and environmental goals. Water companies must be stewards of freshwater no less than public agencies are.

Few water companies are members of the major water stewardship alliances. None are currently members of the CEO Water Mandate or the 2030 Water Resources Group. A handful—Royal HaskoningDHV, Veolia, Water Foundry Advisors, and WaterSmart Solutions—are part of the Alliance for Water Stewardship. Because corporate water consumers developed their stewardship alliances to help them reduce and mitigate the impact of their water use, the small number of members from the water sector may not be surprising. Water consumers and members of the water sector have different goals and problems.

Larger water companies have often, but not always, developed and implemented their own sustainability programs even if they are not members of a stewardship alliance. Few of these sustainability programs, however, explicitly commit to promoting the United Nations Sustainable Development Goals in water, the human right to water, or the public trust. Most programs also lack outside advisory groups to help ensure that companies aggressively pursue greater responsibility. While a handful of companies, like Veolia, have external stakeholder committees, the committees generally serve more as sounding boards than as monitors and advisors.

The human right to water imposes special responsibilities on water companies. Under the UN's Guiding Principles on Business and Human Rights and its Protect, Respect, Remedy Framework, businesses have a responsibility to respect human rights. Investor-owned water utilities and other water companies therefore must avoid taking any action that could potentially harm the human right to water.[6]

Multiple ethical and practical factors, in short, mandate that water companies make strong and genuine commitments to protect the public interests inherent in water. Water companies should work with civic organizations to develop meaningful codes of conduct and implementation plans for their operations. These codes will vary depending on each company's size and market sector. Corporations that receive a high percentage of their revenue from water or that are more directly involved with water deliveries, such as investor-owned utilities, will typically need more detailed and protective codes and plans. Although the water sector is diverse, it also would benefit from its own industry-wide stewardship alliance or a sector-specific program in an existing alliance, with active participation by governmental water agencies and civic groups. Water companies should also measure their progress toward achieving public water goals and hold themselves accountable for their performance. Finally, larger water companies should create stakeholder advisory groups, with active and regular engagement with management, to help monitor compliance, advise the corporation on specific ethical questions that arise in the course of the company's work, and recommend steps for further strengthening the corporation's commitment to public interests.[7]

THE NEED FOR STRONGER PUBLIC-PRIVATE COLLABORATION

The growing role of private organizations in water management tends to attract strong views about the comparative merits of the private and public sectors. Critics often see the private water sector as commodifying water to the detriment of the inherent public interests in water. These critics generally would prefer more public management and less private involvement. Proponents, by contrast, see the private water sector as injecting efficiency into an area long dominated by public incompetence and even corruption. Such proponents therefore generally want more private and less public. Both critics and proponents pit private against public.[8]

Today's freshwater crisis, however, calls for private *and* public. Solutions will require more effective collaboration between the two sectors. Private organizations can best contribute to more effective water management when working together with public agencies. Singapore's active partnership with private technology companies is an example. As Chapter 7 described, Singapore has used public-private partnerships to design and construct its recycling and desalination facilities, funded both basic and applied research on innovative technologies, and created a global "hydrohub" to encourage collaboration across the technology sector. This collaboration has led to a formidable water technology sector that has both allowed Singapore to meet its water needs and created a business growth area for the island nation.[9]

The proven success of active collaboration between the private and public sectors does not end with the Singapore example. DC Water's successful Environmental Impact Bond was the result of a collaboration between DC Water and the finance sector. Technology companies in the United States often overcome regulatory hurdles and develop successful business models by collaborating with public water suppliers. Public-private partnerships allow cities to engage private expertise, obtain private financing, and offload risks, all without the potential challenges of full privatization. California's implementation of SGMA is also an example of effective public-private collaboration. Water trusts often help governmental agencies acquire instream flows, through their greater nimbleness and relationships with local water users, and they fill gaps in the work of the governmental programs. In all these settings, public agencies and private organizations work in tandem to accomplish more than they could separately achieve.

Partnerships do not always work. To be effective, for example, formal partnerships must have clear accountability for decisions. The partnership between the Pittsburgh Water and Sewage Authority and Veolia, for example, failed in part because it was not clear which organization was responsible for what decisions. Where carefully and thoughtfully structured, however, partnerships can combine the best features of both the private and public sectors.

Ultimately, government and the private sector can best address the freshwater crisis by working together. The private sector must recognize that its most effective role is to supplement and enhance rather than replace the public sector, working in partnership with public agencies to provide the tools, skills, resources, and innovation needed to solve the growing water challenges facing the world. The public sector, in turn, must recognize the immense ingenuity and value that the private sector can bring and integrate it into the overall fabric of water management. By actively collaborating and supporting each other, the private and public sectors stand the best chance of solving the growing freshwater challenges confronting the United States and the world today.

NOTES

Introduction

1. Stephen R. Carpenter, Emily H. Stanley, and M. Jake Vander Zanden, "State of the World's Freshwater Ecosystems: Physical, Chemical, and Biological Changes," *Annual Review of Environment and Resources* 36 (2011): 75; UN Convention to Combat Desertification, *Drought in Numbers 2022: Restoration for Readiness and Resilience*, Abidjan, Ivory Coast, 2022, 4, 18; David Hannah et al., "Illuminating the 'Invisible Water Crisis' to Address Global Water Pollution Challenges," *Hydrological Processes* 36, no. 3 (2022): 1; World Health Organization, UNICEF, and World Bank, *State of the World's Drinking Water* (Geneva: WHO, 2022), 11; World Wildlife Fund, *A Deep Dive into Freshwater: Living Planet Report 2020* (Washington, DC: WWF, 2020), 14.

2. Barton H. Thompson, Jr. et al., *Legal Control of Water Resources*, 6th ed. (St. Paul, MN: West Academic, 2018), 769–777.

3. Newsha K. Ajami, Barton H. Thompson, and David G. Victor, *The Path to Water Innovation* (Washington, DC: Brookings Institution, 2014); Xavier Leflaive, Ben Krieble, and Harry Smythe, "Trends in Water-Related Technological Innovation: Insights from Patent Data," OECD Environment Working Paper No. 161, OECD Publishing, Paris, France, April 2020.

4. Howard Chong and David Sunding, "Water Markets and Trading," *Annual Review of Environment and Resources* 31 (2006): 244–246; Janet C. Neuman, "Beneficial Use, Waste, and Forfeiture: The Inefficient Search for Efficiency in Western Water Use," *Environmental Law* 28, no. 4 (1998): 923–962; Thompson, *Legal Control*, 306–307.

5. Bipartisan Infrastructure Law, Public Law 117–58 (2021); N. Grigg, "Aging Water Infrastructure in the United States," in *Resilient Water Services and Systems:*

The Foundation of Well-Being, ed. Petri Juuti et al. (London: IWA Publishing, 2019), 31–46; Bastien Simeon, "The Financing Gap: Re-examining the Role of Private Financing and P3s," *Water Finance and Management,* October 26, 2021.

6. Andrea Cominola, Ian Monks, and Rodney A. Stewart, "Smart Water Metering and AI for Utility Operations and Customer Engagement: Disruption or Incremental Innovation?" *HydroLink* 4 (2020): 114–119; Nathan Huttner, Kathy Francis, and John Whitney, *Sustainable Governance and Funding for Open Water Data in California,* Redstone, May 2018; Aspen Institute, *Internet of Water: Sharing and Integrating Water Data for Sustainability,* Washington, D.C., 2017; Forrest S. Melton et al., "OpenET: Filling a Critical Data Gap in Water Management for the Western United States," *JAWRA: Journal of the American Water Resources Association* 58, no. 6 (December 2021): 971–994 (originally published November 2, 2021).

7. Eloise Kendy et al., "Water Transactions for Streamflow Restoration, Water Supply Reliability, and Rural Economic Vitality in the Western United States," *JAWRA: Journal of the American Water Resources Association* 54, no. 2 (2018): 487–504; Shyama V. Ramani, Shuan SadreGhazi, and Suraksha Gupta, "Catalysing Innovation for Social Impact: The Role of Social Enterprises in the Indian Sanitation Sector," *Technological Forecasting and Social Change* 121 (2017): 216–227; Water Funders Initiative and Water Table, "Overview," March 2021.

8. See Colo. Const., Art. XVI, § 5; Mark Squillace, "Restoring the Public Interest in Western Water Law," *Utah Law Review* 2020, no. 3 (2020): 627.

9. Patrick Trent Greiner, "Community Water System Privatization and the Water Access Crisis," *Sociology Compass* 14, no. 5 (2020); Donald Worster, *Rivers of Empire: Water, Aridity, and the Growth of the American West* (Oxford: Oxford University Press, 1985).

10. The Human Right to Water and Sanitation, G.A. Res. 64/292, § 1, U.N. Doc. A/RES.64/292 (July 28, 2010); S. Afr. Const. § 27(1)–(2), 1996; *Narmada Bachao Andolan v. Union of India,* 10 S.C.C. 644 (2000); Cal. A.B. 685 (2012); Mike Muller, "Free Basic Water—A Sustainable Instrument for a Sustainable Future in South Africa," *Environment and Urbanization* 20, no. 1 (2008): 67; Barton H. Thompson, Jr., "Water as a Public Commodity," *Marquette Law Review* 95 (2011): 17.

11. National Water Act 36 of 1998 § 3(1) (S. Afr.); *National Audubon Society v. Superior Court,* 658 P.2d 709 (1983); David A. Callies and Katie L. Smith, "The Public Trust Doctrine: A United States and Comparative Analysis," *Journal of International and Comparative Law* 7 (2020): 41; Philippe Cullet, "Water Law in a Globalised World: The Need for a New Conceptual Framework," *Journal of Environmental Law* 23, no. 2 (2011): 233; Thompson, "Water as a Public Commodity."

12. "The Cochabamba Declaration, December 8, 2000," in *¡Cochabamba! Water War in Bolivia,* ed. Oscar Olivera (Cambridge, MA: South End Press, 2004); Maude Barlow, *Blue Covenant: The Global Water Crisis and the Coming Battle for the Right to Water* (New York: New Press, 2007); Vandana Shiva, *Water Wars: Privatization, Pollution, and Profit* (Cambridge, MA: South End Press, 2002).

13. International Conference on Water and the Environment, *The Dublin Statement on Water and Sustainable Development,* Dublin, Ireland, 1992.

14. Thompson, "Water as a Public Commodity."

15. Jennifer Davis, "Private-Sector Participation in the Water and Sanitation Sector," *Annual Review of Environment and Resources* 30 (2005): 145; Thompson, "Water as a Public Commodity."

16. United Nations, "Guiding Principles on Business and Human Rights: Implementing the United Nations 'Protect, Respect, and Remedy' Framework," 2011; Noura Barakat, "The UN Guiding Principles: Beyond Soft Law," *Hastings Business Law Journal* 12, no. 3 (2016): 591; Jernej Letnar Cernic, "Corporate Obligations Under the Human Right to Water," *Denver Journal of International Law and Policy* 39, no. 2 (2011): 303; John Ruggie, "The Corporate Responsibility to Respect Human Rights," *Harvard Law School Forum on Corporate Governance*, Cambridge, Massachusetts, May 15, 2010.

17. Ajami, Thompson, and Victor, *Path to Water Innovation*; Michael Kiparsky et al., "The Innovation Deficit in Urban Water: The Need for an Integrated Perspective on Institutions, Organizations, and Technology," *Environmental Engineering Science* 30, no. 8 (2013): 395; Geoff Mulgan and David Albury, "Innovation in the Public Sector," Strategy Unit, United Kingdom Cabinet Office, London, 2003; Barton H. Thompson, Jr., "Institutional Perspectives on Water Policy and Markets," *California Law Review* 81, no. 3 (1993): 671.

18. Ajami, Thompson, and Victor, *Path to Water Innovation*; Melissa S. Kearney et al., *In Times of Drought: Nine Economic Facts about Water in the United States* (Washington, DC: Brookings Institute, 2014).

19. Ajami, Thompson, and Victor, *Path to Water Innovation*; Kearney et al., *In Times of Drought*.

20. John C. Morris, "Planning for Water Infrastructure: Challenges and Opportunities," *Public Works Management and Policy* 22, no. 1 (2016): 24; Ajami, Thompson, and Victor, *Path to Water Innovation*.

Chapter One

1. Norimitsu Onishi and Somini Sengupta, "Dangerously Low on Water, Cape Town Now Faces 'Day Zero,'" *New York Times*, January 30, 2018; Robbie Parks et al., "Experiences and Lessons in Managing Water from Cape Town," Grantham Briefing Paper No. 29, Grantham Institute, Imperial College London, February 2019; Salvatore Pascale et al., "Increasing Risk of Another Cape Town 'Day Zero' Drought in the 21st Century," *Proceedings of the National Academy of Sciences* 117, no. 47 (2020): 29495.

2. G. Thomas LaVanchy, Michael W. Kerwin, and James K. Adamson, "Beyond 'Day Zero': Insights and Lessons from Cape Town (South Africa)," *Hydrogeology Journal* 27 (2019): 1537; Scott Waldman, "Cape Town Won Awards on Climate. Here's What Went Wrong," *E&E News*, February 5, 2018.

3. Peter Gleick, Gary Hartman Wolff, and Katherine Kao Cushing, *Waste Not, Want Not: The Potential for Urban Water Conservation in California*, Pacific Institute, Oakland, California, 2003, 1; Mike Muller, "Understanding the Origins of Cape Town's Water Crisis," *Civil Engineering*, June 2017, 11–13.

4. Zeeshan Aleem, "Cape Town Is Bracing for 'Day Zero'—The Day It Cuts Off Running Water for 4 Million People," *Vox*, February 22, 2018; Zaheer Cassim, "Cape Town Could Be the First Major City in the World to Run Out of Water," *USA Today*,

January 22, 2018; Johan P. Enqvist and Gina Ziervogel, "Water Governance and Justice in Cape Town: An Overview," *WIREs Water* 6, no. 4 (July/August 2019); LaVanchy, Kerwin, and Adamson, "Beyond 'Day Zero'"; Godwell Nhamo and Adelaide O. Agyepong, "Climate Change Adaptation and Local Government: Institutional Complexities Surrounding Cape Town's Day Zero," *Jàmbá: Journal of Disaster Risk Studies* 11, no. 3 (2019): 1; Parks et al., "Experiences and Lessons"; Lucy Rodina, "Water Resilience Lessons from Cape Town's Water Crisis," *WIREs Water* 6, no. 6 (November/December 2019).

5. Natalie J. Burls et al., "The Cape Town 'Day Zero' Drought and Hadley Cell Expansion," *Climate and Atmospheric Science* 2, no. 27 (2019): 1; Mike Muller, "Understanding the Origins," 15–16; Pascale et al., "Increasing Risk"; Rodina, "Water Resilience Lessons"; Pedro M. Sousa et al., "The 'Day Zero' Cape Town Drought and the Poleward Migration of Moisture Corridors," *Environmental Research Letters* 13, no. 12 (December 2018): 124025.

6. M. J. Booysen, M. Visser, and R. Burger, "Temporal Case Study of Household Behavioural Response to Cape Town's 'Day Zero' Using Smart Meter Data," *Water Research* 149 (2019): 414; LaVanchy, Kerwin, and Adamson, "Beyond 'Day Zero'"; Parks et al., "Experiences and Lessons."

7. Parks et al., "Experiences and Lessons"; Tim Smedley, "The Outrageous Plan to Haul Icebergs to Africa," BBC, September 21, 2018.

8. Nate Millington and Suraya Scheba, "Day Zero and the Infrastructures of Climate Change: Water Governance, Inequality, and Infrastructural Politics in Cape Town's Water Crisis," *International Journal of Urban and Regional Research* 45, no. 1 (January 2021): 116; Steven Robins, "'Day Zero,' Hydraulic Citizenship and the Defence of the Commons in Cape Town: A Case Study of the Politics of Water and its Infrastructures (2017–2018)," *Journal of Southern African Studies* 45, no. 1 (2019): 5.

9. Burls et al., "Cape Town 'Day Zero'"; LaVanchy, Kerwin, and Adamson, "Beyond 'Day Zero'"; Pascale et al., "Increasing Risk"; Robins, "'Day Zero'"; Rodina, "Water Resilience Lessons"; Derek Van Dam, "After Nearly Running Out of Water in 2018, Cape Town Dams Are Now Overflowing," CNN, October 5, 2020.

10. Mike Muller, "Lessons from Cape Town's Drought," *Nature*, vol. 559, July 12, 2018, 174; Robins, "'Day Zero'"; Nick Shepherd, "Making Sense of 'Day Zero': Slow Catastrophes, Anthropocene Futures, and the Story of Cape Town's Water Crisis," *Water* 11, no. 9 (2019): 1744.

11. Robins, "'Day Zero.'"

12. Robins, "'Day Zero.'"

13. WWF, "Agricultural Water File: Farming for a Drier Future," July 19, 2018, wwf.org.za; Parks et al., "Experiences and Lessons"; Muller, "Lessons," 175; Bekezela Phakathi, "Farmers Lose R14bn as Cape Drought Bites," *Business Day* (South Africa), February 5, 2018; Robins, "'Day Zero.'"

14. Tom Freyberg, "Day Zero: GrahamTek Offers $2.1m Temporary Desalination Plant to Cape Town," *WaterWorld*, February 1, 2018; Steve Kretzman, "Cape Town Gears Up for Day Zero," *news24*, January 28, 2018; Amy McIntosh, "Coping in Cape Town," *Water Quality Products*, April 25, 2018.

15. Pascale et al., "Increasing Risk."

16. Patricia Gonzales and Newsha Ajami, "An Integrative Regional Resilience Framework for the Changing Urban Water Paradigm," in "Urban Resiliency to Extreme Climate," ed. Girma Bitsuamlak, special issue, *Sustainable Cities and Society* 30 (April 2017): 128; LaVanchy, Kerwin, and Adamson, "Beyond 'Day Zero'"; Lucy Rodina, "Planning for Water Resilience: Competing Agendas Among Cape Town's Planners and Water Managers," in "Knowledge Systems for Urban Resilience," ed. Mathieu Feagan et al., special issue, *Environmental Science and Policy* 99 (September 2019): 10; Kevin Winter, "5 Lessons Learnt from Cape Town's Water Crisis," *Umthombo*, no. 1 (2018): 20–21.

17. City of Cape Town, "Our Shared Water Future: Cape Town's Water Strategy," March 2020; Enqvist and Ziervogel, "Water Governance"; Geordin Hill-Lewis, "Cape Town: Lessons from Managing Water Scarcity," Brookings Institute, Washington, D.C., March 22, 2023; Shem Oirere, "After Avoiding 'Day Zero,' Cape Town Looks to Bolster Water System," *Engineering News-Record*, July 17, 2020.

18. Amy Crawford, "Cliff Hanger: After Nearly Running Out of Water in 2018, the South African City of Cape Town Aims to Rid Its Watersheds of Thirsty Non-Native Trees," *Nature Conservancy Magazine*, August 28, 2020.

19. Robins, "'Day Zero'"; Shepherd, "Making Sense."

20. LaVanchy, Kerwin, and Adamson, "Beyond 'Day Zero'"; Muller, "Lessons," 174; Robins, "'Day Zero'"; Kalpana Sunder, "How to Stop Another 'Day Zero,'" BBC, January 5, 2021; Craig Welch, "Why Cape Town Is Running Out of Water, and Who's Next," *National Geographic*, March 5, 2018.

21. Pascale et al., "Increasing Risk."

22. Minister for Water, Government of Western Australia, "$320m Investment Doubles Perth's Rainfall-Independent Water Source," press release, August 23, 2022.

23. Smedley, "Outrageous Plan"; Caroline Winter, "Towing an Iceberg: One Captain's Plan to Bring Drinking Water to 4 Million People," *Bloomberg Businessweek*, June 5, 2019.

24. Henry Fountain, "Researchers Link Syrian Conflict to a Drought Made Worse by Climate Change," *New York Times*, March 2, 2015; Christopher A. Scholz et al., "East African Megadroughts Between 135 and 75 Thousand Years Ago and Bearing on Early-Modern Human Origins," *Proceedings of the National Academy of Sciences* 104, no. 42 (2007): 16416.

25. Ian James, "New Push to Shore Up Shrinking Colorado River Could Reduce Water Flow to California," *Los Angeles Times,* October 28, 2022.

26. Stefanie Deinet et al., "The Living Planet Index (LPI) for Migratory Freshwater Fish," World Wildlife Fund, 2020.

27. Scott Tong, "From (Un)Happy, Texas — Where the Water Ran Out," *Marketplace*, August 10, 2012; Kate Vandy, "Welcome to Happy, Texas," *The Guardian*, January 24, 2014.

28. Dorany Pineda and Gabrielle Lamarr Lemee, "Household Water Wells Are Drying Up in Record Numbers as California Drought Worsens," *Los Angeles Times*, December 8, 2022.

29. United States Geological Survey, "Land Subsidence in the San Joaquin Valley," October 17, 2018; Megan M. Miller and Manoochehr Shirzaei, "Land Subsidence in

Houston Correlated with Flooding from Hurricane Harvey," *Remote Sensing of Environment* 225 (2019): 368; Meg Rudolph, "Sinking of a Titanic City," *Geotimes*, July 2001; Michelle Sneed, Justin Brandt, and Mike Solt, *Land Subsidence Along the Delta-Mendota Canal in the Northern Part of the San Joaquin Valley, California, 2003–10*, Scientific Investigations Report 2013-5142, United States Geological Survey.

30. Paul M. Barlow and Eric G. Reichard, "Saltwater Intrusion in Coastal Regions of North America," *Hydrogeology Journal* 18, no. 1 (2010): 247; Tara Moran, Janny Choy, and Carolina Sanchez, "The Hidden Costs of Groundwater Overdraft," Water in the West, Stanford, California, September 2014.

31. Moran, Choy, and Sanchez, "Hidden Costs."

32. Bruce Pengra, "A Glass Half Empty: Regions at Risk Due to Groundwater Depletion," UNEP Global Environmental Alert Service, January 2012.

33. Zeke Hausfather, "Explainer: What Climate Models Tell Us About Future Rainfall," *Carbon Brief*, January 19, 2018.

34. Hausfather, "Explainer."

35. Jiawei Bao et al., "Future Increases in Extreme Precipitation Exceed Observed Scaling Rates," *Nature Climate Change* 7, no. 2 (2017): 128; Hausfather, "Explainer"; Angeline G. Pendergrass et al., "Precipitation Variability Increases in a Warmer Climate," *Science Reports* 7, no. 1 (2017): 1; Jim Robbins, "Climate Whiplash: Wild Swings in Extreme Weather Are on the Rise," *Yale Environment 360*, November 14, 2019.

36. Noah S. Diffenbaugh, Daniel L. Swain, and Daniella Touma, "Anthropogenic Warming Has Increased Drought Risk in California," *Proceedings of the National Academy of Sciences* 112, no. 13 (2015): 3931.

37. Bradley Udall and Jonathan Overpeck, "The Twenty-First Century Colorado River Hot Drought and Implications for the Future," *Water Resources Research* 53, no. 3 (2017): 2404.

38. Udall and Overpeck, "Twenty-First Century Colorado River Hot Drought."

39. Toby R. Ault et al., "Relative Impacts of Mitigation, Temperature, and Precipitation on 21st-Century Megadrought Risk in the American Southwest," *Science Advances* 2, no. 10 (2016); Hoerling et al., "Causes for the Century-Long Decline in Colorado River Flow," *Journal of Climate* 32, no. 23 (2019): 8181; Udall and Overpeck, "Twenty-First Century Colorado River Hot Drought."

40. Sarah Kapnick and Alex Hall, "Causes of Recent Changes in Western North, American Snowpack," *Climate Dynamics* 38, no. 9 (2012): 1885; Philip W. Mote et al., "Dramatic Declines in Snowpack in the Western US," *NPJ Climate and Atmospheric Science* 1, no. 1 (2018): 1; Xubin Zeng, Patrick Broxton, and Nicholas Dawson, "Snowpack Change from 1982 to 2016 over Conterminous United States," *Geophysics Research Letters* 45, no. 23 (2018): 12940.

41. R. W. Dudley et al., "Trends in Snowmelt-Related Streamflow Timing in the Conterminous United States," *Journal of Hydrology* 547 (2017): 208; Diana R. Gergel et al., "Effects of Climate Change on Snowpack and Fire Potential in the Western USA," *Climatic Change* 141, no. 2 (2017): 287.

42. Tobias Bolch, "Asian Glaciers Are a Reliable Water Source," *Nature*, May 11, 2017; Jing Gao et al., "Collapsing Glaciers Threaten Asia's Water Supplies," *Nature*, January 2, 2019; Zhaofei Liu, Rui Wang, and Zhijun Yao, "Climate Change and Its

Impact on Water Availability of Large International Rivers over the Mainland Southeast Asia," *Hydrological Processes* 32, no 26 (2018): 3966.

43. Rubens Gondim et al., "Climate Change Impacts on Water Demand and Availability Using CMIP5 Models in the Jaguaribe Basin, Semi-Arid Brazil," *Environmental Earth Sciences* 77, no. 15 (2018): 1.

44. Mohsen M. Sherif and Vijay P. Singh, "Effect of Climate Change on Sea Water Intrusion in Coastal Aquifers," *Hydrological Processes* 13, no. 8 (1999): 1277.

45. UNICEF, "Child Survival Fact Sheet: Water and Sanitation," www.unicef.org; Shizuki Fukuda, Keigo Noda, and Taikan Oki, "How Global Targets on Drinking Water Were Developed and Achieved," *Nature Sustainability* 2, no. 5 (2019): 429; René P. Schwarzenbach et al., "Global Water Pollution and Human Health," *Annual Review of Environment and Resources* 35 (2010): 109; James C. Winter, Gary L. Darmstadt, and Jennifer Davis, "The Role of Piped Water Supplies in Advancing Health, Economic Development, and Gender Equality in Rural Communities," *Social Science and Medicine* 270 (2021): 113599.

46. Aniruddha Deshpande et al., "Mapping Geographical Inequalities in Access to Drinking Water and Sanitation Facilities in Low-Income and Middle-Income Countries, 2000–17," *Lancet Global Health* 8, no. 9 (2020); Fukuda, Noda, and Oki, "How Global Targets."

47. Fukuda, Noda, and Oki, "How Global Targets"; Pedro Martinez-Santos, "Does 91% of the World's Population Really Have 'Sustainable Access to Safe Drinking Water'?" *International Journal of Water Resources Development* 33, no. 4 (2017): 514.

48. Deshpande et al., "Mapping"; Fukuda, Noda, and Oki, "How Global Targets."

49. Robert Bain, Rick Johnston, and Tom Slaymaker, "Drinking Water Quality and the SDGs," *NPJ Clean Water* 3, no. 1 (2020): 1.

50. Dig Deep and US Water Alliance, "Closing the Water Access Gap in the United States: A National Action Plan," 2019; Erin Riggs et al., "An Overview of Clean Water Access Challenges in the United States," Environmental Finance Center, University of North Carolina, Chapel Hill, North Carolina, 2017.

51. Dig Deep and US Water Alliance, "Closing the Water Access Gap."

52. Nina Lakhani, "Millions in US Face Losing Water Supply as Coronavirus Moratoriums End," *The Guardian*, August 14, 2020; Manuel P. Teodoro and Robin Rose Saywitz, "Water and Sewer Affordability in the United States: A 2019 Update," *AWWA Water Science* 2, no. 2 (2020); US Water Alliance, *The Path to Universally Affordable Water Access: Guiding Principles for the Water Sector,* 2022, 8.

53. Riggs et al., "Overview"; Justin Worland, "America's Clean Water Crisis Goes Far Beyond Flint. There's No Relief in Sight," *Time*, February 20, 2020.

54. Sanjana Alex et al., "Why Bengaluru Lakes Catch Fire, and How to Prevent This," *Citizen Matters*, June 23, 2020; Lorraine Boissoneault, "The Cuyahoga River Caught Fire at Least a Dozen Times, but No One Cared Until 1969," *Smithsonian Magazine*, June 19, 2019.

55. Richard Damania et al., *Quality Unknown: The Invisible Water Crisis* (Washington, DC: World Bank, 2019); "'Invisible' Crisis of Water Quality Threatens Human and Environmental Well-Being: World Bank Report," *UN News*, August 20, 2019; Schwarzenbach et al., "Global Water Pollution."

56. Damania et al., *Quality Unknown*.

57. Damania et al., *Quality Unknown*; "Water Quality and Wastewater," UN Water, United Nations, 2018.

58. Melissa Denchak, "Water Pollution: Everything You Need to Know," Natural Resources Defense Council, February 14, 2018; "Water Quality and Wastewater."

59. Denchak, "Water Pollution"; Schwarzenbach et al., "Global Water Pollution."

60. US Environmental Protection Agency, *National Water Quality Inventory Report to Congress*, 2017.

61. Value of Water Campaign and American Society of Civil Engineers, "The Economic Benefits of Investing in Water Infrastructure," 2020.

62. American Society of Civil Engineers, "2021 Report Card on America's Infrastructure," infrastructurereportcard.org; Value of Water Campaign and American Society of Civil Engineers, "Economic Benefits."

63. Martin Allen et al., "Drinking Water and Public Health in an Era of Aging Distribution Infrastructure," *Public Works Management and Policy* 23, no. 4 (July 2018).

64. W. Neil Adger, "Vulnerability," *Global Environmental Change* 16, no. 3 (2006); Javier Fluixá-Sanmartín et al., "Climate Change Impacts on Dam Safety," *Natural Hazards and Earth System Sciences* 18, no. 9 (2018); Value of Water Campaign and American Society of Civil Engineers, "Economic Benefits."

65. Value of Water Campaign and American Society of Civil Engineers, "Economic Benefits."

Chapter Two

1. Michael Agnew, "The Thirsty Business of Beer: How Breweries Are Confronting the Industry's Water Problem," *The Growler*, March 2, 2016; Leon Kaye, "Breweries Across the World Strive to Decrease Beer's Water Footprint," *The Guardian*, August 16, 2011.

2. John Palmer, "Classic Brewing Cities and the Dogma of Virgin Water," *All About Beer*, April 9, 2014.

3. *Russian River Watershed and Drought* (San Diego: University of California at San Diego, 2018), available at https://cw3e.ucsd.edu/wp-content/uploads/2018/09/CW3E_RussianRiverDroughtReadinessReport.pdf, accessed May 9, 2023.

4. Agnew, "Thirsty Business"; Alastair Bland, "California Brewers Fear Drought Could Leave Bad Taste in Your Beer," NPR, February 20, 2014; Kevin Fagan, "California Drought: Beer Helps Tiny Wine Country Town," *SFGate,* January 30, 2014; Brianna Sacks, "State Craft Brewers Fear Drought Could Alter Business, and the Beer," *Los Angeles Times*, July 29, 2014; Grace Sell, "California Drought Puts Pressure on California's Craft Breweries," *The Growler*, March 19, 2014.

5. Peter Cohan, "Will Cambrian Innovation Revolutionize Waste Water Treatment?" *Forbes*, July 10, 2012; Kristine Wong, "The Californian Craft Beer Brewed from Waste Water," *The Guardian*, March 14, 2016.

6. Katherine Tweed, "A PPA Model for Spent Brew Water and More," *Greentechmedia*, November 30, 2015.

7. Kathleen M. Wilburn and Ralph Wilburn, "Achieving Social License to Operate Using Stakeholder Theory," *Journal of International Business Ethics* 4, no. 2 (2011): 4.

8. Matt Mace, "Why Heineken Is Championing Water Circularity as Its Contribution to the SDGs," *Edie.net*, March 22, 2019.

9. David Agren, "Mexican City Rejects Plans for Giant US-Owned Brewery amid Water Shortages," *The Guardian*, March 23, 2020; Santiago Pérez, "Mexican City's Residents Reject Constellation Brewery in Referendum," *Wall Street Journal*, March 23, 2020; David Shortell and Lorena Rios, "How Drought in Mexico Could Shape the Future of the Beer Industry," *New York Times*, November 13, 2022.

10. McKinsey and Company, "Water: A Human and Business Priority," May 2020.

11. Barton H. Thompson, Jr., "Water Institutions and Agriculture," in *The Evolving Sphere of Food Security*, ed. Rosamond L. Naylor (Oxford: Oxford University Press, 2014).

12. Arthur Guarino, "The Economic Implications of Global Water Scarcity," *Global Risk Insights*, December 8, 2016; Josué Medellín-Azuara et al., "Economic Analysis of the 2016 California Drought on Agriculture," University of California at Davis Center for Watershed Sciences, Davis, California, 2016; World Economic Forum, "Global Risks 2014," 9th ed., Geneva, Switzerland, 2014.

13. Peter H. Gleick, "Impacts of California's Ongoing Drought: Hydroelectricity Generation 2015 Update," Pacific Institute, Oakland, California, 2016; Jesse Kathan, "Decline in Hydropower Hampered by Drought Will Impact Utility Costs," *Mercury News*, August 9, 2020.

14. Kathan, "Decline in Hydropower"; McKinsey and Company, "Water."

15. Candise L. Henry and Lincoln F. Pratson, "Differentiating the Effects of Climate Change-Induced Temperature and Streamflow Changes on the Vulnerability of Once-Through Thermoelectric Power Plants," *Environmental Science and Technology* 53, no. 7 (2019): 3969; Jack McClamrock, Lihuan Zhou, and Giulia Christianson, "More Water Shortages Mean Energy Investors Need New Ways to Manage Drought Risk," World Resources Institute, October 2019; Lesley Poch, Guenter Conzelmann, and Tom Veselka, "An Analysis of the Effects of Drought Conditions on Electric Power Generation in the Western United States," in *Dams, Drought, and Energy-Water Interdependencies*, ed. Daniel L. Calzi (New York: NOVA, 2013).

16. Keith Schneider, Brett Walton, and Codi Kozacek, "Stranded Assets: Water Stress Is Factor in Global Mining Slump—Floods. Dam Failures, Public Opposition Batter Big Hard Rock Mines," *Circle of Blue*, December 15, 2016.

17. Thomas Andrew Gustafson, "How Much Water Actually Goes into Making a Bottle of Water," NPR, October 30, 2013; McKinsey and Company, "Water."

18. Agren, "Mexican City Rejects"; Barie Carmichael and Brian Moriarty, "How Coca-Cola Came to Terms with Its Own Water Crisis," *Washington Post*, May 31, 2018; McKinsey and Company, "Water"; Pérez, "Mexican City's Residents Reject"; Tom Perkins, "The Fight to Stop Nestlé from Taking America's Water to Sell in Plastic Bottles," *The Guardian*, October 29, 2019.

19. A. Y. Hoekstra and A. K. Chapagain, "Water Footprints of Nations: Water Use by People as a Function of Their Consumption Pattern," *Water Resources Management* 21 (2007): 35; "The Water Footprint of the Blue Jean," *Fluence*, July 6, 2020.

20. Julia Rosen, "Thirsty Business: How the Tech Industry Is Bracing for a Water-Scarce Future," *Earth*, September 13, 2016; Nikitha Sattiraju, "The Secret Cost of Google's Data Centers: Billions of Gallons of Water to Cool Servers," *Time*, April 2, 2020.

21. Marc Reisner, *Cadillac Desert: The American West and Its Disappearing Water* (New York: Penguin Books, 1993).

22. Carly Cassella, "Nearly 25% of the World's Population Faces a Water Crisis, and We Can't Ignore It," *ScienceAlert*, August 6, 2019; CreditSuisse Research Institute, "Water Scarcity: Addressing the Key Challenges," 2020; Rutger Willem Hofste, Paul Reig, and Leah Schleifer, "17 Countries, Home to One-Quarter of the World's Population, Face Extremely High Water Stress," World Resources Institute, commentary, August 2019; McKinsey and Company, "Water."

23. CDP Water Security, "Cleaning Up Their Act," London, 2020; World Economic Forum, "Global Risks 2014," 9th ed., Geneva, Switzerland, 2014.

24. Arjen Y. Hoekstra and Mesfin M. Mekonnen, "The Water Footprint of Humanity," *Proceedings of the National Academy of Sciences* 109, no. 9 (2012): 3232.

25. Hoekstra and Mekonnen, "Water Footprint"; John Ramos, "Small Winery Operators Fear New California Wastewater Rules Will Cork Profits," KPIX, January 23, 2021; CDP Worldwide, "CDP Non-Disclosure Campaign: Measuring the Impact of Investor Engagement on Corporate Environmental Disclosure," London, England, 2020.

26. Becky Hammer, "Craft Brewers to EPA: Keep Protecting Clean Water," Natural Resources Defense Council, June 2017.

27. Alessandro Galli et al., "Integrating Ecological, Carbon and Water Footprint into a 'Footprint Family' of Indicators: Definition and Role in Tracking Human Pressure on the Planet," *Ecological Indicators* 16 (2012): 100.

28. BCC Research, "Water and Wastewater Treatment Technologies: Global Markets," 2018; Mordor Intelligence, "Smart Water Management: Growth, Trends, Forecasts," 2020; Reese Tisdale, "Top Water Trends to Watch in 2020," *WaterWorld*, December 12, 2019.

29. Edouard Pérard, "Water Supply: Public or Private? An Approach Based on Cost of Funds, Transaction Costs, Efficiency and Political Costs," *Policy and Society* 27, no. 3 (2009): 193.

30. Donald E. Wolf, *Big Dams and Other Dreams: The Six Companies Story* (Norman: University of Oklahoma Press, 1996).

31. Value of Water Campaign and American Society of Civil Engineers, "The Economic Benefits of Investing in Water Infrastructure," 2020.

32. Abby Schultz, "Investing in Water for Impact," *Barron's Penta*, March 27, 2019.

33. Frost & Sullivan, "Digitalization Powering the Global Water Market," November 9, 2020.

Chapter Three

1. Maura Allaire, Haowei Wu, and Upmanu Lall, "National Trends in Drinking Water Quality Violations," *Proceedings of the National Academy of Sciences* 115, no. 9 (2018): 2078; Bipartisan Policy Center, "America's Aging Water Infrastructure," Washington, D.C., September 2016; Food and Water Watch, "Water Privatization: Facts and Figures," updated August 11, 2022, www.foodandwaterwatch.org; National Association of Water Companies, "Regulated Water Companies," www.nawc.org; Glenn Thrush, "Justice Dept. Strikes Deal to Address Struggling Water System in Jackson," *New York Times*, November 30, 2022.

2. Morris A. Pierce, "Documentary History of American Water-Works: Pittsburgh, Pennsylvania," www.waterworkshistory.us; Pittsburgh Water and Sewer Authority, "Our History," www.pgh2o.com.

3. Allegheny Institute for Public Policy, "A New Chapter Begins in the Long Running PWSA Saga," December 13, 2017, alleghenyinstitute.org; Allegheny Institute for Public Policy, "Water, Water Everywhere But No Accountability," September 12, 2011, alleghenyinstitute.org; Mike Bucsko, "Authority Manager's Close Ties to Contractor at Center of Federal Sewer Investigation," *Pittsburgh Post-Gazette*, October 25, 2000; Julia Lurie, "This Major City's Drinking Water Was Fine. Then Came the Private Water Company," *Mother Jones*, October 26, 2016; Oliver Morrison, "Introduction—The Untold Story of Pittsburgh's Water Crisis and the Likely Future of $300 Water Bills," *PublicSource*, October 18, 2021; Oliver Morrison, "Part 2—The Pittsburgh Mayor Who Spent PWSA's Money on Development Projects and the Pittsburgh Mayor Who Underfunded It," *PublicSource*, October 18, 2021; Oliver Morrison, "Part 3—Cronyism: Was PWSA Overrun with Unqualified Political Hires?" *PublicSource*, October 18, 2021; Oliver Morrison, "Part 4—A New Board: PWSA's Crisis Hit Slowly and Then All at Once," *PublicSource*, October 18, 2021; Marcela González Rivas and Caitlin Schroering, "Pittsburgh's Translocal Social Movement: A Case of the New Public Water," *Utilities Policy* 71, no. 3 (August 2021); Amy McConnell Schaarsmith, "Major Inadequacies Reported at PWSA," *Pittsburgh Post-Gazette*, September 11, 2011; Carrie Sloan, "The Unexpected Cause of Water Crises in American Cities," *Talk Poverty*, March 9, 2016.

4. Morrison, "Part 2"; Pittsburgh Water and Sewer Authority, "$167,390,000 Water and Sewer System Revenue Refinancing Bonds, Series of 2003," bond statement, September 23, 2003.

5. Morrison, "Part 2"; Rivas and Schroering, "Pittsburgh's Translocal Social Movement."

6. Leana Hosea and Sharon Lerner, "From Pittsburgh to Flint, the Dire Consequences of Giving Private Companies Responsibility for Ailing Public Water Systems," *The Intercept*, May 20, 2018; Lurie, "This Major City's Drinking Water"; Morrison, "Part 2"; Morrison, "Part 3"; PWSA and Veolia, "Pittsburgh Water and Sewer Authority: 2012 Executive Report," 2012; Rivas and Schroering, "Pittsburgh's Translocal Social Movement"; Veolia, "160 Years of History," www.veolia.com; Veolia, "Offering a Range of Solutions for Utilities Across North American," www.veolia.com.

7. Hosea and Lerner, "From Pittsburgh to Flint"; Morrison, "Part 4"; Rivas and Schroering, "Pittsburgh's Translocal Social Movement"; PWSA and Veolia, *2012 Executive Report*; Veolia, "The Truth about Veolia's Role and Work for the Pittsburgh Water and Sewer Authority," www.veolia.com; Veolia, "160 Years"; Veolia, "Offering a Range."

8. Hosea and Lerner, "From Pittsburgh to Flint"; Morrison, "Part 4"; Oliver Morrison, "Part 11—A Quick Primer on the Ups and Downs of the Pittsburgh Water and Sewer Authority," *PublicSource*, October 21, 2021; Veolia, "160 Years"; Veolia, "Offering a Range."

9. Hosea and Lerner, "From Pittsburgh to Flint"; Linnea Warren May, Jordan R. Fischbach, and Michele Abbott, "Informing Pittsburgh's Options to Address Lead in Water," Rand Perspective, 2017; Adam Smeltz, "PWSA Alleges Management Failures in Filing against Firm," *Pittsburgh Post-Gazette*, October 12, 2016; Alissa Weinman, "Pittsburgh Mayor Bill Peduto Denounces Water Privatization," *Corporate Accountability*, June 7, 2019.

10. Lurie, "This Major City's Drinking Water"; Morrison, "Part 2."

11. Hosea and Lerner, "From Pittsburgh to Flint"; May, Fischbach, and Abbott, "Informing Pittsburgh's Options"; Oliver Morrison, "Part 5—The Lead Crisis in Retrospect: The Main Problem Wasn't PWSA's Corporate Management," *PublicSource*, October 19, 2021; Smeltz, "PWSA Alleges Management Failures"; Veolia, "160 Years."

12. "Veolia North America Finds New Strategies for Growth After PPS Fails to Make Headway," *Global Water Intelligence Magazine*, February 2018; Morrison, "Part 4"; Morrison, "Part 5"; Morrison, "Part 11"; PWSA and Veolia, "PWSA and Veolia: A Partnership at Glance," apps.pittsburghpa.gov; Veolia, "Offering a Range."

13. Oliver Morrison, "Part 6—The Key Moment: How Three PWSA Board Members Ignited the Authority's Turnaround," *PublicSource*, October 19, 2021.

14. Oliver Morrison, "Part 7—A Coalition of Activists Helped Begin the Turnaround at PWSA," *PublicSource*, October 19, 2021; Oliver Morrison, "Part 8—Privatization Pitch: How Close PWSA Came to Being Privatized," *PublicSource*, October 19. 2021.

15. American Water, "Pennsylvania American Water Announces $2 Million Greater Pittsburgh Water System Upgrade," press release, September 23, 2021; American Water, "Pennsylvania American Water Systems Recognized for Excellent Tap Water Quality," press release, September 27, 2021; Morrison, "Part 8"; Adam Smeltz, "Pennsylvania American Eyes PWSA for Acquisition, Pitches Consolidation," *Pittsburgh Post-Gazette*, July 2, 2018.

16. Tom Hoffman, "Privatization by Any Other Name . . . Is Still Privatization," Sierra Club Pennsylvania, February 22, 2019; Morrison, "Part 7"; Rivas and Schroering, "Pittsburgh's Translocal Social Movement"; Doug Shields, "The Stealthy Corporate Scheme to Privatize Pittsburgh's Water System," *In These Times*, January 14, 2019.

17. Morrison, "Part 7"; Rivas and Schroering, "Pittsburgh's Translocal Social Movement"; Weinman, "Pittsburgh Mayor Bill Peduto."

18. Rivas and Schroering, "Pittsburgh's Translocal Social Movement."

19. Morrison, "Part 8."

20. Tom Davidson, "PWSA Seeks Regulatory Approval for Rate Increases in 2022, 2023," *TribLive*, April 12, 2021; Morrison, "Introduction"; Morrison, "Part 9"; Oliver Morrison, "Part 10—The Retirement of an Old-School Public Servant Will Test the Durability of PWSA's Turnaround," *PublicSource*, October 21, 2021; Pennsylvania Public Utility Commission, "PUC Approves Pittsburgh Water and Sewer Authority Rate Settlement for Water, Wastewater, and Stormwater Sewers," press release, November 18, 2021; "PWSA Cellibrates 10,000 Lead Service Line Replacements with Federal, State, and Local Leaders," Pittsburgh Water and Sewage Authority, March 24, 2023.

21. Rivas and Schroering, "Pittsburgh's Translocal Social Movement."

22. David Lloyd Owen, *Pinsent Masons Water Yearbook 2012–2013*, Pinsent Masons, London, 2012; "The World's Top 50 Private Water Operators," *Global Water Intelligence Magazine*, August 22, 2019.

23. Mohammed Yousef Al-Madfaei, "The Impact of Privatisation on the Sustainability of Water Resources," IWA Publishing, iwapublishing.com; American Water, "The Benefits of Investor-Owned Water Utilities," white paper, 2014, calwaterassn. com; Andrea Kopaskie, "Public v. Private: A National Overview of Water Systems," *UNC Environmental Finance Center*, October 19, 2016; US Government Accountability Office, "Private Water Utilities: Actions Needed to Enhance Ownership Data," GAO-21-291, April 26, 2021.

24. "Investor-Owned Utilities Served 72% of U.S. Electricity Customers in 2017," *EIA: Today in Energy*, August 15, 2019; Norbert Michel and James Gattuso, "Are U.S. Telecom Networks Public Property?" Heritage Foundation, April 8, 2004; "U.S. Homes and Businesses Receive Natural Gas Mostly from Local Distribution Companies," *EIA: Today in Energy*, July 31, 2020.

25. Nelson Manfred Blake, *Water for the Cities: A History of the Urban Water Supply Problem in the United States* (Syracuse, NY: Syracuse University Press, 1956); James Salzman, *Drinking Water: A History* (New York: Abrams Press, 2012); Barton H. Thompson, Jr. et al., *Legal Control of Water Resources*, 6th ed. (St. Paul, MN: West Academic, 2018).

26. Blake, *Water for the Cities*; Robert Carlisle, *Water Ways: A History of the Elizabethtown Water Company* (Elizabeth, NJ: Elizabethtown Water Company, 1982); David A. McDonald, "Remunicipalization: The Future of Water Services?" *Geoforum* 91 (May 2018): 47; Martin Melosi, "Pure and Plentiful: The Development of Modern Waterworks in the United States, 1801–2000," *Water Policy* 2, no. 4 (December 2000): 243; Brian Phillips Murphy, "'A Very Convenient Instrument': The Manhattan Company, Aaron Burr, and the Election of 1800," *William and Mary Quarterly* 65, no. 2 (April 2008): 233; Salzman, *Drinking Water*; Thompson et al., *Legal Control*.

27. Karen Bakker, *Privatizing Water: Governance Failure and the World's Urban Water Crisis* (Ithaca, NY: Cornell University Press, 2010); Evans Clark, *Municipal Ownership in the United States* (New York: Intercollegiate Socialist Society, 1916); McDonald, "Remunicipalization"; Thompson et al., *Legal Control*.

28. Bakker, *Privatizing Water*; McDonald, "Remunicipalization"; Salzman, *Drinking Water*; Thompson et al., *Legal Control*.

29. Fionn MacKillop, "The Los Angeles 'Oligarchy' and the Governance of Water and Power Networks: The Making of a Municipal Utility Based on Market Principles (1902–1930)," *Flux* 60 (2005): 23; Thompson et al., *Legal Control.*

30. Paula Baker, "Politics in the Gilded Age and Progressive Era," in *The Oxford Handbook of American Political History*, ed. Paula Baker and Donald T. Critchlow (Oxford: Oxford University Press, 2020); Bakker, *Privatizing Water*; Jules P. Gehrke, "A Radical Endeavor: Joseph Chamberlain and the Emergence of Municipal Socialism in Birmingham," *American Journal of Economics and Sociology* 75, no. 1 (January 2016): 23; McDonald, "Remunicipalization"; Gail Radford, "From Municipal Socialism to Public Authorities: Institutional Factors in the Shaping of American Public Enterprise," *Journal of American History* 90, no. 3 (December 2003): 863.

31. Blake, *Water for the Cities*; "Los Angeles Aqueduct," The History Channel, updated March 7, 2019; Melosi, "Pure and Plentiful"; Martin Melosi, *The Sanitary City: Urban Infrastructure in America from Colonial Times to the Present (Creating the North American Landscape)* (Baltimore, MD: John Hopkins University Press, 2000); Rachael Myrow, "The Not-So-Crystal Clean History of San Francisco's Drinking Water," KQED, May 16, 2019.

32. Marta Suárez-Varela et al., "Ownership and Performance in Water Services Revisited: Does Private Management Really Outperform Public?" *Water Resources Management* 31, no. 8 (2017).

33. Bakker, *Privatizing Water*; David Harvey, *A Brief History of Neoliberalism* (Oxford: Oxford University Press, 2005); McDonald, "Remunicipalization"; World Bank, *Water Resources Management* (Washington, DC: World Bank, 1993).

34. Karen Bakker, *An Uncooperative Commodity: Privatizing Water in England and Wales* (Oxford: Oxford University Press, 2004); Chris Edwards, "Margaret Thatcher's Privatization Legacy," *Cato Journal* 37, no. 1 (2017): 89; Karma Loveday, "England's Water Industry Is About to Get Competitive," *Raconteur*, December 8, 2016; Maitreyee Mukherjee and Olivia Jensen, "Open Water: Impacts of Retail Competition on Service Performance and Water-Use Efficiency in England," *Utilities Policy* 79 (2022): 101429.

35. California Water Service, "2015 Urban Water Management Plan: City of Hawthorne District," 2016; National Research Council, *Privatization of Water Services in the United States: An Assessment of Issues and Experience* (Washington, DC: National Academies Press, 2002); Barton H. Thompson, Jr., "Privatization of Municipal Water Supplies," *Looking Ahead*, May/June 1999.

36. Douglas Jehl, "As Cities Move to Privatize Water, Atlanta Steps Back," *New York Times*, February 10, 2003; Geoffrey Segal, "What Can We Learn from Atlanta's Water Privatization," Reason Foundation, January 21, 2003; Suez, "Jersey City and Suez Extend Water Service Partnership," *TAPintoEdison*, April 1, 2019; Thompson et al., *Legal Control*; "City of Buffalo Renews Drinking Water Contract for Veolia NA," *WaterWorld*, August 6, 2020.

37. "Houston—The Contract Operations Capital of Texas," *Global Water Intelligence Magazine*, August 26, 2021; Veolia, "Innovative Technology at Honolulu's Reclamation Plant," www.veolianorthamerica.com; Thompson et al., *Legal Control.*

38. Thompson et al., *Legal Control.*

39. Kimberly Scism Eagle, "New Public Management in Charlotte, North Carolina: A Case Study of Managed Competition," PhD diss., Virginia Polytechnic Institute and State University, 2005; Geoff Greenough et al., "Public Works Delivery Systems in North America: Private and Public Approaches, including Managed Competition," *Public Works Management and Policy* 4, no. 1 (1999); Thompson et al., *Legal Control.*

40. Satoko Kishimoto, Olivier Petitjean, eds., *Reclaiming Public Services: How Cities and Citizens Are Turning Back Privatisation* (Amsterdam and Paris: Transnational Institute, 2017); McDonald, "Remunicipalization"; Mildred E. Warner, "Key Issues in Water Privatization and Remunicipalization," *Utilities Policy* 73 (December 2021).

41. Hoffman, "Privatization"; Oliver E. Williamson, "Public and Private Bureaucracies: A Transaction Cost Economics Perspective," *Journal of Law, Economics, and Organization* 15, no. 1 (1999): 306.

42. Germà Bel and Mildred Warner, "Does Privatization of Solid Waste and Water Services Reduce Costs? A Review of Empirical Studies," *Resources, Conservation, and Recycling* 52, no. 12 (2008): 1337; Germà Bel, Xavier Fageda, and Mildred E. Warner, "Is Private Production of Public Services Cheaper than Public Production? A Meta-Regression Analysis of Solid Waste and Water Services," *Journal of Policy Analysis and Management* 29, no. 3 (2010): 553; Germà Bel, "Trends and Comparisons of Outcomes Between Public and Privately Owned Utilities," in *Routledge Handbook of Urban Water Governance,* ed. Megan Farrelly (Oxford: Routledge, 2021); McDonald, "Remunicipalization"; Suarez-Varela, "Ownership and Performance Outperform Public?"; Warner, "Key Issues."

43. Martin Allen et al., "Drinking Water and Public Health in an Era of Aging Distribution Infrastructure," *Public Works Management and Policy* 23, no. 4 (July 2018): 301; American Water, "Benefits"; Neil S. Grigg, "Water Infrastructure: Does the US Need a National Policy?" *Public Works Management and Policy* 26 (August 2021): 2010; Neil S. Grigg, "Water Infrastructure: Does the US Need a National Policy?" *Public Works Management and Policy* 26 (August 2021): 2010; US Environmental Protection Agency, "Drinking Water Infrastructure Needs Survey and Assessment: Sixth Report to Congress," Washington, D.C., 2018; US Environmental Protection Agency, "Clean Watersheds Needs Survey 2012: Report to Congress," Washington, D.C., 2012.

44. American Water, "Benefits"; Thompson et al., *Legal Control.*

45. Elizabeth Douglass, "Towns Sell Their Public Water Systems—And Come to Regret It," *Washington Post,* July 8, 2017; Morrison, "Part 10"; Thompson et al., *Legal Control;* US Government Accountability Office, "Private Water Utilities."

46. Melissa S. Kearney et al., *In Times of Drought: Nine Economic Facts about Water in the United States* (Washington, DC: Brookings Institute, 2014); Jhih-Shyang Shih et al., "Economies of Scale in Community Water Systems," *Journal of American Water Works Association* 98, no. 9 (2006): 100.

47. Douglass, "Towns Sell"; Lauren Joca, "Three Strategies to Reduce Costs: Purchasing Partnerships for Water Systems," UNC Environmental Finance Center, August 4, 2016; Thompson, *Legal Control;* US Government Accountability Office, "Private Water Utilities."

48. Joca, "Three Strategies."

49. Thompson et al., *Legal Control.*

50. Suarez-Varela, "Ownership and Performance Outperform Public?"

51. Hoffman, "Privatization"; Ryan Honeyman and Tiffany Jana, *The B Corp Handbook: How You Can Use Business as a Force for Good,* 2d ed. (Oakland, CA: Berrett-Koehler Publishers, 2019), 1–2; Martin Lipton, Karessa L. Cain, and Kathleen C. Iannone, "Stakeholder Governance and the Fiduciary Duties of Directors," *Harvard Law School Forum on Corporate Governance,* August 24, 2019; Shields, "Stealthy Corporate Scheme."

52. Isaac Wait and William Adam Petrie, "Comparison of Water Pricing for Publicly and Privately Owned Water Utilities in the United States," *Water International* 42, no. 8 (2017); X. Zhang et al., "Water Pricing and Affordability in the US: Public vs. Private Ownership," *Water Policy* 24, no. 3 (2022).

53. Zhang et al., "Water Pricing."

54. Thomas M. Hanna and David A. McDonald, "From Pragmatic to Politicized? The Future of Water Remunicipalization in the United States," *Utilities Policy* 72 (October 2021); McDonald, "Remunicipalization."

55. George Homsy and Mildred Warner, "Does Public Ownership of Utilities Matter for Local Government Water Policies?" *Utilities Policy* 64 (June 2020); McDonald, "Remunicipalization"; Rivas and Schroering, "Pittsburgh's Translocal Social Movement"; Joanna L. Robinson, *Contested Water: The Struggle Against Water Privatization in the United States and Canada* (Cambridge, MA: MIT Press, 2013).

56. World Bank, *Approaches to Private Participation in Water Services: A Toolkit* (Washington, DC: World Bank, 2006).

57. Hanna and McDonald, "From Pragmatic to Politicized?"; McDonald, "Remunicipalization"; Rivas and Schroering, "Pittsburgh's Translocal Social Movement"; Robinson, *Contested Water.*

58. Douglass, "Towns Sell"; McDonald, "Remunicipalization"; "U.S. Water and Wastewater Contract Operations Market Report Shows Sector Continues to Build Momentum in Growth and Popularity," National Association of Water Companies, press release, June 30, 2021.

59. "MSCI ACWI Water Utilities Index (USD)," Index Factsheet, MSCI, April 28, 2023; Nikolaos Sismanis, "Let Your Profits Flow with These Top 5 Water Stocks," *Forbes,* July 22, 2021.

60. Sismanis, "Let Your Profits."

61. Neil Gupta, "Veolia and Suez Merger Directly Threatens Human Right to Water," *Corporate Accountability,* June 30, 2021; Sismanis, "Let Your Profits"; Sarah White and Sudip Kar-gupta, "Veolia, Suez Agree $15 Billion Utilities Merger after Bitter Spat," Reuters, April 12, 2021.

62. Eric Cheng, "China's Water Industry Is Still Attractive with Strong Fundamentals," *Natixis,* November 9, 2020; "China's Private Water Operators Diversify Their Exposure," *Global Water Intelligence Magazine,* August 22, 2019; Sismanis, "Let Your Profits"; Nusa Tukic and Meryl Burgess, "China's Role in Africa's Water Sector: Mapping the Terrain," *Waterlines* 35, no. 1 (2016): 18.

63. Terry Cowgill, "Sheffield Water Company Acquired by Energy Giant Eversource," *Berkshire Edge*, April 8, 2021; Andrew Maykuth, "Pa. Approves Aqua America's $4.3 Billion Expansion into Natural Gas. Now It Wants to Be Essential," *Inquirer*, January 16, 2020; US Government Accountability Office, "Private Water Utilities."

64. Thomas Peyton Lyon, A. Wren Montgomery, and Dan Zhao, "A Change Would Do You Good: Privatization, Municipalization, and Drinking Water Quality," *Academy of Management*, October 2017.

65. American Water Works, "Environment, Social, and Governance (ESG)," ir.amwater.com; California Water Services Group, "ESG Report," www.calwater.com; California Water Services Group, "Human Rights Policy," www.calwater.com; Veolia, "Corporate Social Responsibility," www.veolia.com.

66. American Water Works, "Environment, Social, and Governance (ESG)"; California Water Services Group, "Human Rights Policy"; Veolia, "Corporate Social Responsibility."

67. Tracxn, "Acquisitions by Veolia," tracxn.com.

68. Ky. Rev. Stat. §§ 107.700 et seq.; N.J. Rev. Stat. §§ 58-30-1 et seq.; Utah Code §§ 73-10d-1 et seq.

69. Cory L. Mann and Mildred E. Warner, "Power Asymmetries and Limits to Eminent Domain: The Case of Missoula Water's Municipalisation," *Water Alternatives* 12, no. 2 (2019); Douglass, "Towns Sell"; Kevin G. Glade, "CP National Corp. v. Public Service Commission: The Jurisdictional Ambiguity Surrounding Municipal Power Systems," *Utah Law Review* 1982, no. 4 (1982); "Judge Tentatively Rules Against Town in Water Trial," *Apple Valley News*, May 11, 2021; Shelley Ross Saxer, "Government Power Unleashed: Using Eminent Domain to Acquire a Public Utility or Other Ongoing Enterprise," *Indiana Law Review* 38, no. 1 (2005); Rodney T. Smith, "Superior Court Dismisses City of Claremont Complaint to Condemn Golden State Water Company System," *Journal of Water*, January 31, 2017; Thompson et al., *Legal Control*.

70. Douglass, "Towns Sell."

71. American Water Works, "Environment, Social, and Governance (ESG)"; California Services Group, "Human Rights Policy"; US Government Accountability Office, "Private Water Utilities."

72. American Water Works, "Environment, Social, and Governance (ESG)"; Morrison, "Part 10."

73. S.B. 1469, 2021–2022 Reg. Sess. (Cal. 2022); California Public Utilities Commission, *2010 Water Action Plan* (October 2010); California Public Utilities Commission, "CPUC Approves Pilot Program to Provide Rate Discounts to Qualified Cal-Am Water Customers in San Diego," press release, June 2, 2022; California Public Utilities Commission, "CPUC Continues Efforts to Address Affordability of Utility Rates," press release, August 4, 2022.

74. Zhang et al., "Water Pricing"; Warner, "Key Issues."

Chapter Four

1. Peter Debaere et al., "Water Markets as a Response to Scarcity," *Water Policy* 16, no. 4 (2014): 625.

2. National Research Council, *Water Transfers in the West: Efficiency, Equity, and the Environment* (Washington, DC: National Academies Press, 1992).

3. Imperial Irrigation District, "IID History," www.iid.com; National Research Council, *Water Transfers*; Tony Perry, "Proposal to Sell Imperial Valley Water Stirs Anger," *Los Angeles Times*, October 2, 1995.

4. Peter Passell, "A Gush of Profits from Water Sale?" *New York Times*, April 23, 1998.

5. Thomas J. Graff, "Water Planning and Conservation, California Won't Go Dry in 1985," *Los Angeles Times*, September 27, 1981; Passell, "Gush of Profits"; Robert Stavins, *Trading Conservation Investments for Water* (Berkeley, CA: Environmental Defense Fund, 1983).

6. Graff, "Water Planning"; Passell, "Gush of Profits"; Stavins, *Trading Conservation Investments*.

7. Barton H. Thompson, Jr., "Institutional Perspectives on Water Policy and Markets," *California Law Review* 81, no. 3 (1993): 671.

8. Karl Anderson, *The Salton Sea* (Charleston, SC: Arcadia Publishing, 2011); David Owen, *Where the Water Goes: Life and Death Along the Colorado River* (New York: Riverhead Books, 2017).

9. *Imperial Irrigation District: Alleged Waste and Unreasonable Use of Water*, Water Rights Decision 1600 (California Water Resources Control Board, 1984); Steven P. Erie and Harold David Brackman, *Beyond Chinatown: The Metropolitan Water District, Growth, and the Environment in Southern California* (Stanford, CA: Stanford University Press, 2006); Samantha Spangler, "Imperial Irrigation District v. State Water Resources Control Board: Board as Arbiter of Reasonable and Beneficial Use of California Water," *Pacific Law Journal* 19, no. 4 (1988): 1565.

10. Erie and Brackman, *Beyond Chinatown*; National Research Council, *Water Transfers*; "Imperial Irrigation District Order to Submit Plan and Implementation Schedule for Conservation Measures," Water Rights Order 88-20, California Water Resources Control Board, 1988.

11. Erie and Brackman, *Beyond Chinatown*; Perry, "Proposal to Sell."

12. Jedidiah Brewer, Robert Glennon, Alan Ker, and Gary B. Libecap, "Water Markets in the West: Prices, Trading, and Contractual Forms," *Economic Inquiry* 46, no. 2 (2008): 91.

13. Passell, "Gush of Profits"; Perry, "Proposal to Sell."

14. "Boulder Canyon Project Agreement Requesting Apportionment of California's Share of the Waters of the Colorado River Among the Applicants in the State," August 18, 1931; Passell, "Gush of Profits"; Imperial Irrigation District, "History of the QSA and Related Agreements," www.iid.com.

15. Erie and Brackman, *Beyond Chinatown*; John Gibler, *Water for People and Place: Moving Beyond Markets in California Water Policy* (Washington, DC: Public Citizen, 2005); Perry, "Proposal to Sell."

16. National Research Council, *Water Transfers*; "Hot Water," *Forbes*, June 10, 2002.

17. "Hot Water," *Forbes*; Imperial Irrigation District, "IID History"; Denise Zapata, "Water Politics Fuel San Diego Election," *iNewsource*, June 4, 2010.

18. Antoine Abou-Diwan, "Western Farms Case Against IID Dismissed by Judge," *Imperial Valley Press*, March 6, 2013; Richard Montenegro Brown, "After 16 Years, Kuhn to Depart IID; Potential Successors Quickly Emerge," *Calexico Chronicle*, December 6, 2019; Congressional Research Service, *Salton Sea Restoration* (updated July 28, 2021); Erie and Brackman, *Beyond Chinatown*; "Hot Water," *Forbes*; Passell, "Gush of Profits"; Zapata, "Water Politics."

19. Joshua Parthow, "Water Cuts Could Save the Colorado River. Farmers Are in the Crossbars," *Washington Post*, April 16, 2023; Joshua Parthow, "As the Colorado River Dries Up, States Can't Agree on Saving Water," *Washington Post*, February 1, 2023.

20. National Research Council, *Water Transfers*.

21. K. William Easter and Qiuqiong Huang, *Water Markets for the 21st Century: What Have We Learned?* (Dordrecht, Germany: Springer, 2014); K. William Easter, Mark W. Rosegrant, and Ariel Dinar, "Formal and Informal Markets for Water: Institutions, Performance, and Constraints," *World Bank Research Observer* 14, no. 1 (1999): 107–10; Takahiro Endo et al., "Are Water Markets Globally Applicable?" *Environmental Research Letters* 13 (2018); R. Quentin Grafton et al., "An Integrated Assessment of Water Markets: A Cross-Country Comparison," *Review of Environmental Economics and Policy* 5, no. 2 (2011): 219–220; Amelie Joseph, "Implementing Water Markets in the Jordan Valley to Insure Environmental Flows in Drought Periods," working paper, Friends of the Earth Middle East, January 2013; Greenwell Matchaya, Luxon Nhamo, Sibusiso Nhlengethwa, and Charles Nhemachena, "An Overview of Water Markets in Southern Africa: An Option for Water Management in Times of Scarcity," *Water* 11 (2019): 1006; Vanessa Casado-Pérez, *The Role of Government in Water Markets* (Oxford: Routledge, 2016); Joan Pujol, Meri Raggi, and Davide Viaggi, "The Potential Impact of Markets for Irrigation Water in Italy and Spain: A Comparison of Two Study Areas," *Australian Journal of Agricultural and Resource Economics* 5 (2006): 361; Jesper Svensson et al., "How Does Hybrid Environmental Governance Work? Examining Water Rights Trading in China (2000–2019)," *Journal of Environmental Management* 288 (2021): 112333; Sarah A. Wheeler, ed., *Water Markets: A Global Assessment* (Northampton, MA: Edward Elgar Press, 2021).

22. Endo et al., "Are Water Markets"; Wheeler, ed., *Water Markets*.

23. T. E. Lauer, "Reflections on Riparianism," *Missouri Law Review* 35 (1970): 1; Kenneth R. Wright, ed., *Water Rights of the Eastern States* (Denver, CO: American Water Works Association, 1998).

24. Olivia S. Choe, "Appurtenancy Reconceptualized: Managing Water in an Era of Scarcity," *Yale Law Journal* 113 (2004): 1909; Joseph Dellapenna, "Displacing Riparian Rights with Comprehensive Non-Temporal Permit Systems," in *Waters and Water Rights*, ed. Amy K. Kelley, 3rd ed. (Newark, NJ: Matthew Bender, 2017); Joseph W. Dellapenna, "Special Challenges to Water Markets in Riparian States," *Georgia State University Law Review* 21 (2004): 305; Phyllis Isley and Robert J. Middleton, Jr., "Water Markets in Georgia: An Overview of Ongoing Sales of Water," Water Policy Working Paper Series No. 2003-006, Georgia Water Planning and Policy Center, 2003; Logan Elizabeth Pike, "Opening Water Markets in Florida," *The Journal*, Fall/Winter 2017.

25. Wheeler, ed., *Water Markets*; Endo et al., "Are Water Markets"; George A. Gould, "Water Rights Systems," in *Water Rights,* ed. Wright.

26. Andrew Ayres et al., "Improving California's Water Market: How Water Trading and Banking Can Support Groundwater Management," Public Policy Institute of California, San Francisco, September 2021; Nicholas Schupbach, "How to Invest in Water So We Don't Run Out," Barings Investment Institute, February 2020.

27. Peter Debaere and Tianshu Li, "The Effects of Water Markets: Evidence from the Rio Grande," *Advances in Water Resources* 145 (2020): 103700; R. Quentin Grafton, James Horne, and Sarah Ann Wheeler, "On the Marketisation of Water: Evidence from the Murray-Darling Basin, Australia," *Water Resources Management* 30 (2016): 923; Grafton et al., "Integrated Assessment," 235; Charles Meyers and Richard Posner, *Market Transfers of Water Rights: Toward an Improved Market in Water Resources* (Washington, DC: National Water Commission, 1971).

28. Jesus Arellano-Gonzalez et al., "The Adaptive Benefits of Agricultural Water Markets in California," *Environmental Resource Letters* 16 (2021); Debaere and Li, "Effects of Water Markets"; Grafton, Horne, and Wheeler, "On the Marketisation of Water," 923; Grafton et al., "Integrated Assessment," 235; Richard Howitt, Nancy Moore, and Rodney Smith, *A Retrospective on California's 1991 Emergency Drought Water Bank* (Sacramento: California Department of Water Resources, 1992).

29. Andrew B. Ayres, Kyle C. Meng, and Andrew J. Plantinga, "Do Environmental Markets Improve on Open Access? Evidence from California Groundwater Rights," *Journal of Political Economy* 129, no. 10 (2021): 2817; Andrew Ayres et al., "Improving California's Water Market: How Water Trading and Banking Can Support Groundwater Management," Public Policy Institute of California, San Francisco, September 2021; Ellen Bruno, "The Economic Impacts of Agricultural Groundwater Markets," *ARE Update* 21, no. 6 (2018): 9.

30. Peter W. Culp, Robert Glennon, and Gary Libecap, *Shopping for Water: How the Market Can Mitigate Water Shortages in the American West* (Washington, DC: The Hamilton Project/Stanford Woods Institute, 2014); Gary D. Libecap, "The West Needs Water Markets," *Defining Ideas*, February 7, 2018.

31. Stavins, *Trading Conservation Investments*; Graff, "Water Planning"; Grafton, Horne, and Wheeler, "On the Marketisation of Water," 923.

32. James Kluger, *Turning on Water with a Shovel: The Career of Elwood Mead* (Albuquerque, NM: University of New Mexico Press, 1992); Elwood Mead, *Irrigation Institutions* (New York: Macmillan, 1903).

33. Mead, *Irrigation Institutions.*

34. 1909 Wyo. Sess. Laws, ch. 68, § 1; Barton H. Thompson, Jr. et al., *Legal Control of Water Resources*, 6th ed. (St. Paul, MN: West Academic, 2018).

35. Kurt Schwabe, Mehdi Nemati, Clay Landry, and Grant Zimmerman, "Water Markets in the Western United States: Trends and Opportunities," *Water* 12 (2020): 233; Thompson et al., *Legal Control.*

36. *Colorado River Water Conservation District v. Vidler Tunnel Water Company,* 594 P.2d 566 (Colo. 1979); Sandra Zellmer, "The Anti-Speculation Doctrine and its Implications for Collaborative Water Management," *Nevada Law Journal* 8, no. 3 (2008): 994.

37. Adam Loch et al., "Markets, Mis-Direction, and Motives: A Factual Analysis of Hoarding and Speculation in Southern Murray-Darling Basin Water Markets," *Australian Journal of Agricultural and Resource Economics* 65, no. 2 (2021): 291.

38. *Central Delta Water Agency v. State Water Resources Control Board*, 124 Cal. App. 4th 245 (Cal. Ct. App. 2004); Peter Fimrite, "The Delta's Sinking Islands," *S.F. Chronicle*, January 12, 2020.

39. *Central Delta Water Agency v. State Water Resources Control Board*; Bettina Boxall, "MWD Considers Buying 4 Delta Islands to Solve Some Water Problems," *Los Angeles Times*, November 10, 2015; Matt Hamilton, "Southern California Water District Completes $175-Million Purchase of Delta Islands," *Los Angeles Times*, July 18, 2016.

40. N.M. Stat. § 72-1-9; Utah Code § 73-1-4(2)(f); *Pagosa Area Water & Sanitation District v. Trout Unlimited*, 170 P.3d 307 (Colo. 2007).

41. Australian Competition and Consumer Commission, *Murray-Darling Basin Water Markets Inquiry: Final Report* (February 2021); Grafton et al., "Integrated Assessment," 235.

42. *Farmers Highline Canal & Reservoir Co. v. City of Golden*, 272 P.2d 629 (Colo. 1954); Grafton et al., "Integrated Assessment," 235; David C. Taussig, "The Devolution of the No-Injury Standard in Changes of Water Rights," *University of Denver Water Law Review* 18, no. 1 (2014): 116.

43. Cal. Water Code § 386; National Research Council, *Water Transfers*; Barton H. Thompson, Jr., "Water as a Public Commodity," *Marquette Law Review* 95 (2011): 17.

44. National Research Council, *Water Transfers*.

45. William L. Kahrl, *Water and Power* (Berkeley: University of California Press, 1982); Gary D. Libecap, *Owens Valley Revisited: A Reassessment of the West's First Great Water Transfer* (Stanford, CA: Stanford University Press, 2007); National Research Council, *Water Transfers*; Panel for Independent Assessment of Social and Economic Conditions in the Murray-Darling Basin, *Final Report* (April 2020); Les Standiford, *Water to the Angels: William Mulholland, His Monumental Aqueduct, and the Rise of Los Angeles* (New York: Ecco, 2015).

46. Davide Castellani, "In Praise of Pecuniary Externalities," *European Journal of Development Research* 24, no. 1 (2012): 15; Randall G. Holcombe and Russell S. Sobel, "Public Policy toward Pecuniary Externalities," *Public Finance Review* 29, no. 4 (2001): 304; James J. Murphy et al., "Mechanisms for Addressing Third-Party Impacts Resulting from Voluntary Water Transfers," in *Using Experimental Methods in Environmental and Resource Economics* 91 (2006); National Research Council, *Water Transfers*; Joseph Sax, "Understanding Transfers: Community Rights and the Privatization of Water," *West-Northwest* 14 (1994): 13; Barton H. Thompson, Jr., "Water Law as a Pragmatic Exercise: Professor Joseph Sax's Water Scholarship," *Ecology Law Quarterly* 25 (1998): 363.

47. Cal. Water Code §§ 386, 1736, 1810(d); Neb. Rev. Stat. § 46–289; Nev. Rev. Stat. §§ 533.040, 533.438, 533.4385; Okl. Stat. § 105.22; Wyo. Stat. Ann. § 41-3-104; Michael Elizabeth Sakas, "San Luis Valley Water Will Not Flow to Thirsty Douglas County, At Least for Now," *CPR News*, May 25, 2022; Schupbach, "How to Invest"; David Takacs, "South Africa and the Human Right to Water: Equity, Ecology, and the Public Trust

Doctrine," *Berkeley Journal of International Law* 34 (2016): 55; Thompson, "Water as a Public Commodity."

48. Christine Souza, "Irrigation Districts Look to Transfers as Water Dwindles," *AgAlert*, May 19, 2021; Thompson, "Institutional Perspectives."

49. Britt Banks and Peter Nichols, "A Roundtable Discussion on the No-Injury Rule of Colorado Water Law," *The Colorado Lawyer* 44, no. 7 (2015): 87; Donna Brennan, "Water Policy Reform in Australia: Lessons from the Victorian Seasonal Water Market," *Australian Journal of Agricultural and Resource Economics* 50, no. 3 (2006): 403; Brian Gray, "The Shape of Transfers to Come: A Model Water Transfer Act for California," *West-Northwest* 4 (1996): 23; Murphy et al., "Mechanisms for Addressing"; National Research Council, *Water Transfers*.

50. Greg Avery, "City of Aurora Buys Companies to Secure Industrial, Farm Water for Future Growth," *Denver Business Journal*, August 28, 2020; Patricia Nelson Limerick, *Ditch in Time: The City, the West, and Water* (Golden, CO: Fulcrum Publishing, 2012); Tony Perry, "Palo Verde Valley Farmers and MWD Find Fallowing Deal a Win-Win So Far," *Los Angeles Times*, August 15, 2015; Bonnie Saliba, David B. Bush, and William Edwin Martin, "Water Marketing in the Southwest: Can Market Prices Be Used to Evaluate Water Supply Augmentation Projects?" technical report, US Dept. of Agriculture, Forest Service, Rocky Mountain Forest and Range Experiment Station, Fort Collins, Colorado, 1987.

51. Ayres et al., "Improving California's Water Market"; Lisa M. Krieger, "California Drought Pits Farmer Against Farmer in Water Bidding Wars," *Los Angeles Daily News*, July 20, 2014.

52. Carrie Cabral, "Azurix Water Supply and the Fall of Enron International," *Shortform*, August 24, 2020; Matt Dotray, "Remembering the Water Race Between T. Boone Pickens and West Texas Cities," *Lubbock Avalanche-Journal*, September 22, 2019; Timothy Egan, "Near Vast Bodies of Water, Land Lies Parched," *New York Times*, August 12, 2001; Abrahm Lustgarten and ProPublica, "A Free-Market Plan to Save the American West from Drought," *The Atlantic*, March 2016; Joe Nick Patoski, "Boone Pickens Wants to Sell You His Water," *Texas Monthly*, August 2001; Perry, "Proposal to Sell."

53. Bill Alpert, "Water Asset Management: Hunting Liquid Assets," *Barron's*, April 25, 2015; Schupbach, "How to Invest."

54. Brian O'Connell, "How to Invest in Water Commodities," *TheStreet*, February 12, 2020; Nelson Harvey, "Betting on Water Shortages? A Hedge Fund Buys Water Rights in Grand Valley," *Water Education Colorado*, August 8, 2018; Chris Janiec, "Water Asset Management Deals Prompt Colorado Water Law Review," *AgriInvestor*, September 9, 2021; Schupbach, "How to Invest"; Joy Wiltermuth, "Water Funds Attract $35 Billion as Drought Drains Reservoirs. A New Report Asks If They Are Worth It," *MarketWatch*, August 24, 2021; "Is the Drought in Water Stocks About to End?" *Investing Whisperer*, n.d.; Water Asset Management, "Investment Vehicles," www.waterinv.com.

55. Australian Competition and Consumer Commission, *Murray-Darling Basin Water Markets Inquiry*; Adam Courtenay, "Water Rights, Trading and the New Water

Barons," *InTheBlack*, November 1, 2017; Anne Davies, "Water Investment Companies Score Bumper Year as Farmers Hit by Drought," *The Guardian*, May 28, 2019; Brent Loeskow and Nick Waters, "Australian Water Entitlements: A Unique Alternative Asset Class," *Enterprising Investor*, October 29, 2019; Greg Wilkinson, "Water Markets Are Key to Properly Valuing Water," in *Water Disruption: Investment Risk from Multiple Angles*, Franklin Templeton, October 2020, 23.

56. Christina Babbitt et al., *Groundwater Trading as a Tool for Implementing California's Sustainable Groundwater Management Act* (New York: Environmental Defense Fund, 2017); Sarah Heard et al., *SGMA's First Groundwater Market: An Early Case Study from Fox Canyon* (San Francisco, CA: The Nature Conservancy, 2019); Mammoth Water, "Who We Are," www.mammothwater.com; MCubed, "Considerations for Designing Water Markets," blog, www.mcubedecon.com.

57. CME Group, "Understanding the Nasdaq Veles California Water Index," www.cmegroup.com; Courtenay, "Water Rights"; WestWater Research, www.water-exchange.com.

58. Australian Competition and Consumer Commission, *Murray-Darling Basin Water Markets Inquiry*.

59. Bonnie G. Colby, Katie Pittenger, and Lana Jones, "Voluntary Irrigation Forbearance to Mitigate Drought Impacts: Economic Considerations," working paper, March 2007; Sina Fazeli et al., "Introducing Water Banks: Principles and Importance," in *Economic, Political, and Social Issues in Water Resources*, ed. Omid Bozorg-Haddad (Amsterdam: Elsevier, 2021), 83; Schupbach, "How to Invest."

60. Australian Competition and Consumer Commission, *Murray-Darling Basin Water Markets Inquiry*; Ellen Bruno and Heidi Schweizer, "Why Wall Street Investors' Trading California Futures Is Nothing to Fear—And Unlikely to Work Anyway," *The Conversation*, April 15, 2021; Cora Kammeyer, *California's Water Futures Market: Explained*, Pacific Institute, (Oakland, California, February 24, 2021; Karl Plume, "Water Futures Market Fails to Make a Splash with California Farmers," Reuters, June 29, 2021.

61. Anne Davies, "Water Investment Companies Score Bumper Year as Farmers Hit by Drought," *The Guardian*, May 28, 2019; Scott Hamilton and Stuart Kells, *Sold Down the River: How Robber Barons and Wall Street Traders Cornered Australia's Water Market* (Melbourne, Australia: Text Publishing, 2021); Scott Hamilton and Stuart Kells, "Robber Barons and High-Speed Traders Dominate Australia's Water Market," *The Conversation*, August 30, 2021; Scott Hamilton and Stuart Kells, "Australia's Water Tragedy Has Urgent Lessons for America," *Pursuit*, June 29, 2021; Ben Ryder Howe, "Wall Street Eyes Billions in the Colorado's Water," *New York Times*, January 3, 2021.

62. A.B. 1205 (Cal. 2023); S.B. 20-048 (Colo. 2020); Neal Hughes, "Water Markets Are Not Perfect, But Vital to the Future of the Murray-Darling Basin," *The Conversation*, March 1, 2021; letter from California State Senators Melissa Hurtado and David Cortese to US Attorney General Merrick Garland, May 17, 2022.

63. Australian Competition and Consumer Commission, *Murray-Darling Basin Water Markets Inquiry*; Loch et al., "Markets."

64. Australian Competition and Consumer Commission, *Murray-Darling Basin Water Markets Inquiry*; Kelly Brown, "Researchers Debunk Claims of Water Hoarding and Speculative Behavior in Water Markets," *Phys.org*, March 15, 2021; Loch et al., "Markets."

65. Australian Competition and Consumer Commission, *Murray-Darling Basin Water Markets Inquiry*.

66. Australian Competition and Consumer Commission, *Murray-Darling Basin Water Markets Inquiry*.

67. "SB 20-048: Report of the Work Group to Explore Ways to Strengthen Current Water Anti-Speculation Law," submitted to the Interim Water Resources Review Committee of the Colorado General Assembly as required by Section 37-98-103, C.R.S., August 13, 2021.

68. Ayres et al., "Improving California's Water Market."

Chapter Five

1. Nick C. Davidson, "How Much Wetlands Has the World Lost? Long-Term and Recent Trends in Global Wetland Area," *Marine and Freshwater Research* 65, no. 10 (2014).

2. Julian Smith, "After the Big Dry," *The Nature Conservancy Magazine*, May 30, 2017; The Nature Conservancy, "Balancing Water in the Murray-Darling," www.nature.org.

3. Murray-Darling Basin Authority, "Sustainable Rivers Audit 2: Summary," 2012, 24; Smith, "After the Big Dry"; The Nature Conservancy, "Balancing Water."

4. Murray Darling Wetlands Working Group, "Project: Yambuna Lagoon on the Lower Goulburn River, VIC," mdwwg.com.au; "Donated Water Floods Lagoon," *Pressreader*, November 7, 2017; Victorian Environmental Water Holder, "Goulburn Wetlands," www.vewh.vic.gov.au.

5. Murray Darling Wetlands Working Group, "Project: Yambuna Lagoon"; Emma Nobel, "Yambuna Beef Producer Finds Watering Private Wetlands Does Not Have to Cost the Farm," *ABC Rural*, September 25, 2017; Melanie Tranter et al., "Greiner's Lagoon Environmental Watering Plan," Jacobs Group, Australia, November 18, 2020.

6. Nobel, "Yambuna Beef Producer."

7. Ben Carr et al., "The Murray-Darling Basin Balanced Water Fund and the Environmental Water Trust—Using Markets and Innovative Financing to Restore Wetlands and Floodplains in the Murray-Darling Basin for Financial, Social and Environmental Outcomes," *Proceedings of the 8th Australian Stream Management Conference* (2016): 269–271; The Nature Conservancy, "Balancing Water."

8. Carr et al., "Murray-Darling Basin Balanced Water Fund"; The Nature Conservancy, "Balancing Water."

9. The Nature Conservancy Australia, "Creating A Sustainable Murray-Darling," www.natureaustralia.org.au.

10. Kilter Rural, "The Murray-Darling Basin Balanced Water Fund Information Memorandum," kilterrural.com.

11. Carr et al., "Murray-Darling Basin Balanced Water Fund," 270–271; Kilter Rural, "Murray-Darling Basin Balanced Water Fund Information Memorandum."

12. Carr et al., "Murray-Darling Basin Balanced Water Fund," 271; Nobel, "Yambuna Beef Producer."

13. Barton H. Thompson, Jr. et al., *Legal Control of Water Resources*, 6th ed. (St. Paul, MN: West Academic, 2018), 220–221.

14. Peter B. Moyle, Jacob V. E. Katz, and Rebecca M. Quiñones, "Rapid Decline of California's Native Inland Fishes: A Status Assessment," *Biological Conservation* 144, no. 10 (2011): 2414; Kelly Miller Reed and Brian Czech, "Causes of Fish Endangerment in the United States, or the Structure of the American Economy," *Fisheries* 30, no. 7 (2005): 36; Brian D. Richter et al., "Water Scarcity and Fish Imperilment Driven by Beef Production," *Nature Sustainability* 3 (2020): 319; Brian D. Richter et al., "A Presumptive Standard for Environmental Flow Protection," *River Research and Applications* 28, no. 8 (2012): 1318; Brian D. Richter et al., *Protection and Restoration of Freshwater Ecosystems* (London: Taylor & Francis Group, 2016).

15. J. Patrick Donnelly et al., "Climate and Human Water Use Diminish Wetland Networks Supporting Continental Waterbird Migration," *Global Change Biology* 26, no. 4 (2020): 2042; Richard T. Kingsford, Alberto Basset, and Leland Jackson, "Wetlands: Conservation's Poor Cousins," *Aquatic Conservation: Marine and Freshwater Ecosystems* 26, no. 5 (2016): 892, 901.

16. Janet C. Neuman, "The Good, the Bad, and the Ugly: The First Ten Years of the Oregon Water Trust," *Nebraska Law Review* 83, no. 2 (2004): 438; Brian D. Richter et al., "Buy Me a River: Purchasing Water Rights to Restore River Flows in the Western USA," *Journal of the American Water Resources Association* 56, no. 1 (2020): 2; Thompson et al., *Legal Control*, 223–224.

17. Eloise Kendy et al., "Water Transactions for Streamflow Restoration, Water Supply Reliability, and Rural Economic Vitality in the Western United States," *JAWRA: Journal of the American Water Resources Association* 54, no. 2 (2018): 489; Thompson et al., *Legal Control*, 700–739.

18. Jeffrey Mount et al., *Managing Water for the Environment during Drought: Lessons from Victoria, Australia* (San Francisco, CA: Public Policy Institute of California, June 2016): 6; Neuman, "The Good, the Bad," 438; Leon F. Szeptycki et al., "Environmental Water Rights Transfers: A Review of State Laws," Water in the West, Stanford, California, August 31, 2015, 2.

19. Richard Brewer, *Conservancy: The Land Trust Movement in America* (Hanover, NH: University Press of New England, 2003).

20. Janet C. Neuman and Cheyenne Chapman, "Wading into the Water Market: The First Five Years of the Oregon Water Trust," *Journal of Environmental Law and Litigation* 14 (1999): 135; The Freshwater Trust, "The Lostine," www.thefreshwatertrust.org.

21. Australian River Restoration Centre, "Water Trust Alliance: Non-Government Options for Managing Environmental Water," arrc.com.au; Dustin Garrick, Chelsea Lane-Miller, and Amy L. McCoy, "Institutional Innovations to Govern Environmental Water in the Western United States: Lessons for Australia's

Murray-Darling Basin," *Economic Papers: A Journal of Applied Economics and Policy* 30, no. 2 (2011): 176.

22. Bryan David, "Environmental Water Markets: Growth, Trends, and Outlook," master's project, Nicholas School, Duke University, 2020; Leon Szeptycki et al., "Environmental Water Transactions in the Colorado River Basin: A Closer Look," Water in the West, Stanford, California, November 2018.

23. Colorado Water Trust, "Colorado River—15-Mile Reach," coloradowatertrust. org; David, "Environmental Water Markets," 18; Kendy et al., "Water Transactions," 489; Szeptycki et al., "Environmental Water Rights Transfers," 3.

24. Seema Jayachandran, "Using the Airbnb Model to Protect the Environment," *New York Times*, December 29, 2017; Mark Reynolds, "Dynamic Conservation for Migratory Species," *Science Advances* 3 (2017).

25. Genevieve Bennett, "In the Colorado Delta, A Little Water Goes a Long Way," *Ecosystem Marketplace*, September 6, 2013; Lucas Isakowitz, "Restoring the Colorado River Delta," *The Nature Conservancy*, July 31, 2019; Philip Womble, Allen Townsend, and Leon F. Szeptycki, "Decoupling Environmental Water Markets from Water Law," *Environmental Research Letters* 17, no. 6 (2022).

26. Kendy et al., "Water Transactions," 489; Mount et al., *Managing Water*, 6; Barton H. Thompson, Jr., "Conservation Options: Toward a Greater Private Role," *Virginia Environmental Law Journal* 21, no. 2 (2002): 273–276.

27. David, "Environmental Water Markets," 16–18; Thompson, "Conservation Options," 310; Womble, Townsend, and Szeptycki, "Decoupling."

28. Kendy et al., "Water Transactions," 501; Neuman, "The Good, the Bad"; Szeptycki et al., "Environmental Water Rights Transfers," 2–3.

29. Neuman, "The Good, the Bad," 475–484.

30. Alex Bennett et al., "Factors Influencing the Expansion of Environmental Water Markets," group master's project, Bren School, University of California, Santa Barbara, 2016, 4; David, "Environmental Water Markets," 14–15.

31. Paul Brest and Kelly Born, "When Can Impact Investing Create Real Impact?" *Stanford Social Innovation Review* 11, no. 4 (2013): 22; Ariane Volk, *Investing for Impact: The Global Impact Investing Market 2020* (Washington, DC: International Finance Corporation, 2021).

32. Eric Hallstein and Charlotte Kaiser, "Bridging the Nature Funding Gap," The Nature Conservancy, perspective, May 12, 2021.

33. Peter Culp et al., "Liquid Assets: Investing for Impact in the Colorado River Basin," Encourage Capital and Squire Patton Boggs, 2015.

34. *The Liquid Assets Project: Year Three—Lessons Learned* (August 2019); *The Liquid Assets Project: Year Two—Lessons Learned* (August 2018).

35. Brian Richter, "Water Share: Using Markets and Impact Investors to Drive Sustainability," The Nature Conservancy, Arlington, Virginia, 2016, 48–53; The Nature Conservancy, "Investing Our Way Out of the Global Water Crisis," August 24, 2016.

36. Renewable Resources Group and The Nature Conservancy, "Sustainable Water Impact Fund: 2020 Impact Report," May 2021; Hallstein and Kaiser, "Bridging."

37. Beatrice L. Gordon et al., "Existing Accessible Modeling Tools Offer Limited Support to Evaluation of Impact Investment in Rangeland Ecosystem Services," *Frontiers in Sustainable Food Systems* 3 (2019): 77.

Chapter Six

1. Philip A. M. Bachand et al., "On-Farm Flood Capture Could Reduce Groundwater Overdraft in Kings River Basin," *California Agriculture* 70, no. 4 (2016): 200; City of Los Angeles, "LADWP Water Supply in Acre Feet," data.lacity.org; Ellen Hanak et al., "Water and the Future of the San Joaquin Valley," Public Policy Institute of California, San Francisco, February 2019, 10; RMC Water and Environment, "A New Opportunity: Groundwater Recharge through Winter Flooding of Agricultural Land in the San Joaquin Valley," 2015, 1; United States Geologic Survey, "Location of Maximum Levels of Subsidence in the U.S.: Levels at 1925 and 1977," www.usgs.gov.

2. American Farmland Trust, "Terranova Ranch, Inc.," stewards.farmland.org.

3. Bachand et al., "On-Farm Flood Capture," 200–201.

4. American Farmland Trust, "Terranova Ranch, Inc."; Jesse Roseman et al., "Introduction to Groundwater Recharge," Almond Board of California, Modesto, California, 2021, 3–4.

5. American Farmland Trust, "Terranova Ranch, Inc."

6. Janny Choy, Geoff McGhee, and Melissa Rohde, "Recharge: Groundwater's Second Act," article from series "Understanding California's Groundwater," Water in the West, Stanford University, December 19, 2014; RMC Water and Environment, "New Opportunity," 2.

7. Bachand et al., "On-Farm Flood Capture," 202, 204–206; "Accelerating On-Farm Recharge in the San Joaquin Valley," *Maven's Notebook,* February 8, 2016, mavensnotebook.com; RMC Water and Environment, "New Opportunity," 2.

8. Bachand et al., "On-Farm Flood Capture," 205; Leigh Martinez, "Farmers Hope to Divert Potential El Nino Floodwaters to Irrigate Crops before They Bloom," CBS13 (Lodi), November 25, 2015.

9. California Department of Water Resources, "Flood-Managed Aquifer Recharge," water.ca.gov; Hannah Waterhouse et al., "Agricultural Managed Aquifer Recharge—Water Quality Factors to Consider," *California Agriculture* 74, no. 3 (2020): 145; Roseman et al., "Introduction."

10. Choy, McGhee, and Rohde, "Recharge."

11. Will Sarni and Hugh Share, "From Corporate Water Risk to Value Creation," *Global Water Intelligence,* August 1, 2019, www.globalwaterintel.com.

12. Martin Doyle, "Trading Agriculture's Most Valuable Asset," *The Source IWA,* February 22, 2019; Reed Watson and Brandon Scarborough, "Flint River Basin: Wireless Water for Biodiversity," Property and Environment Research Center, Bozeman, Montana, September 28, 2010.

13. Choy, McGhee, and Rohde, "Recharge"; Debra Perrone and Melissa Rohde, "Benefits and Economic Costs of Managed Aquifer Recharge in California," *San Francisco Estuary and Watershed Science* 14, no. 2 (2016); Debra Perrone and Melissa Rohde, "Research Brief: Storing Water in California: What Can $2.7 Billion Buy Us?" Water in the West, Stanford, California, 2014.

14. D. E. Wendt et al., "Managed Aquifer Recharge as a Drought Mitigation Strategy in Heavily-Stressed Aquifers," *Environmental Research Letters* 16, no. 1 (2021).

15. Kathleen Miller, Andrew T. Fisher, and Michael Kiparsky, "Incentivizing Groundwater Recharge in the Pajaro Valley through Recharge Net Metering (ReNeM)," *Case Studies in the Environment* 5, no. 1 (2021); Kathleen Miller, Anita Millman, and Michael Kiparsky, "Introduction to the Special Collection: Institutional Dimensions of Groundwater Recharge," *Case Studies in the Environment* 5, no. 1 (2021); Anita Millman et al., "Groundwater Recharge to Support Wildlife and Water Users: The Heyborne Ponds Project, Sedgwick County, Colorado," *Case Studies in the Environment* 5, no. 1 (2021).

16. Laura Tam, "SF's Latest Tool to Save More Water: Pay Building Owners to Recycle It," *SPUR News*, October 26, 2015; "The Westin Cape Town Hotel Shows Off Flagship Projects," *Cape Business News*, March 6, 2019; "Westin Gets On-Site Desalination Plant," *cape{town}etc.*, March 5, 2019.

17. Carolyn M. Cooper et al., "Oil and Gas Produced Water Reuse: Opportunities, Treatment, Needs, and Challenges," *ACES EST Engineering* 2, no. 3 (2022): 347; Cloelle Danforth et al., "Alternative Management of Oil and Gas Produced Water Requires More Research on its Hazards and Risks," *Integrated Environmental Assessment and Management* 15, no. 5 (2019): 677–678; Flannery C. Dolan, Tzahi Y. Cath, and Terri S. Hogue, "Assessing the Feasibility of Using Produced Water for Irrigation in Colorado," *Science of the Total Environment* 640 (2018): 620; Bridget R. Scanlon et al., "Can We Beneficially Reuse Produced Water from Oil and Gas Extraction in the U.S.," *Science of the Total Environment* 717 (2020): 2–3.

18. Thor Benson, "Mini Desalination Plants Could Refresh the Parched West: A Historic Drought Calls for New Ideas," *Popular Science*, April 3, 2022.

19. Cooper et al., "Oil and Gas Produced," 348; Danforth et al., "Alternative Management," 678; Scanlon et al., "Can We Beneficially Reuse," 3.

20. Joshua G. Mahoney and Rebecca T. Asami, "Food Safety Project White Paper: On the Reuse of Oil Field Produced Water for Irrigation of Food Crops in Central Kern County, California," California Regional Water Quality Control Board, Fresno, California, 2016; Liza Gross, "A California Water Board Assured the Public That Oil Wastewater Is Safe for Irrigation. Experts Say Evidence Is Flimsy," *Grist*, April 9, 2022; Jennifer Redmon et al., "Is Food Irrigated with Oilfield-Produced Water in the California Central Valley Safe to Eat? A Probabilistic Human Health Risk Assessment Evaluating Trace Metals Exposure." *Risk Analysis* 41, no. 8 (2021): 1463.

21. Danforth et al., "Alternative Management," 677–679; Scanlon et al., "Can We Beneficially Reuse," 11.

22. Sarah Fakhreddine et al., "Mobilization of Arsenic and Other Naturally Occurring Contaminants During Managed Aquifer Recharge: A Critical Review," *Environmental Science and Technology* 55, no. 4 (2021): 2208; Nisha Marwaha et al., "Identifying Agricultural Managed Aquifer Recharge Locations to Benefit Drinking Water Supply in Rural Communities," *Water Resources Research* 57, no. 3 (2021); Mary H. Ward et al., "Drinking Water Nitrate and Human Health: An Updated Review," *International Journal of Environmental Research and Public Health* 15, no. 7 (2018): 1557; Hannah Waterhouse et al., "Influence of Agricultural Managed Aquifer Recharge

(AgMAR) and Stratigraphic Heterogeneities on Nitrate Reduction in the Deep Subsurface," *Water Resources Research* 57, no. 5 (2021); Waterhouse et al., "Agricultural Managed Aquifer Recharge."

23. Ellen Hanak et al., "Myths of California Water—Implications and Reality," *Hastings West Northwest Journal of Environmental Law and Policy* 16, no. 1 (2010): 3; Vanessa Casado-Pérez, "Inefficient Efficiency: Crying Over Spilled Water," *Environmental Law Reporter* 46, no. 12 (2016): 11046.

24. Ellen Hanak, *Who Should Be Allowed to Sell Water in California? Third-Party Issues and the Water Market* (San Francisco: Public Policy Institute of California, 2003); Barton H. Thompson, Jr. et al., *Mind the Gaps: The Case for Truly Comprehensive Sustainable Groundwater Management* (Stanford, CA: Water in the West, 2021).

25. Hannah Waterhouse et al., *Management Considerations for Protecting Groundwater Quality Under Agricultural Managed Aquifer Recovery* (San Francisco: Sustainable Conservation, June 2021).

Chapter Seven

1. Michael D. Barr, *Singapore: A Modern History* (London: I.B. Tauris, 2019); Andrew Maddocks, Robert Samuel Young, and Paul Reig, "Ranking the World's Most Water-Stressed Countries in 2040," World Resources Institute, commentary, August 26, 2015, www.wri.org; John Curtis Perry, *Singapore: Unlikely Power* (New York: Oxford University Press, 2017); Cecilia Tortajada, Yugal Joshi, and Asit K. Biswas, *The Singapore Water Story: Sustainable Development in an Urban City-State* (London: Routledge, Taylor & Francis Group, 2013), 1, 6.

2. Tortajada, Josh, and Biswas, *Singapore Water Story*, 9–14.

3. Valerie Chew, "Singapore-Malaysia Water Agreements," *Singapore Infopedia*, last modified July 2019, eresources.nlb.gov.sg/infopedia; Wahab Jumrah, "The 1962 Johor-Singapore Water Agreement: Lessons Learned," *The Diplomat*, September 20, 2021; Danton Liem, "Water Security for a City-State: Growing Pains," December 9, 2020, storymaps.arcgis.com/stories; Public Utilities Board, "Singapore Water Story," last modified January 10, 2022, www.pub.gov.sg; Nur Asyiqin Mohamed Salleh, "Parliament: Water an Issue of National Security and Must Be Priced Fully," *The Straits Times*, March 1, 2017; Tortajada, Joshi, and Biswas, *Singapore Water Story*, 1, 10–29.

4. Jeremy Grant, "Singapore Seeks Sustainable Water Supply," *Financial Times*, April 10, 2014; Kim Irvine, Lloyd Chua, and Hans S. Eikass, "The Four National Taps of Singapore: A Holistic Approach to Water Resources Management from Drainage to Drinking Water," *Journal of Water Management Modeling* 22 (2014); Liz Neisloss, "How Singapore Is Making Sure It Doesn't Run Out of Water," CNN, April 7, 2011; "Four National Taps," *Singapore Infopedia*, last modified July 2019, eresources.nlb.gov.sg/infopedia; Tortajada, Joshi, and Biswas, *Singapore Water Story*, 1–2.

5. Cynthia Barnett, *Blue Revolution: Unmaking America's Water Crisis* (Boston: Beacon Press, 2011); Singapore PUB, "Innovation in Water Singapore," vol. 9, Singapore, July 2017, 5; Singapore PUB, "Innovation in Water Singapore," vol. 12, Singapore, January 2022, 19; Micaela Tam, "Singapore National Day: NEWater Case Study," *Asia P3 Hub Updates*, August 29, 2018; Tortajada, Joshi, and Biswas, *Singapore Water Story*, 25–27.

6. Craig Francis Barham, "Public Policy and Strategies to Support Institutional and Technological Innovations in the New Water Economy," PhD diss., University of Louisville, 2018; Singapore PUB, "Innovation in Water Singapore," vol. 9, 5; Singapore PUB, "PUB Pushes the Frontier of Water Technology to Reach Future Energy and Sludge Reduction Targets," July 4, 2018; Tortajada, Joshi, and Biswas, *Singapore Water Story*, 26, 120–122.

7. Selina Ho, "Growing Singapore's Water Industry: From Water Scarcity to Global Hydrohub," Leadership Academy for Development, Stanford, California; Singapore PUB, "PUB Pushes the Frontier."

8. Barham, "Public Policy," 402; Ho, "Growing Singapore's Water Industry"; Singapore PUB, "Innovation in Water Singapore," vol. 9, 7; Singapore PUB, "Partners," www.pub.gov.sg.

9. Barham, "Public Policy," 421; A. M. Dhalla, "Developing a Global Waterhub: Singapore's Leadership in Water Innovation," in *Chemistry and Water: The Science Behind Sustaining the World's Most Crucial Resource*, ed. Satinder Ahuja (Amsterdam: Elsevier, 2017), 541; Chee Kiong Goh, "Singapore the Global Hydrohub," *WaterWorld*, January 31, 2009; Ho, "Growing Singapore's Water Industry"; Singapore PUB, "Innovation in Water Singapore," vol. 9, 5; Michael Toh, "Singapore Water Exchange: A Global Marketplace for Innovative Water Companies," *Water and Wastewater Asia*, July/August 2021.

10. Aquaporin, "Aquaporin Successfully Completed Phase I for Low-Energy Reverse Osmosis Membrane Development Project," July 20, 2020, aquaporin.com; Zahra Jamshed, "How Singapore Is Using Technology to Solve its Water Shortage," *CNN Business,* September 25, 2019; Singapore PUB, "PUB Pushes the Frontier"; Singapore PUB, "Singapore Achieves Breakthrough in Desalination Technology," June 28, 2018; Singapore PUB, "Innovation in Water Singapore," vol. 9, 8.

11. "Aquarious Spectrum to Provide Leak Detection Services in Singapore," *WaterWorld*, July 14, 2021; Chad Henderson, "Smart Water: Leak Detection and Non-Revenue Water," Xylem, October 27, 2018, xylem.com; "Xylem Expands Regional Headquarters in Singapore with New Technology Hub," *BusinessWire*, January 8, 2020.

12. Newsha K. Ajami, Barton H. Thompson, Jr., and David G. Victor, *The Path to Water Innovation* (Washington, DC: Brookings Institution, 2014); Michael Kiparsky et al., "The Innovation Deficit in Urban Water: The Need for an Integrated Perspective on Institutions, Organizations, and Technology," *Environmental Engineering Science* 30, no. 8 (2013): 395; Josselin Rouillard et al., "Governance Regime Factors Conducive to Innovative Uptake in Urban Water Management: Experiences from Europe," *Water* 8, no. 10 (2016): 477; Luke Sherman et al., "Examining the Complex Relationship Between Innovation and Regulation Through a Survey of Wastewater Utility Managers," *Journal of Environmental Management* 260 (2020); Vanessa L. Speight, "Innovation in the Water Industry: Barriers and Opportunities for US and UK Utilities," *WIREs Water* 2 (2015): 301.

13. James Salzman, *Drinking Water: A History* (New York: Abrams Press, 2012), 72–112; David L. Sedlak, *Water 4.0: The Past, Present, and Future of the World's Most Vital Resource* (New Haven, CT: Yale University Press, 2014).

14. Ajami, Thompson, and Victor, *Path to Water Innovation*; Meenu EG, "The Promise of Artificial Intelligence in Water Management," *Analytics Insight*, February 17, 2021; "Global Non-Revenue Water Losses of About $40 Billion Is Driving Growth Opportunities for Smart Water Leakage Management Solutions," *GlobeNewswire*, October 24, 2018; Speight, "Innovation"; Chunyang (Sophie) Su, "Water Tech Spotlight: The Latest Technology Developments in the Water Industry—December 2021," International Water Association, December 16, 2021, iwa-network.org; Chunyang (Sophie) Su, "Water Tech Spotlight: The Latest Technology Developments in the Water Industry—October 2021," International Water Association, October 21, 2021, iwa-network.org; "Xylem Expands."

15. Ajami, Thompson, and Victor, *Path to Water Innovation*; Speight, "Innovation."

16. Diego J. Rodriguez et al., *From Waste to Resource Shifting Paradigms for Smarter Wastewater Interventions in Latin America and the Caribbean* (Washington, DC: World Bank, 2020); Su, "October 2021 Spotlight"; Office of Water, "Promoting Technological Innovation for Clean and Safe Water: Water Technology Innovation Blueprint—Version 2," Doc. 820-R-14-006, US Environmental Protection Agency, Washington, D.C., 2014.

17. Ajami, Thompson, and Victor, *Path to Water Innovation*; Michael Kiparsky et al., "Barriers to Innovation in Urban Wastewater Utilities: Attitudes of Managers in California," *Environmental Management* 57, no. 6 (2016): 1204; Kiparsky et al., "Innovation Deficit."

18. Markus J. Kalmutzki, Christian S. Diercks, and Omar M. Yaghi, "Metal-Organic Frameworks for Water Harvesting from the Air," *Advanced Materials* 30 (2018).

19. Peter Kaecki, "Two Designers Just Won $1.5 Million for Creating a Device that Can Pull Clean Drinking Water Out of Thin Air," *Business Insider*, October 23, 2018; Kalmutzki, Diereks, and Yaghi, "Metal-Organic Frameworks"; Matthew W. Logan, Spencer Langevin, and Zhiyong Xia, "Reversible Atmospheric Water Harvesting Using Metal-Organic Frameworks," *Science Reports* 10 (2020); Jackson Lord et al., "Global Potential for Harvesting Drinking Water from Air Using Solar Energy," *Nature* 598 (2021): 611; Nina Natman, "Atmospheric Water Harvesting," *Chemistry World*, July 6, 2020.

20. Ajami, Thompson, and Victor, *Path to Water Innovation*; Jeanette Howard et al., "Developing Tools to Model Impaired Streamflow in Streams Throughout California," *California Water Blog*, September 26, 2021; H. T. Samboko et al., "Evaluation and Improvement of Remote Sensing-Based Methods for River Flow Management," *Physics and Chemistry of the Earth* 117 (2020).

21. Achilles D. Boursianis et al., "Internet of Things (IoT) and Agricultural Unmanned Aerial Vehicles (UAVs) in Smart Farming: A Comprehensive Review," *Internet of Things* 18 (2022); Richard Koech and Philip Langat, "Improving Irrigation Water Use Efficiency: A Review of Advances, Challenges and Opportunities in the Australian Context," *Water* 10 (2018); Samboko et al., "Evaluation and Improvement"; Su, "October 2021 Spotlight"; Su, "December Spotlight"; Office of Water, "Promoting Technological Innovation"; Willie Vogt, "Imagery Can Be Used to Manage Water Use," *Western Farm Press*, January 5, 2022.

22. Ajami, Thompson, and Victor, *Path to Water Innovation*; EG, "Promise of Artificial Intelligence"; Sarah Fletcher, "Adaptive Water Infrastructure Planning for a Changing World," *All ECSTATIC Materials*, Paper 91, https://digitalcommons.usu.edu/ecstatic_all/91; Kiparsky et al., "Innovation Deficit"; Munir Ahmad Nayak, Jonathan D. Herman, and Scott Steinschneider, "Balancing Flood Risk and Water Supply in California: Policy Search Integrating Short-Term Forecast Ensembles with Conjunctive Use," *Water Resources Research* 54, no. 10 (2018): 7557; Chunyang (Sophie) Su, "Water Tech Spotlight: The Latest Technology Developments in the Water Industry—August 2021," International Water Association, August 26, 2021, wa-network.org; Alexander Y. Sun and Bridget R. Scanlon, "How Can Big Data and Machine Learning Benefit Environment and Water Management: A Survey of Methods, Applications, and Future Directions," *Environmental Research Letters* 14 (2019): 073001.

23. Alvar Escriva-Bou, "A Water Sector Energy Hog," Public Policy Institute of California, blog, December 20, 2016, www.ppic.org; Speight, "Innovation."

24. Menachem Elimelech and William A. Phillip, "The Future of Seawater Desalination: Energy, Technology, and the Environment," *Science* 333 (2011): 712; Yaniv D. Scherson and Craig S. Criddle, "Recovery of Freshwater from Wastewater: Upgrading Process Configurations to Maximize Energy Recovery and Minimize Residuals," *Environmental Science and Technology* 48 (2014): 8420.

25. Farah Elaz Ahmed, Abdullah Khalil, and Nidal Hilal, "Emerging Desalination Technologies: Current Status, Challenges and Future Trends," *Desalination* 517 (2021): 115183; Ajami, Thompson, and Victor, *Path to Water Innovation*; Ahmad Al Amoudi and Nikolay Voutchkov, "Innovation in Desalination—The Path Forward," *International Desalination Association Global Connections*, Fall 2021; Kiparsky et al., "Barriers to Innovation"; Nora Savage and Mamadou S. Diallo, "Nanomaterials and Water Purification: Opportunities and Challenges," *Journal of Nanoparticle Research* 7 (2005): 331; Office of Water, "Promoting Technological Innovation."

26. Nadeem A. Khan et al., "Applications of Nanotechnology in Water and Wastewater Treatment: A Review," *Asian Journal of Water, Environment, and Pollution* 16, no. 4 (2019): 81; "Latest Water Purification Technologies—Top Five," *Water Technology*, February 5, 2021, www.water-technology.net.

27. Ajami, Thompson, and Victor, *Path to Water Innovation*; Bipartisan Policy Center Executive Council on Infrastructure Water Task Force, "Increasing Innovation in America's Water Systems," Washington, D.C., 2017; Henry Grabar, "Why Is There So Little Innovation in Water Infrastructure?" *Bloomberg CityLab*, September 13, 2013; Kiparsky et al., "Innovation Deficit"; London Economics, "Innovation in the Water Industry in England and Wales: Final Report," Cave Review of Competition and Innovation in Water Markets, London, 2009, available at https://londoneconomics.co.uk/wp-content/uploads/2011/09/40-Innovation-in-the-Water-Industry-in-England-and-Wales.pdf, accessed May 9, 2023; Jason Potts, "The Innovation Deficit in Public Services: The Curious Problem of Too Much Efficiency and Not Enough Waste and Failure," *Innovation: Organization and Management* 11, no. 1 (2009): 34; Sherman et al., "Examining the Complex Relationship," 1; Duncan A. Thomas and Roger R. Ford, *The Crisis of Innovation in Water and Wastewater* (Cheltenham, U.K.: Edward Elgar Publishing, 2005).

28. Xavier Leflaive, Ben Krieble, and Harry Smythe, "Trends in Water-Related Technological Innovation: Insights from Patent Data," OECD Environment Working Paper No. 161, OECD Publishing, Paris, France, April 2020.

29. Ajami, Thompson, and Victor, *Path to Water Innovation.*

30. Ajami, Thompson, and Victor, *Path to Water Innovation.*

31. Ajami, Thompson, and Victor, *Path to Water Innovation*; Kiparsky et al., "Barriers to Innovation"; Sherman et al., "Examining the Complex Relationship," 1–3.

32. Ajami, Thompson, and Victor, *Path to Water Innovation*; Barham, "Public Policy"; Declan Conway et al., "Invention and Diffusion of Water Supply and Water Efficiency Technologies: Insights from a Global Patent Dataset," *Water Economics and Policy* 1, no. 4 (2015): 40; Gregory F. Nemet and Daniel M. Kammen, "U.S. Energy Research and Development: Declining Investment, Increasing Need, and the Feasibility of Expansion," *Energy Policy* 35, no. 1 (2007): 746; Gregory Tassey, "Underinvestment in Public Good Technologies," *Journal of Technology Transfer* 30, no. 1–2 (2004): 89.

33. Ajami, Thompson, and Victor, *Path to Water Innovation*

34. Ajami, Thompson, and Victor, *Path to Water Innovation*; Kiparsky et al., "Innovation Deficit"; James J. Porter and Kamal Birdi, "22 Reasons Why Collaborations Fail: Lessons from Water Innovation Research," *Environmental Science and Policy* 89 (2018): 101; Christian Walder, "Identification of Innovation Barriers in the Water Industry," MBA thesis, University of Vienna, 2017, 34, 48.

35. Paul O'Callaghan, "Dynamics of Water Innovation: Insights into the Rate of Adoption, Diffusion and Success of Emerging Water Technologies Globally," PhD diss., Wageningen University, 2020, 86–87; Clayton M. Christensen, *The Innovator's Dilemma: When New Technologies Cause Great Firms to Fail* (Boston, MA: Harvard Business School Press, 1997); Kiparsky et al., "Innovation Deficit."

36. Ajami, Thompson, and Victor, *Path to Water Innovation*; Kiparsky et al., "Innovation Deficit"; Porter and Birdi, "22 Reasons," 101.

37. Kiparsky et al., "Barriers to Innovation"; Kiparsky et al., "Innovation Deficit"; Jan Hendrik Trapp, Heide Kerber, and Engelbert Schramm, "Implementation and Diffusion of Innovative Water Infrastructures: Obstacles, Stakeholder Networks and Strategic Opportunities for Utilities," *Environmental Earth Sciences* 76, no. 4 (2017): 5.

38. Kiparsky et al., "Innovation Deficit."

39. Jason T. Carter et al., "A Framework for Driving Innovation in Your Water and Wastewater Utility," *Journal American Water Works Association* 109, no. 12 (2017): 32–33; Kiparsky et al., "Barriers to Innovation"; Speight, "Innovation."

40. Ajami, Thompson, and Victor, *Path to Water Innovation*; Kiparsky et al., "Innovation Deficit"; Sherman et al., "Examining the Complex Relationship"; Speight, "Innovation"; Wes Strickland, "The Organization of Water Utilities in California," Private Water Law (blog), September 25, 2013, privatewaterlaw.com; U.S. Environmental Protection Agency, "Clean Watersheds Needs Survey 2008: Report to Congress," Washington, D.C., 2009.

41. Ajami, Thompson, and Victor, *Path to Water Innovation*; Carter et al., "Framework," 32; Kiparsky et al., "Barriers to Innovation"; Lionel Nesta, Francesco Vona, and Francesco Nicolli, "Environmental Policies, Competition and Innovation in Renewable Energy," *Journal of Environmental Economics and Management* 67, no.

3 (2014): 396; Sherman et al., "Examining the Complex Relationship," 2; Joe Tidd and John R. Bessant, *Managing Innovation: Integrating Technological, Market, and Organizational Change*, 6th ed. (Chichester, U.K.: John Wiley & Sons, 2018).

42. Ajami, Thompson, and Victor, *Path to Water Innovation*; Gil Forer and Christine Staub, "The U.S. Water Sector on the Verge of Transformation," white paper, Global Cleantech Center, Ernst & Young, 2013, available at https://www.yumpu.com/en/document/read/14398889/the-us-water-sector-on-the-verge-of-transformation, accessed May 9, 2023; Kiparsky et al., "Barriers to Innovation"; Arti Patel and Sheeraz Haji, "Trends in the U.S. Water Market Shaping Technology Innovations," US Environmental Protection Agency, Washington, D.C., 2015; Porter and Birdi, "22 Reasons," 101; Kimberly J. Quesnel and Newsha K. Ajami, "Advancing Water Innovation Through Public Benefit Funds: Examining California's Approach for Electricity," *Journal American Water Works Association* 110, no. 2 (2018): E18.

43. Ajami, Thompson, and Victor, *Path to Water Innovation*; W. Michael Hanemann, "The Economic Conception of Water", in *Water Crisis: Myth or Reality?* ed. Peter P. Rogers, M. Ramon Llamas, and Luis Martinez Cortina (London: Routledge, Taylor & Francis Group, 2006); Kiparsky et al., "Barriers to Innovation"; Kiparsky et al., "Innovation Deficit"; Patel and Haji, "Trends"; Quesnel and Ajami, "Advancing Water Innovation."

44. Jennifer Kho, "Water Acquisitions Rise: Will Venture Capital Follow?" *Forbes*, February 28, 2012; Kiparsky et al., "Innovation Deficit"; Patel and Haji, "Trends"; Rouillard et al., "Governance Regime Factors," 3.

45. Ajami, Thompson, and Victor, *Path to Water Innovation*; Conway et al., "Invention and Diffusion," 40; Kiparsky et al., "Innovation Deficit"; Speight, "Innovation."

46. Kiparsky et al., "Innovation Deficit"; Dennis Wichelns, "Agricultural Water Pricing," in "Sustainable Management of Water Resources in Agriculture," Organization for Economic Cooperation and Development, Paris, March 15, 2010.

47. Kiparsky et al., "Barriers to Innovation"; Peiyuan Liu, Yuxiong Huang, and Slav W. Hermanowicz, "Shifting Entrepreneurial Landscape and Development Performance of Water Startups in Emerging Water Markets," *PLOS One* 16, no. 2 (2021): 7; Speight, "Innovation."

48. Carter et al., "Framework," 35; Damian Dominguez et al., "Closing the Credibility Gap: Strategic Planning for the Infrastructure Sector," *California Management Review* 51, no. 2 (2009): 30; Kiparsky et al., "Barriers to Innovation"; Kiparsky et al., "Innovation Deficit"; Walder, "Identification of Innovation Barriers."

49. Ajami, Thompson, and Victor, *Path to Water Innovation*; Black & Veatch, *2012 Strategic Directions in the U.S. Water Utility Industry,* Kansas City, 2012; Forer and Staub, "U.S. Water Sector"; Hanemann, "Economic Conception of Water"; Kiparsky et al., "Barriers to Innovation"; Kiparsky et al., "Innovation Deficit"; Sharlene Leurig, *Water Ripples: Expanding Risks for U.S. Water Providers* (Boston: Ceres, 2012).

50. Ajami, Thompson, and Victor, *Path to Water Innovation*; Kiparsky et al., "Innovation Deficit"; O'Callaghan, "Dynamics of Water Innovation," 86–87; Allison H. Roy et al., "Impediments and Solutions to Sustainable, Watershed-Scale Urban Stormwater Management: Lessons from Australia and the United States,"

Environmental Management 42 (2008): 344; Trapp, Kerber, and Schramm, "Implementation and Diffusion," 4; Walder, "Identification of Innovation Barriers."

51. Kiparsky et al., "Innovation Deficit"; Speight, "Innovation."

52. Hana Askren and Marlene Givant Star, "Capital Flowing to Water Technology Startups from Big Corporations," *Forbes*, March 7, 2019.

53. Askren and Star, "Capital Flowing."

54. Brian V. Iverson, "Why Venture Capital Is Failing in Water," *Oxford Business Review*, October 9, 2021; Liu, Huang, and Hermanowicz, "Shifting Entrepreneurial Landscape"; O'Callaghan, "Dynamics of Water Innovation," 10, 43–44, 103; Patel and Haji, "Trends"; Walder, "Identification of Innovation Barriers," 33; Antoine Walker, "Is the Unicorn's Recipe to Success Useful in the Water Industry?" *(Don't!) Waste Water*, June 28, 2021, dww.show.

55. Askren and Star, "Capital Flowing"; Krzysztof Smalec, "Smart Water Strategy Should Widen Xylem's Moat," *Morningstar*, January 21, 2019.

56. Conway et al., "Invention and Diffusion," 4; Luke J. L. Eastin, "An Assessment of the Effectiveness of Renewable Portfolio Standards in the United States," *The Electricity Journal* 27, no. 7 (2014): 126; David E. McNabb, "Managing Recycled Water" in *Water Resource Management* (London: Palgrave Macmillan, 2017), 283; Panchali Saikia et al., "City Water Resilience Framework: A Governance Based Planning Tool to Enhance Urban Water Resilience," *Sustainable Cities and Society* 77 (2022): 103497.

57. Alida Cantor et al., "Regulators and Utility Managers Agree about Barriers and Opportunities for Innovation in the Municipal Wastewater Sector," *Environmental Research Communications* 3, no. 3 (2021): 031001; Sherman et al., "Examining the Complex Relationship."

58. Shyama Ratnasiri et al., "Effectiveness of Two Pricing Structures on Urban Water Use and Conservation: A Quasi-Experimental Investigation," *Environmental Economics and Policy Studies* 20, no. 3 (2018): 547.

59. Quesnel and Ajami, "Advancing Water Innovation," E19, E26–27.

60. Megan Mullin, "The Effects of Drinking Water Service Fragmentation on Drought-Related Water Security," *Science* 368, no. 6488 (2020): 274; Gregory Pierce, Larry Lai, and J. R. DeShazo, "Identifying and Addressing Drinking Water System Sprawl, Its Consequences, and the Opportunity for Planners' Intervention: Evidence from Los Angeles County," *Journal of Environmental Planning and Management* 62, no. 12 (2019): 2080.

61. Barham, "Public Policy"; Jonas Gabrielsson et al., "Promoting Water-Related Innovation Through Networked Acceleration: Insights from the Water Innovation Accelerator," *Journal of Cleaner Production* 171 (2018): S130; Walder, "Identification of Innovation Barriers."

62. Carter et al., "Framework," 37; Rouillard et al., "Governance Regime Factors," 11; Walder, "Identification of Innovation Barriers."

63. John Randolph, "Inventory of Current State Energy Activities," in *State Energy Policy*, ed. Stephen W. Sawyer and John R. Armstrong (New York: Routledge, 2019), 27; Guido Schmidt et al., "The European Innovation Partnership on Water (EIP Water): Approach and Results to Date (2012–2015)," *Journal of Cleaner Production* 171 (2018): S147.

64. Barham, "Public Policy"; Teng Chye Khoo, "Singapore Water: Yesterday, Today and Tomorrow," in *Water Management in 2020 and Beyond*, ed. Asit K Biswas, Cecilia Tortajada, and Rafel Izquierdo (Berlin: Springer, 2009), 237; Ivy Ong Bee Luan, "Singapore Water Management Policies and Practices," *International Journal of Water Resources Development* 26, no. 1 (2010): 65.

Chapter Eight

1. Katie Henderson et al., "The Economic Benefits of Investing in Water Infrastructure: How a Failure to Act Would Affect the US Economic Recovery," American Society of Civil Engineers and Value of Water of Campaign, Reston, Virginia, 2020, 12.

2. Claudia Copeland, "Green Infrastructure and Issues in Managing Urban Stormwater," Congressional Research Service, Washington, D.C., May 2, 2016.

3. Copeland, "Green Infrastructure"; Henderson et al., "Economic Benefits," 10; Diana Kruzman, "Cities Are Investing Billions in New Sewage Systems. They Are Already Obsolete," *Grist*, March 8, 2022; Megan Ulrich, "Cleaning Up the Capital's Rivers: Solving the Problem of Combined Sewer Overflows in Washington, D.C.," *Journal of Science Policy and Governance* 4, no. 1 (2014).

4. Joshua Cousins and Dustin T. Hill, "Green Infrastructure, Stormwater, and the Financialization of Municipal Environmental Governance," *Journal of Environmental Policy and Planning* 23, no. 5 (2021): 1–2; DC Water, "Clean Rivers Project," www.dcwater.com; Ulrich, "Cleaning Up."

5. Copeland, "Green Infrastructure"; Chunhui Li et al., "Mechanisms and Applications of Green Infrastructure Practices for Stormwater Control: A Review," *Journal of Hydrology* 568 (2019).

6. Jennifer North and Gloria Gong, "DC Water Environmental Impact Bond," Government Performance Lab, Harvard Kennedy School, Cambridge, Massachusetts, 2017.

7. Water Infrastructure and Resiliency Finance Center, "DC Water's Environmental Impact Bond: A First of Its Kind," US Environmental Protection Agency, Washington, D.C., April 2017.

8. North and Gong, "DC Water"; Water Infrastructure and Resiliency Finance Center, "DC Water's Environmental Impact Bond."

9. DC Water, "DC Water's Pioneering Environmental Impact Bond a Success," press release, May 27, 2021, www.dcwater.com; Quantified Ventures, "Atlanta's Department of Watershed Management," case study, n.d.

10. Barton H. Thompson, Jr. et al., *Legal Control of Water Resources*, 6th ed. (St. Paul, MN: West Academic, 2018), 769–777.

11. American Society of Civil Engineers, "2021 Report Card for America's Infrastructure," Reston, Virginia, 2022, 34–42; Henderson et al., "Economic Benefits," 12.

12. Robert A. Greer, "A Review of Public Water Infrastructure Financing in the United States," *WIREs Water* 7, no. 5 (2020): 2–3; Justin Marlowe, "Municipal Bonds and Infrastructure Development—Past, Present, and Future," International City/County Management Association, Washington, D.C., August 2015, 11.

13. Greer, "Review," 3–6; Jonathan L. Ramseur and Mary Tiemann, "Water Infrastructure Financing: History of EPA Appropriations," Congressional Research Service, Washington, D.C., April 10, 2019; Erika Smull, Lauren Patterson, and Martin Doyle, "Rising Market Risk Exposure of Municipal Water Service Providers in Distressed Cities," *Journal of Water Resource Planning and Management* 148, no. 2 (2022).

14. Naeem Qureshi, "US Water Infrastructure Investment Long Overdue," *Opflow* 48, no. 3 (2022); Sridhar Vedachalam and R. Richard Geddes, "The Water Infrastructure Finance and Innovation Act of 2014: Structure and Effects," *Journal American Water Works Association* 109, no. 4 (2017).

15. California Water Boards, "Budget Act of 2021—Drinking Water Infrastructure Appropriation," factsheet, January 6, 2022; Anabelle Rosser and Caitrin Chappelle, "How Water Bonds Plug Spending Holes," *Public Policy Institute of California* (blog), June 7, 2021, www.ppic.org; Vedachalam and Geddes, "Water Infrastructure," E100.

16. X. Zhang et al., "Water Pricing and Affordability in the US: Public vs. Private Ownership," *Water Policy* 24, no. 3 (2022).

17. John Godfrey and Phyllis E. Currie, "The Importance of, and Outlook for, Municipal Bonds and Public Power," *Electricity Journal* 26, no. 6 (2013): 67; Marlowe, "Municipal Bonds," 4–5; Smull, Patterson, and Doyle, "Rising Market Risk," 4; Vedachalam and Geddes, "Water Infrastructure," E100.

18. Ashwini Agrawal and Daniel Kim, "Municipal Bond Insurance and Public Infrastructure: Evidence from Drinking Water," draft manuscript, February 14, 2022.

19. Scott Crist, "Increasing Use of Private Placements in the Issuance of Bonds," *UMB Financial Corporation* (blog), June 9, 2020, blog.umb.com; Greer, "Review," 7.

20. Matthew Willi Brand et al., "Environmental Impact Bonds: A Common Framework and Looking Ahead," *Environmental Research: Infrastructure and Sustainability* 1, no. 2 (2021); Greer, "Review," 7; Water Infrastructure and Resiliency Finance Center, "The Forest Resilience Bond: Structural Design and Contribution to Water Management in Collaborative Forest Restoration Projects," US Environmental Protection Agency, Washington, D.C., March 2021.

21. Barry Bosworth and Sveta Milusheva, "Innovations in U.S. Infrastructure Financing: An Evaluation," Brookings Institution, Washington, D.C., October 20, 2011, 12; Alissa Dubetz and Matt Norton, "Sharing the Cost: Accelerating Water Resilience through Infrastructure Finance in California," Milken Institute, Los Angeles, California, 2022, 20; Robert A. Greer et al., "Public-Private Partnerships in the Water Sector: The Case of Desalination," *Water Resources Management* 35, no. 11 (2021): 3499–3500; Michael Kiparsky et al., "Barriers to Innovation in Urban Wastewater Utilities: Attitudes of Managers in California," *Environmental Management* 57, no. 6 (2016); Marlowe, "Municipal Bonds," 12; Water Infrastructure and Resiliency Finance Center, "Perspective: 'The Financial Impact of Alternative Water Project Delivery Models' in the Water Sector," US Environmental Protection Agency, Washington, D.C., February 2017; American Water, "The Benefits of Investor-Owned Water Utilities," white paper, 2014, calwaterassn.com.

22. Allan T. Marks, "Vista Ridge to Deliver 20% More Water," *Project Finance International Yearbook 2017*, Thomson Reuters.

23. Marks, "Vista Ridge"; "Vista Ridge P3 Closes Wildly Successful Refinancing," *Global Water Intelligence*, December 23, 2020.

24. Robert A. Greer et al., "Public-Private Partnerships," 3505–3506; Marlowe, "Municipal Bonds," 12; Poseidon Water, "Carlsbad Desalination Plant," slide presentation, August 30, 2016.

25. Marlowe, "Municipal Bonds," 11.

26. Bosworth and Milusheva, "Innovations," 12; Brian Budden, "The Debate Over Private Infrastructure Financing in the United States," McKinsey & Company, April 12, 2017, mckinsey.com; Marlowe, "Municipal Bonds," 12.

27. Bosworth and Milusheva, "Innovations," 13; Dubetz and Horton, "Sharing the Cost," 21.

28. Dale Bonner and Caitlin MacLean, "Public-Private Infrastructure Financing Solutions," Milken Institute, Santa Monica, California, November 2014, 11; West Coast Infrastructure Exchange, "West Coast Infrastructure Exchange Final Report," CH2MHill, November 2012, 12; Brandon Pho, "Is Poseidon's Huntington Beach Desal Plant Proposal Gone for Good?" *Voice of OC*, July 14, 2022.

29. Aaron Bielenberg et al., "US Water Infrastructure: Making Funding Count," McKinsey & Company, November 24, 2021, mckinsey.com.

30. Bosworth and Milusheva, "Innovations," 9–10; Gao Liu and Dwight Denison, "Indirect and Direct Subsidies for the Cost of Government Capital: Comparing Tax Exempt Bonds and Build America Bonds," *National Tax Journal* 67, no. 3 (2014).

31. Bosworth and Milusheva, "Innovations"; Liu and Denison, "Indirect and Direct Subsidies."

32. Newsha Ajami et al., "Water Finance: The Imperative for Water Security and Economic Growth," Water in the West, Stanford, California, July 1, 2018, 8–9.

33. Greer, "Review," 2–3; Qureshi, "US Water"; Moonshot Missions, "Moonshot Shifts Focus to Helping Disadvantaged Communities Access Federal and State Funding," www.moonshotmissions.org; Vedachalam and Geddes, "Water Infrastructure," E100; Water Finance Exchange, "Water Finance Exchange: No Community Left Behind," https://waterfx.org.

34. Ajami et al., "Water Finance," 13; Maria Carmen Lemos et al., "Public-Private Partnerships as Catalysts for Community-Based Water Infrastructure Development: The Border WaterWorks Program in Texas and New Mexico Colonias," *Environment and Planning C: Government and Policy* 20, no. 2 (2002); Bastien Simeon, "The Financing Gap: Re-examining the Role of Private Financing and P3s," *Water Finance and Management*, October 26, 2021.

Chapter Nine

1. Barton H. Thompson, Jr. et al., *Legal Control of Water Resources*, 6th ed. (St. Paul, MN: West Academic Publishing, 2018), 445–450, 545–556.

2. Joseph L. Sax, "We Don't Do Groundwater: A Morsel of California Legal History," *University of Denver Water Law Review* 6, no. 2 (2003).

3. William A. Blomquist, *Dividing the Waters: Governing Groundwater in Southern California* (San Francisco: ICS Press, 1992); Ellen Hanak et al., *Managing California's Water: From Conflict to Reconciliation* (San Francisco: Public Policy Institute of California, 2011), 191–194.

4. Chris Austin, "Groundwater Problems and Prospects, Part 2: The Story Behind the Passage of the Sustainable Groundwater Management Act," *Maven's Notebook*, March 19, 2005.

5. Austin, "Groundwater Problems."

6. Michael Kiparsky et al., "The Importance of Institutional Design for Distributed Local-Level Governance of Groundwater: The Case of California's Sustainable Groundwater Management Act," *Water* 9, no. 10 (2017).

7. Leslie Dumas, "Implementing the Sustainable Groundwater Management Act in California," *Journal of American Water Works Association* 111, no. 7 (2019).

8. GEI Consultants, "Groundwater Management Solutions," Woburn, Massachusetts, July 16, 2020.

9. Dumas, "Implementing"; Leslie Dumas, "Implementing SGMA—An Update on California's Foray into Groundwater Regulation," in *World Environmental and Water Resources Congress 2017*, ed. Christopher N. Dunn and Brian Van Weele (Reston, VA: American Society of Civil Engineers, 2017).

10. Dumas, "Implementing"; GEI Consultants, "Groundwater Management Solutions," 4. Multiple groundwater sustainability plans are available at sgma.water.ca.gov/portal.

11. Andrew B. Ayres, "Easier Said than Done," *Regulation* 44, no. 3 (2021); Brian German, "Groundwater Accounting Platform to Become Available Statewide," *AgNet*, May 12, 2021; Sarah Heard, Matthew Fienup, and E. J. Remson, "The First SGMA Groundwater Market Is Trading: The Importance of Good Design and the Risks of Getting It Wrong," *California Agriculture* 75, no. 2 (2021).

12. H. Scott Butterfield, T. Rodd Kelsey, and Abigail K. Hart, *Rewilding Agricultural Landscapes: A California Study in Rebalancing the Needs of People and Nature* (Washington, DC: Island Press, 2021); Environmental Defense Fund, "Advancing Strategic Land Repurposing and Groundwater Sustainability in California," New York, March 2021; Ellen Hanak et al., "Water and the Future of the San Joaquin Valley," Public Policy Institute of California, San Francisco, February 2019; Brad Hooker, "EDF and Lawmakers Make Plans for Farmland to Be Fallowed under SGMA," *AgriPulse*, April 14, 2021.

13. Matthias Kipping, "America First: How Consultants Got into the Public Sector," in *Professional Service Firms and Politics in a Global Era*, ed. Chris Hurl and Anne Vogelpohl (London: Palgrave Macmillan, 2021); Christopher D. McKenna, "The Origins of Modern Management Consulting," *Business and Economic History* 24, no. 1 (1995); Matti Ylönen and Hanna Kuusela, "Consultocracy and Its Discontents: A Critical Typology and a Call for a Research Agenda," *Governance* 32, no. 2 (2019).

14. Malcolm Abbott and Bruce Cohen, "Productivity and Efficiency in the Water Industry," *Utilities Policy* 17, no. 3–4 (2009): 239.

15. "$7.79 Billion Water and Waste Management Consulting Services Global Market to 2030—Identify Growth Segments for Investment," *GlobalNewswire*, June 3,

2021; "Global Environmental Consulting Market Set to Surge," *EnvironmentAnalyst*, May 14, 2021; Debra K. Rubin, Mary B. Powers, and Peter Reina, "2021 Top 200 Environmental Firms: Market is Whirlwind of Change," *Engineering News-Record*, July 14, 2021.

16. Tetra Tech, "Delivering Innovative Water Solutions in San Antonio," May 18, 2021, www.tetratech.com; Geosyntec Consultants, "LADWP Stormwater Capture Master Plan," www.geosyntec.com.

17. Cordoba Corporation, "Owens Lake Dust Mitigation Project," cordobacorp .com.

18. Michael L. Dougherty, "Boom Times for Technocrats? How Environmental Consulting Companies Shape Mining Governance," *The Extractive Industries and Society* 6, no. 2 (2019); Dave Owen, "Private Facilitators of Public Regulation: A Study of the Environmental Consulting Industry," *Regulation and Governance* 15, no. 1 (2021); Matthew Wargent, Gavin Parker, and Emma Street, "Public-Private Entanglements: Consultant Use by Local Planning Authorities in England," *European Planning Studies* 28, no. 1 (2020).

19. Ross Beveridge, "Consultants, Depoliticization, and Arena-Shifting in the Policy Process: Privatizing Water in Berlin," *Policy Sciences* 45, no. 1 (2012); Svenja Keele, "Consultants and the Business of Climate Services: Implications of Shifting from Public to Private Science," *Climatic Change* 157, no. 1 (2019): 21; Tyler A. Scott and David P. Carter, "Collaborative Governance or Private Policy Making? When Consultants Matter More than Participation in Collaborative Environmental Planning," *Journal of Environmental Policy and Planning* 21, no. 2 (2019); Wargent, Parker and Street, "Public-Private Entanglements"; Ylönen and Kuusela, "Consultocracy," 248–250, 252.

20. Beveridge, "Consultants"; Ylönen and Kuusela, "Consultocracy," 251.

21. S. D. Bechtel, Jr. Foundation, "Water Solutions That Meet the Needs of People and Nature," *Issue Lab*, December 9, 2020.

22. S. D. Bechtel, Jr. Foundation, "Water Solutions."

23. S. D. Bechtel, Jr. Foundation, "Water Solutions."

24. Michele M. Betsill et al., "Philanthropic Foundations as Agents of Environmental Governance: A Research Agenda," *Environmental Politics* 31, no. 4 (2022); Edward W. Wilson, Carol Bromer, and David LaRoche, "Balancing the Competing Demands of Strategic Philanthropy: The Case of the Delaware River Watershed Initiative," *Foundation Review* 11, no. 4 (2019).

25. Peter Colohan and Kyle Onda, "Water Data for Water Science and Management: Advancing an Internet of Water (IoW)," *PLOS Water* 1, no. 3 (2022); Water Funder Initiative, "Toward Water Sustainability: A Blueprint for Philanthropy," March 2016.

26. Colohan and Onda, "Water Data"; Ted Kowalski, "Keeping the Colorado Flowing," *Irrigation Today*, October 1, 2020; Forrest S. Melton et al., "OpenET: Filling a Critical Data Gap in Water Management for the Western United States," *JAWRA: Journal of the American Water Resources Association* 58, no. 6 (December 2021): 971–994 (originally published November 2, 2021); Dana Rollison et al., "OpenET: Enabling Science-Based Water Management through Open Data Services and User-Driven

Design," in *AGU Fall Meeting Abstracts* (Washington, DC: American Geophysical Union, 2020).

27. Gina G. Gilson and Dustin E. Garrick, "Can Philanthropy Enable Collective Action to Conserve Rivers? Insights from a Decade of Collaboration in the Colorado River Basin," *Conservation and Society* 19, no. 3 (2021); Scott Patterson, "The Colorado River Is in Crisis: The Walton Family Is Pushing a Solution," *Wall Street Journal,* October 2, 2021; Carol D. Rugg, *Great Lakes: A Stewardship Left Untended* (Flint, MI: Mott Foundation, 1988); Wilson, Bromer, and LaRoche, "Balancing."

28. Gina Gilson, "Funding Flows for Freshwater: The Role of Philanthropy in Market-Based Freshwater Conservation," MSc and MPhil diss., University of Oxford, 2018; Gilson and Garrick, "Can Philanthropy"; San Diego Foundation, "The San Diego Foundation Grants $230,462 to Increase Regional Resilience to Climate Change and a Drought-Prone Future," press release, December 22, 2017; Water Funder Initiative, "Toward Water Sustainability."

29. Gilson, "Funding Flows," 41; Gilson and Garrick, "Can Philanthropy."

30. Betsill et al., "Philanthropic Foundations"; Gilson, "Funding Flows," 37–38, 41; Gilson and Garrick, "Can Philanthropy."

31. Betsill et al., "Philanthropic Foundations"; Gilson and Garrick, "Can Philanthropy"; George Holmes, "Biodiversity for Billionaires: Capitalism, Conservation and the Role of Philanthropy in Saving/Selling Nature," *Development and Change* 43, no. 1 (2012); Rob Reich, "Repugnant to the Whole Idea of Democracy? On the Role of Foundations in Democratic Societies," *PS: Political Science and Politics* 49, no. 3 (2016); Rob Reich, Chiara Cordelli, and Lucy Bernholz, eds., *Philanthropy in Democratic Societies: History, Institutions, Values* (Chicago: University of Chicago Press, 2016); Wilson, Bromer, and LaRoche, "Balancing."

32. Josh Eagle, James Salzman, and Barton H. Thompson, Jr., *Natural Resources Law and Policy* (St. Paul, MN: West Academic Publishing, 2017), 7–9.

33. AB 252, 2021–2022 Sess. (Cal. 2021); Environmental Defense Fund, "Advancing Strategic Land Repurposing and Groundwater Sustainability in California," New York, March 2021.

34. Jon P. Devine, Jr., "Comment on the Proposed Rule Titled 'Definition of "Waters of the United States"—Recodification of Preexisting Rules,'" comment letter to US Environmental Protection Agency, Washington, D.C., September 27, 2017; Sandi Matsumoto et al., "Groundwater Sustainability Plan for the Westside Subbasin," comment letter to the California Department of Water Resources, May 15, 2020.

35. *TVA v. Hill,* 437 U.S. 153 (1978); *National Audubon Society v. Superior Court,* 658 P.2d 709 (Cal. 1983).

36. Kate A. Brauman et al., "Water Funds," in *Green Growth That Works,* ed. Lisa Mandle et al. (Washington, DC: Island Press, 2019); Sara H. Nelson et al., "The Political Life of Natural Infrastructure: Water Funds and Alternative Histories of Payments for Ecosystem Services in Valle Del Cauca, Colombia," *Development and Change* 51, no. 1 (2020).

37. Thompson et al., *Legal Control,* 1030–1037; Lourdes Medrano, "The Colorado River Runs Again," *Yes! Magazine,* August 24, 2021.

38. AB 685, 2011–2012 Sess. (Cal. 2012); SB 200, 2019–2020 Sess. (Cal. 2019); Alesandra Najera and Alex Paxton, "Water Boards: Pathways to Community Power," *Water Foundation Currents*, December 15, 2020.

39. Ilma Ibrisevic, "Top 10 Nonprofits Fighting the Global Water Crisis," *donorbox* (blog), May 13, 2022, donorbox.org; Water.org, *Unleashing Capital to Make Safe Water and Sanitation Available for All*, May 2019; Keith B. Waterhouse, "Acknowledging the Good Work of Water-Aid Organizations," *Journal American Water Works Association* 110, no. 9 (2018).

Chapter Ten

1. Barnali Chaklader and Neeran Gautam, "Efficient Water Management Through Public-Private Partnership Model: An Experiment in CSR by Coca-Cola India," *Vikalpa* 38, no. 4 (2013): 98; Aneel Karnani, "Corporate Social Responsibility Does Not Avert the Tragedy of the Commons. Case Study: Coca-Cola India," *Economics, Management, and Financial Markets* 9, no. 3 (2014): 19–21.

2. Chaklader and Gautam, "Efficient Water Management," 99; Karnani, "Corporate Social Responsibility," 21–24.

3. Georgina Drew, "Coca-Cola and the Moral Economy of Rural Development in India," *South Asia: Journal of South Asian Studies* 44, no. 3 (2021): 482–494; Sonu Goyal and N. Linthoingambi, "Coca-Cola India: Losing Its Fizz," *Market Forces* 5, no. 3 (2009): 196–197; Karnani, "Corporate Social Responsibility," 17; Gayatri Raghunandan, "A Look at the Legal Issues Plachimada's Struggle for Water Against Coca-Cola Has Brought Up," *The Wire*, August 20, 2017; K. A. Shaji, "People Power Shut Coke Down in Plachimada, But Wells Are Still Dry," *Huffington Post*, January 22, 2019.

4. Goyal and Linthoingambi, "Coca-Cola India," 198; Denise Gül Holzendorff, "Living on the Coke Side of Thirst: The Coca-Cola Company and Responsibility for Water Shortage in India," *Journal of European Management and Public Affairs Studies* 1, no. 1 (2013); Karnani, "Corporate Social Responsibility," 17–18; Steve Stecklow, "How a Global Web of Activists Gives Coke Problems in India," *Wall Street Journal*, June 7, 2005.

5. Coca-Cola Company, "Our Company," www.coca-colacompany.com; Coca-Cola Company and The Nature Conservancy, "Product Water Footprint Assessments: Practical Application in Corporate Water Stewardship," Atlanta, Georgia, September 2010, 11–15; Bartow J. Elmore, *Citizen Coke: The Making of Coca-Cola Capitalism* (New York: W.W. Norton & Company, 2015); Christine MacDonald, "Coke Claims to Give Back as Much Water as It Uses. An Investigation Shows It Isn't Even Close," *The Verge*, May 31, 2018.

6. Coca-Cola Company, "2020 Business, Environmental, Social, and Governance Report," Atlanta, Georgia, April 2021, 21; Coca-Cola Company, "Water Stewardship," www.coca-colacompany.com; Karnani, "Corporate Social Responsibility," 24; Therese Rudebeck, *Corporations as Custodians of the Public Good? Exploring the Intersection of Corporate Water Stewardship and Global Water Governance* (Cham, Switzerland: Springer Nature, 2019), 60.

7. Coca-Cola Company, "Water Stewardship"; MacDonald, "Coke Claims."

8. Chaklader and Gautam, "Efficient Water Management," 100–102; Goyal and Linthoingambi, "Coca-Cola India," 198–200; Karnani, "Corporate Social Responsibility," 26.

9. Coca-Cola Company, *2020 Business, Environmental, Social, and Governance Report*, 21; John Kell, "Coca-Cola Just Hit a Major Environmental Milestone," *Fortune*, August 29, 2016; POMA, "Coca-Cola: Sustainability Visionary or Villain?" Harvard Business School, November 15, 2017, digital.hbs.edu; Joe Rozza et al., "Corporate Water Stewardship: Achieving a Sustainable Balance," *Journal of Management and Sustainability* 3, no. 4 (2013).

10. MacDonald, "Coke Claims"; POMA, "Coca-Cola."

11. Coca-Cola Company, *2020 Business, Environmental, Social, and Governance Report*, 21–22; Coca-Cola Company, "Coca-Cola Unveils 2030 Water Security Strategy," March 22, 2021, www.coca-colacompany.com; Coca-Cola Company, "Improving Our Water Efficiency," August 28, 2018, www.coca-colacompany.com; Amy Mayer, "Ceres Ranks Companies for Water Sustainability Efforts," *AgriPulse*, October 28, 2021.

12. Coca-Cola Company, *2020 Business, Environmental, Social, and Governance Report*, 21; Coca-Cola Company, "Water Quality and Wastewater Management," www.coca-colacompany.com.

13. Coca-Cola Company, *2020 Business, Environmental, Social, and Governance Report*, 25; Rudebeck, *Corporations as Custodians*, 88; Clean River Trust, "Things Flow Better with Coke," www.cleanriverstrust.co.uk.

14. Coca-Cola Company, *2020 Business, Environmental, Social, and Governance Report*, 21–23.

15. Coca-Cola Company, "2018 Business and Sustainability Report," Atlanta, Georgia, 2018, 26; Shaju Philip, "Coca-Cola Bottling Plant at Heart of Kerala Agitation 20 Years Ago Will Now Be a 600-Bed Covid Hospital," *Indian Express*, June 24, 2021.

16. Mayer, "Ceres Ranks."

17. MacDonald, "Coke Claims"; POMA, "Coca-Cola"; Rudebeck, *Corporations as Custodians*.

18. Peter Newborne and James Dalton, "Water Management and Stewardship: Taking Stock of Corporate Water Behaviour," International Union for Conservation of Nature and Overseas Development Institute, Gland, Switzerland, 2016, 9–10; Rudebeck, *Corporations as Custodians*, 89, 95, 102.

19. Ross Hamilton, "From Water Management to Water Stewardship—A Policy Maker's Opinion on the Progress of the Mining Sector," *Water* 11, no. 3 (2019): 2; Nick Hepworth, "Open for Business or Opening Pandora's Box? A Constructive Critique of Corporate Engagement in Water Policy: An Introduction," *Water Alternatives* 5, no. 3 (2012): 548; Rudebeck, *Corporations as Custodians*, 2, 86–88.

20. Nick Hepworth, "Tackling the Global Water Crisis: The Role of Water Footprints and Water Stewardship," Institute of Development Studies, Brighton, U.K., August 2021, 4; Rudebeck, *Corporations as Custodians*, 91–92; H. Yu, "Water

Conservation in Beverage Production: Examining Corporate Water Stewardship Programs," *IOP Conference Series: Earth and Environmental Science* 776 (2021): 3.

21. Hannah Northey, "Questions Trail Big Business' 'Water Positive' Pledges," *Greenwire*, August 25, 2021; Amanda Schupak, "Corporations Are Pledging to Be 'Water Positive.' What Does That Mean?" *The Guardian*, October 14, 2021.

22. WaterAid, "Strengthening the Business Case for Water, Sanitation, and Hygiene," London, July 2018, 13–15; USAID, "Women + Water Alliance," www.global waters.org.

23. AB InBev, "Co-Investing in Water Solutions for Measurable Impact in Jaguariuna, Brazil," June 5, 2021, www.ab-inbev.com; Hepworth, "Tackling," 4; Yu, "Water Conservation," 3–4.

24. Alexis Morgan, "Water Stewardship Revisited: Shifting the Narrative from Risk to Value Creation," WWF-Germany, Berlin, 2018, 10–11; Newborne and Dalton, "Water Management," 9.

25. Global Reporting Initiative, "Standard 303: Water and Effluents," Amsterdam, 2018; Ross Hamilton and Ruth Thomas, "A Practical Guide to Consistent Water Reporting," International Council on Mining and Metals, London, 2017, 26–29; Stephen A. Northey et al., "Sustainable Water Management and Improved Corporate Reporting in Mining," *Water Resources and Industry* 21 (2019): 3.

26. Carbon Disclosure Project, "Cleaning Up Their Act: Are Companies Responding to the Risks and Opportunities Posed by Water Pollution?" London, 2019; Enok Chinyenze and Francesca Recanati, "Water Risks: Why Investors Care About Sustainability," *Climate Disclosure Standards Board* (blog), September 29, 2021, www.cdsb.net; World Economic Forum, "Global Risks 2014," 9th ed., Geneva, Switzerland, 2014; Hui-Cheng Yu, Lopin Kuo, and Beiling Ma, "The Drivers of Corporate Water Disclosure in Enhancing Information Transparency," *Sustainability* 12, no. 1 (2020).

27. Chinyenze and Recanati, "Water Risks"; Thomas Hundertmark, Kun Lueck, and Brent Packer, "Water: A Human and Business Priority," *McKinsey Quarterly*, May 5, 2020; Rudebeck, *Corporations as Custodians*, 59–60.

28. WaterAid, "Strengthening the Business Case," 13–15.

29. Hamilton, "From Water Management," 2; Tom Perkins, "The Fight to Stop Nestlé from Taking America's Water to Sell in Plastic Bottles," *The Guardian*, October 29, 2019.

30. Hamilton, "From Water Management," 2; Hepworth, "Open for Business," 550.

31. Hepworth, "Open for Business," 550; Rudebeck, *Corporations as Custodians*, 65–66.

32. Carbon Disclosure Project, "Cost of Water Risks to Business Five Times Higher Than Cost of Taking Action," March 19, 2021, www.cdp.net; Rick J. Hogeboom, Ilja Kamphuis, and Arjen Y. Hoekstra, "Water Sustainability of Investors: Development and Application of an Assessment Framework," *Journal of Cleaner Production* 202 (2018); Hepworth, "Open for Business," 550; Rudebeck, *Corporations as Custodians*, 65–66; US Securities and Exchange Commission, "Commission Guidance Regarding Disclosure Related to Climate Change," February 8, 2010; Dylan Waldhuetter, "What Does Water Stewardship Mean, Anyway?" *ESG Investor*, January 14, 2022; Yu, Kuo, and Ma, "Drivers," 10.

33. Rudebeck, *Corporations as Custodians*, 61, 65, 112, 119; Will Sarni and Hugh Share, "From Corporate Water Risk to Value Creation," *Global Water Intelligence*, August 1, 2019.

34. Patrick Velte, "Do CEO Incentives and Characteristics Influence Corporate Social Responsibility (CSR) and Vice Versa? A Literature Review," *Social Responsibility Journal* 16, no. 8 (2020).

35. Hepworth, "Open for Business," 547–548; Hepworth, "Tackling," 3–4; Rudebeck, *Corporations as Custodians*, 70–71.

36. Hepworth, "Open for Business," 546; Rutger W. Hofste et al., "Aqueduct 3.0: Updated Decision-Relevant Global Water Risk Indicators," World Resources Institute, Washington, D.C., July 2019; Ariane Laporte-Bisquit, "WWF Water Risk Filter: Assess, Respond, and Value Water Risks," in *Sustainable Industrial Water Use: Perspectives, Incentives, and Tools*, ed. Cheryl Davis and Eric Rosenblum (London: IWA Publishing, 2021), 321.

37. Hepworth, "Open for Business," 548; Hepworth, "Tackling," 4; Newborne and Dalton, "Water Management," 14; Sarni and Share, "From Corporate Water Risk."

38. Rudebeck, *Corporations as Custodians*, 113; Yu, "Water Conservation," 3.

39. Hepworth, "Open for Business," 543; Newborne and Dalton, "Water Management," 9; Rudebeck, *Corporations as Custodians*, 68–69, 136–149.

40. Alliance for Water Stewardship, "About the Alliance for Water Stewardship," a4ws.org; Hepworth, "Tackling," 5; Newborne and Dalton, "Water Management," 11, 13; Adrian Sym and Sarah Wade, "The AWS Standard: A Common Language for the Global Water Stewardship Community," in *Sustainable Industrial Water Use: Perspectives, Incentives, and Tools*, ed. Cheryl Davis and Eric Rosenblum (London: IWA Publishing, 2021).

41. CEO Water Mandate, "Annual Report 2020," 2020, 5, 8–9; Rudebeck, *Corporations as Custodians*, 75; CEO Water Mandate, "Six Commitment Areas," ceowatermandate.org.

42. 2030 Water Resources Group, "Our Impact in Numbers (Cumulative)," www.2030wrg.org; Beth Jenkins, Richard Gilbert, and Jane Nelson, "The 2030 Water Resources Group: Collaboration and Country Leadership to Strengthen Water Security," Harvard Kennedy School Corporate Responsibility Initiative, Cambridge, Massachusetts, 2017, 7–8, 12–16.

43. Hepworth, "Open for Business," 543, 549; Rudebeck, *Corporations as Custodians*, 133.

44. Hepworth, "Open for Business," 543; Waldhuetter, "What Does Water Stewardship Mean, Anyway?"

45. Hepworth, "Open for Business," 544; Hepworth, "Tackling," 2; Rudebeck, *Corporations as Custodians*, 71–72

46. Morgan, "Water Stewardship Revisited," 10; Sarni and Share, "From Corporate Water Risk."

47. Hamilton, "From Water Management," 3; Rudebeck, *Corporations as Custodians*, 120.

48. Hamilton, "From Water Management," 2; Rudebeck, *Corporations as Custodians*, 85; Yu, "Water Conservation," 3–4.

49. Catherine Moncrieff et al., "A Wave of Change: The Role of Companies in Building a Water-Secure World," Carbon Disclosure Project, London, 2021, 23–24.

50. Sarni and Share, "From Corporate Water Risk."

51. Hepworth, "Open for Business," 548; Nora Lanari et al., "In Whose Interests? Water Risk Mitigation Strategies Practiced by the Fruit Industry in South Africa's Western Cape," *Geoforum* 126 (2021), 105, 112; Newborne and Dalton, "Water Management," 9; Rudebeck, *Corporations as Custodians*, 29, 164, 169, 187–188.

52. "Introduction to the AWS Standard," Alliance for Water Stewardship, April 27, 2017, 27; Hepworth, "Open for Business," 542–559; Newborne and Dalton, "Water Management," 12–13; Rudebeck, *Corporations as Custodians*, 133, 166, 184–188; Sym and Wade, "AWS Standard," 314.

53. Newborne and Dalton, "Water Management," 13; Rudebeck, *Corporations as Custodians*, 189–191; Sym and Wade, "AWS Standard," 313.

Chapter Eleven

1. Norman J. Baldwin and Quinton A. Farley, "Comparing the Public and Private Sectors in the United States," in *Handbook of Comparative and Development Public Administration*, ed. Ali Farazmand, 2nd ed. (New York: Routledge, 2001); William J. Baumol, *The Free-Market Innovation Machine: Analyzing the Growth Miracle of Capitalism* (Princeton, NJ: Princeton University Press, 2002); Pietro Micheli, "New Business Models for Public-Sector Innovation," *Research Technology Management* 55, no. 5 (2012).

2. California Water Boards, "Drinking Water Partnerships and Consolidation," waterboards.ca.gov; Katy Hansen, Megan Mullin, and Erin K. Riggs, "Collaboration Risk and the Choice to Consolidate Local Government Services," *Perspectives on Public Management and Governance* 3, no. 3 (2019); Andy Lange, "A Brief History of Water Districts and Water Associations," *Waterproof* (2014); Nell Green Nylen, Camille Pannu, and Michael Kiparsky, "Learning from California's Experience with Small Water System Consolidations," Center for Law, Energy, and the Environment, Berkeley Law, Berkeley, California, May 2018.

3. Gregory Pierce et al., "Solutions to the Problem of Drinking Water Service Affordability: A Review of the Evidence," *Water* 8, no. 4 (2021); Kimberly J. Quesnel and Newsha K. Ajami, "Advancing Water Innovation Through Public Benefit Funds: Examining California's Approach for Electricity," *Journal of American Water Works Association* 110, no. 2 (2018).

4. Dean Gillette, "Impact of Regulations on R&D: How Regulations Encourage and Discourage Innovation," *Research Management* 20, no. 2 (1977).

5. Julian Brookes, "Why Water is the New Oil," *Rolling Stone*, July 7, 2011; Paul B. Farrell, "Water Is the New Gold, A Big Commodity Bet," *MarketWatch*, July 24, 2012.

6. Jernej Letnar Cernic, "Corporate Obligations under the Human Right to Water," *Denver Journal of International Law and Policy* 39, no. 2 (2011); John Ruggie, "The Corporate Responsibility to Respect Human Rights," Harvard Law School Forum on Corporate Governance, Cambridge, Massachusetts, May 15, 2010; United Nations, "Guiding Principles on Business and Human Rights: Implementing the United Nations 'Protect, Respect, and Remedy' Framework," 2011.

7. Alan Jones, "Social Responsibility and the Utilities," *Journal of Business Ethics* 34, no. 3 (2001); Daniel J. Morrissey, "The Promise of Stakeholder Advisory Councils," *University of Pennsylvania Journal of Business Law* 23, no. 2 (2021); J. Haskell Murray, "Adopting Stakeholder Advisory Boards," *American Business Law Journal* 54, no. 1 (2017); Heiko Spitzeck, Erik G. Hansen, and David Grayson, "Joint Management-Stakeholder Committees—A New Path to Stakeholder Governance?" *Corporate Governance* 11, no. 5 (2011).

8. Karen Bakker, *Privatizing Water: Governance Failure and the World's Urban Water Crisis* (Ithaca, NY: Cornell University Press, 2010); Maude Barlow, *Blue Covenant: The Global Water Crisis and the Coming Battle for the Right to Water* (New York: New Press, 2007); Austill Stewart, "Private Sector Water Management Solutions Help Governments Deliver Affordability and Reliability," commentary, Reason Foundation, September 4, 2020, reason.org.

9. Sock Yong Phang, Thomas Kok Kim Lim, and Flocy Joseph, "PUB's PPP Journey: Learning How to Make the Most of a Scarce Resource," Singapore Management University, Singapore, 2021.

INDEX

Australia (*continued*)
116, 118; Murray-Darling Basin, 108,
115–18; Perth drought, 22–23; Victorian Environmental Water Holder,
118; water market, 96, 102, 105, 108;
wetlands, 114–18; Yambuna Wetlands
Complex, 116
Azurix, 107

Baltimore, Maryland, 73
Barcelona, Spain, 22
Bass, Ed and Lee, 93, 95, 107
Bayer, 215
Bay Institute of San Francisco, 200
B Corporation (B Corp), 79–80
Bear Republic Brewing Company,
43–44
Bechtel Foundation. *See* S.D. Bechtel, Jr.
Foundation
beer, 42–46; Brewers for Clean Water,
45, 53–54; Russian River breweries,
43–46; water, importance of, 42–43;
water recycling, 44–45
beverage companies: Cape Town, 19;
corporate water stewardship, 215;
shortage impacts, 52; water use,
50. *See also* beer; *names of specific
companies*
Bipartisan Infrastructure Law, 4, 77, 177,
184
birds, migratory, 119; Bird Returns, 122
Blue Forest Conservation, 179
Bluffdale, Utah, 51
Booz Allen Hamilton, 191
Boulder, Colorado, 104
BP, 215
breweries. *See* beer
Buffalo, New York, 75
Burr, Aaron, 71
Business of Water, 59

California: Central Valley, 5, 30–31, 38,
99, 127; Central Valley Project, 103;
climate change, 32–33; consolidation of suppliers, 233; Department

of Water Resources, 133, 187–89;
droughts, 43–44, 48; Fox Canyon
Groundwater Management Agency,
189; groundwater depletion, 30–31,
185–86; Hetch Hetchy Valley, 199–
200; human right to water, 6, 202;
infrastructure funding, 177; Kings
River Basin, 131–33; Mono Lake, 7,
201; Multibenefit Land Repurposing Program, 200–201; native fish
decline, 28, 119; Open and Transparent Water Data Act, 196; Owens
Lake, 193; Pajaro Valley, 136; public
trust doctrine, 7, 201; public utility
regulation, 80, 87–88; Rosedale-Rio
Bravo Water Storage District, 189;
Russian River breweries, 43–46; Safe
and Affordable Drinking Water
Fund, 196; Salton Sea, 92, 94–95; San
Joaquin Valley, 129–34; speculation
concerns, 111; State Water Project,
103; State Water Resources Control
Board, 92, 133; water markets, 99,
101–2, 105; wheeling legislation, 94.
See also Colorado River; Hawthorne;
Imperial Valley; Los Angeles; San
Diego; San Francisco; Stockton;
Sustainable Groundwater Manage-
ment Act
California Water Foundation. *See* Water
Foundation
California Water Service Company, 75
Calvert Foundation, 171
Cambrian Innovation, 44–45, 55
Cameron, Don, 131–34
Campbell Foundation, 197
Canadian Algonquin Power & Utilities
Corporation, 83
Canadian Public Sector Pension Invest-
ment Board, 108
Cape Town, South Africa: agricultural
water use, 19–20; climate change, 17,
20, 32; conservation efforts, 16–18;
Day Zero, 15–23, 32, 136; desalina-
tion, 18, 20–21, 136; future water

US Securities and Exchange Commission, 221
US Water LLC, 64, 69

Veles Water, 109
Veolia, 55, 57, 71, 75, 83, 85, 164–65, 192, 236; Peer Performance Solutions (PPS) program, 65; Pittsburgh Water and Sewer Authority, 65–69, 239
Vidler Water, 107–8
virtual water, 222
Vista Ridge Regional Water Supply Project, 180–81
Vivendi. *See* Veolia.

Walton Family Foundation, 126, 195–98
Washington Water Trust, 121
wastewater disposal: combined wastewater-stormwater systems, 41, 171; pandemic detection, 152; sewage systems, 171; technological innovation, 151–52; wine industry, 53. *See also* wastewater reclamation
wastewater reclamation, 4; beer, 44–45; Cape Town, 20–21; energy production, 152; energy use, 4, 44–45, 148; resource recovery centers, 151–52; Singapore, 147–49; technological innovation, 4, 56, 148–49, 151–52, 154; water energy purchase agreement, 45
Water Access Acceleration Fund, 55
Water Aid, 223
Water and Tribes Initiative, 198
Water Asset Management (WAM), 55, 107–8, 135
water data, 5, 56; artificial intelligence, 56, 153–54; data needs, 5, 56, 153, 196–97; data reform efforts, 197; foundations, support by, 198; satellite imaging, 5, 56, 153–54; sensors, 56, 153; smart meters, 5, 56, 153. *See also* Internet of Water (IoW) Coalition; Open ET
water distribution, global, 23–28; freshwater versus salt water, 23–24;

glaciers, 23–24; seasonal variation, 25–26
Water Environment Federation, 168
Water Environment Research Foundation, 164
WaterEquity, 55
Water Exchange, 109
Water Finance Exchange (WFX), 184, 233
Waterfind Water Management Specialists, 55
Water Footprint Network, 222
Water for People, 203
Water Foundation, 55, 186–87, 190, 195, 198; groundwater work, 186–87, 190
Water Foundry, 236
Water Funders Initiative (WFI), 195–96
water funds, 59, 202
Water Hub, 196
Water Infrastructure and Resiliency Finance Center, 184
Waterkeeper Alliance, 200
water law: anti-speculation doctrine, 101–3; anti-waste doctrine, 92, 94; environmental protection, 119; environmental water acquisitions, 120, 124; groundwater law, 185–86; growing cities doctrine, 72; instream flow rights, 118–19; no-injury rule, 104; prior appropriation doctrine, 97; public interest standard, 5; public ownership of water, 5; public trust doctrine, 7, 201, 236; regulated riparianism, 98; riparian doctrine, 97–98; "use it or lose it" principle, 120, 124; wild and scenic river acts, 119. *See also* Sustainable Groundwater Management Act; water markets
water management, 232–33
water markets, 2–4, 8–9, 56, 89–113, 230; anti-speculation doctrine, 101–3; Australia, 96, 102, 105, 108; benefits, 99–100; brokers and intermediaries, 109; bundling of water and land,

World Health Organization: drinking
water survey, 36; minimum water
recommendation, 15
WWF: beer study, 42; Coca-Cola collaboration, 212, 226–27; corporate
collaboration, 223, 225, 227; Living
Planet Index, 28; water funds, 202;

water risk filter, 222; water stewardship ladder, 217–18

XPV Water Partners, 55
Xylem, 55, 149, 157, 164–65

Zurich Insurance, 103